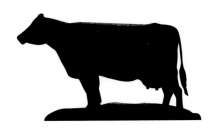

THE COMPLETE BOOK OF

BUTCHERING, SMOKING, CURING, AND SAUSAGE MAKING

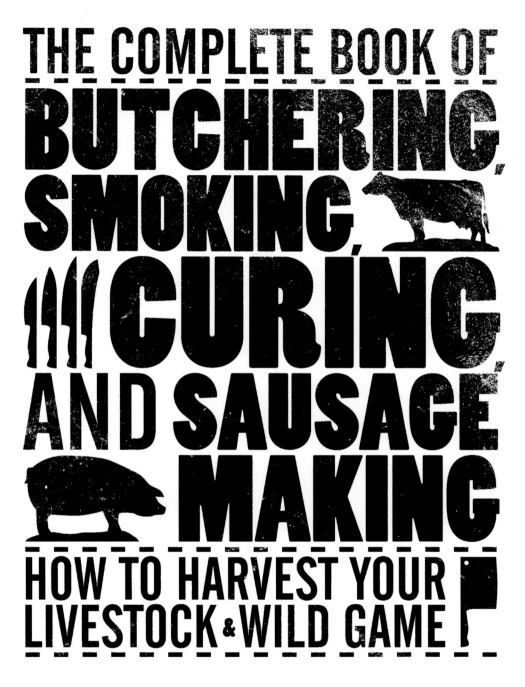

HOW TO HARVEST YOUR LIVESTOCK & WILD GAME

PHILIP HASHEIDER

Voyageur Press

Dedication

This book is dedicated to my grandfather, Herbert Hasheider, who first exposed me
to the butchering process and taught me the basics at a very young age.
He made the best dried beef I've ever tasted.

First published in 2010 by Voyageur Press, an imprint of MBI Publishing Company,
400 First Avenue North, Suite 300, Minneapolis, MN 55401 USA

Voyageur Press titles are also available at discounts in bulk quantity for industrial or sales-promotional use. For details write
to Special Sales Manager at MBI Publishing Company, 400 First Avenue North, Suite 300, Minneapolis, MN 55401 USA.
To find out more about our books, visit us online at www.voyageurpress.com.

Library of Congress Cataloging-in-Publication Data

Hasheider, Philip, 1951-
The complete book of butchering, smoking, curing, and sausage making :
how to harvest your livestock & wild game / Philip Hasheider. — 1st ed.
    p. cm.
Includes index.
ISBN 978-0-7603-3782-0 (flexibound)
1. Slaughtering and slaughter-houses. 2. Meat—Preservation. 3. Cookery
(Sausages) I. Title.
TS1960.H37 2010
664'.902—dc22
                    2010002969

Except where noted all photographs copyright © Marcus Hasheider

Editor: Leah Noel
Design Manager: LeAnn Kuhlmann
Designed by: Chris Fayers
Cover designed by: Matthew Simmons

Printed in China

Contents

It does not require owning a large acreage to raise meat animals. Small pastures of one to two acres would be sufficient to raise several meat goats or sheep for home use.

INTRODUCTION

The vast majority of people today no longer hunts for their food or have the opportunity to do so. The long arc of human civilization across the millennia has seen the transformation of hunter-gatherer societies into ones where consumers routinely purchase their daily meals at supermarkets, restaurants, convenience stores, and a host of other venues where the food, or many of the ingredients, are prepared off-site.

Agriculture, the basis for all domesticated food production, reaches back at least 10,000 years. But in more recent times, industrialization models have been applied to animal agriculture practices with the result that more total food is produced by fewer people than at any time in history. The hunter-gatherer model in present terms may mostly include hunting and gathering in market aisles or at farmer's market stalls, the desire to provide top quality food for the family table. Interest in butchering and processing meat for family use has increased in recent years. This interest may be partly attributed to the numerous broadcast channels highlighting cooking and culinary topics, popular chefs, and food promoters. Equipment that is easy to use and maintain makes do-it-yourself food processing attainable

Historically, home butchering was done in the fall of the year when the weather was cooler. This decreased the chance for meat spoilage before the era of modern refrigeration. Today, with proper care of the meat, home butchering can occur at any time during the year.

and has captured the imagination of even the most inexperienced food aspirant. The opportunities are available to accomplish a safe harvest, fabrication, and food preservation program of your own.

Society Evolution

For our hunter-gatherer ancestors, a successful hunt, in which their prey were killed and subsequently eaten, was a matter of survival; with no success, there was little or nothing to eat. The development of small tribes or clans into cohesive units may have been as much for banding together for hunting purposes as it was for group protection and socializing. The more members who became involved with the hunt, the greater their chances for success. To keep all members satisfied, distribution of the captured prey or food was determined by the group in a manner that was fair and equitable. Food would need to be shared in sufficient quantities to ensure adequate nutrition for the hunters in order to maintain their strength and stamina for future hunts.

As human civilization evolved, community participation was an integral part of its development. Shared concerns helped bind them together as did marriages within groups. This cohesiveness encouraged the sharing of difficult tasks that were made easier with the help of many hands. These included planting, harvesting, and butchering, among others.

A major change in each individual's participation in gathering food occurred during the Industrial Revolution, as people left farms and rural areas for cities in search of better-paying jobs. Many urban areas or cities restricted the raising of animals within their boundaries due to potential health issues and animal-borne illness that could be transferred to humans.

With an inability to raise their own livestock, urban dwellers needed markets to secure their food, particularly meat markets where they could purchase meat cuts and sausages. This led to the rise in the number of butcher shops and local meat markets, which could offer special products based on family or heritage recipes. As time passed, more consumers became disconnected from the farms and livestock their parents or grandparents had known so well.

Diet Evolution

Our distant ancestors often hunted wild game that was available, and this typically included small game, such as birds and fowl, rodents, turtles, rabbits, and anything else that might have wandered across their paths. Some large animals that were hunted often included bison, deer, bear, moose, and elk.

Over time, as the nation's population changed and migrated to urban areas, their diet subsequently changed as well. Today, a large percent of the typical diet in the United States uses four basic groups of animals for the majority of its meat: cattle, sheep, pigs, and domestic fowl. The vast majority of consumers rarely eat any other kind of animal, especially some that we now label as exotics but may have been normal food fare for our ancestors (squirrels, rabbits, frogs, snakes, turtles, or other small animals).

Butchering Evolution

Butchering of the animals at the end of a successful hunt became a family and community activity as group members hurried to deconstruct the carcass before it had a chance to spoil. It took a tremendous amount of effort to handle a large animal, such as a buffalo, moose, or bear; kill and dress it; and then break down the carcass into manageable portions that could be successfully dried and transported. It took several strong members of the group to do a proper job of it. The meat had to be preserved. Before refrigeration, this was accomplished through a variety of methods, including smoking, packing in lard, and, later, through canning.

Fall was typically when the family butchering was done. The weather was cooler, which made working with the carcass easier and helped keep it from spoiling as quickly as it may have in warmer weather. It was also a time when less farm work needed to be done after the crops were harvested. Butchering also could be used as a communal or family social event, where members of an extended family or neighbors gathered as they worked to provide food for the coming winter. It was often a time of thankful harvest for the crops, the animals, and the community as a whole.

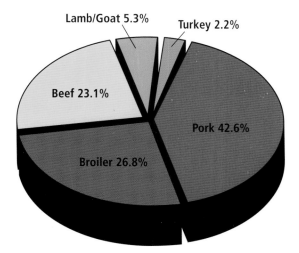

The U.S. Department of Agriculture reported in 2005 that 43 percent of the meat consumed in the United States was pork. Ninety-five percent of the total meat consumed that year came from either pork, beef, or poultry. The chart above represents the percentages in tons consumed.

Great significance was assigned to the butchering of domestic animals for home consumption. Selection of which animal(s) to use was an important decision. These were animals that were often regarded as individuals, each with his or her own unique characteristics. The decision to use a particular animal was not taken lightly.

As the generations passed and fewer people remained on farms, the knowledge of butchering procedures and principles became fractured, and in many families, this knowledge became lost. This loss may have been voluntary because of a lack of interest or the desire to pursue butchering in an urban environment, no longer wanting to contend with the mess, not having access to an animal or equipment, or for a variety of other reasons. Without teaching the procedures and practices of butchering to the next generation, these skills remained dormant or nonexistent.

Human civilization has consumed animal meat products as part of its diet for thousands of years. Today's consumers can choose from a variety of animal species, such as beef cattle, to include as part of their daily diet.

Geese, ducks, and poultry are among the fowl that can provide a distinctive meal for special occasions. Small in size, they require less feeding than large animals and reach target butchering weights in short time periods.

New Markets and Opportunities

The food industry in the United States has evolved to where a few large corporations dominate the markets, but not all. Often large conglomerates involved with animal agriculture control the entire process, from birth to slaughter and processing, distributing their products nationally and internationally. This consolidation and integration of food sources and products have dramatically affected consumer attitudes and inclinations toward production of their own food. Providing a vast array of meat products in a multitude of different forms has offered consumers convenience of meal preparation and food access. There has been little need to provide your own when it is so easily provided to you at a reasonable cost.

In recent years, the trend has been changing as more consumers become aware of the sources of their food and that they have alternative choices. Concerns over animals raised in large units or in confinement housing are being addressed. Also, concerns about the conditions under which animals destined for their dinner tables are raised, their health, and how they are ultimately processed have propelled consumers to seek different sources of food that they can have some connection with and may be more in line with their own philosophy. Small-scale farmers have eased many of these concerns due to the less intensive nature of their businesses. This has, in turn, helped spawn an increasing number of small unit farms for those seeking an alternative to large-scale production.

One consequence of these changes has been the development of on-farm butchering and processing facilities with a venue for their meat products located in a village, town, or city. This provides a new marketing opportunity for those with an interest in butchering and processing meats. A business can be developed that is based on butchering and slaughtering of animals for customers in your area or region.

Heritage beef breeds, such as the Scottish Highland, can be grown for home use. Different species and breeds offer different carcass characteristics and also have different habitat adaptabilities. You should study which ones may suit your situation best.

Ring-necked pheasants are one type of wild game bird that can be used for meat dishes. Game birds are regulated compared to domestically raised fowl, which are not. You should check state rules and regulations before hunting.

The resurgence of interest in locally grown food, whether raised or purchased, can be beneficial to anyone having an interest in home butchering or processing meat cuts and sausages, because it opens up new opportunities for those with an interest in providing those services.

How to Use This Book

The purpose of this book is to provide accurate information on all aspects of butchering, from slaughtering to processing, and the preservation of the meat. Detailed step-by-step instructions—from securing an animal to deconstructing the carcass—will allow you to safely and humanely transform a carcass to a family meal. Both domestically raised animals and wild game are discussed. The principles of home curing and preserving the meat harvested are explained, so it can be used later at the dinner table. Different meat cuts are discussed in each section, and other products, such as sausages, receive attention too. The recipes are included as examples and represent only a fraction of what you can do with each animal.

It is difficult to envision our society reverting to a hunter-gatherer system, regardless of the publicity and support it receives in some circles. There simply is not enough land, space, or wild game populations available to sustain such a dynamic.

Yet butchering and processing your own meat does not need to be the sole province of rural landowners. Many urbanites interested in making their own meat products can do so with a little ingenuity, some resources, and a deliberate plan of action.

The food pyramid guides encourage a daily allowance of carbohydrates, proteins, and fats. These can be provided by cereals, fruits and vegetables, milk, fats, and meats for healthful living. This book is centered on one main food group: meat. It is a resource guide that will allow you to provide food for yourself, your family, or your potential customers.

Beef carcasses can reach and exceed seven feet in length after hanging and pork carcasses five feet. If you hang them for aging, they must not touch the floor or ground to avoid contamination.

Chapter 1

MUSCLES ARE MEAT

In the past, the internal organs of animals were a highly prized part of the carcass. Although many are still used today in a variety of food, pharmaceutical, and health care applications, their value has become secondary to that of the muscles. The decrease in selection choices has resulted from three major changes in our society, namely cultural conditioning, industrial urbanization, and the difficulty in domesticating some wild species and/or their supply.

Cultural conditioning resulted from a lack of variation in available food choices, particularly from wild game. What was familiar and more readily available became the norm of what was eaten, moving away from traditional foods. The movement of rural residents to urban centers during the industrialization period of this country resulted in having to purchase meat from a local market rather than procuring it from your own efforts in raising animals. Some wild species, such as bison, elk, and antelope, were difficult, if not impossible, to domesticate or procure, resulting in fewer being used for meat purposes.

This evolution of eating preferences or choices has not gone unnoticed. In 1997, the World Health Organization (WHO) issued a report that stated that affluent populations habitually consume a diet that was unknown to the human species a mere ten generations ago.

Today's Meat Animals

The animals we use in our diets are either herbivores, such as cattle and sheep, or more or less omnivores, such as pigs and chickens. The texture of the muscles and the fats found in the bodies of different species are largely reflective of their diet. Genetic factors are also involved. Grass-fed domestic animals are the only group that has a fat profile that is similar to wild herbivores. Supplements of grains or

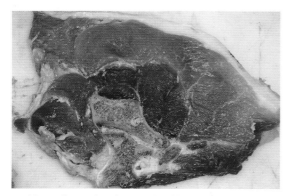

Marbling refers to the white specks of fat within a muscle and seam fat is the streaks that surround the muscle. Fat amounts may vary between animals of the same species due to diet and genetics. Large amounts of fat should be trimmed off the carcass but can be useful for rendering into lard or mixed with wild game to add texture and flavor to sausages.

compounded feeds that are fed to domestic animals will change this fat profile in their bodies to reflect the fats found in those plants. For example, pigs are often fed high grain and soybean diets to produce rapid growth. This produces fat profiles that are typically high in oleic acids and lower in palmitic acids. Because pigs are omnivores, their muscle fat reflects the kinds of fat they are fed. Cattle, however, are natural grass eaters if given the opportunity, and their body fat profile will reflect the influence of plant nutrients.

Consumers are becoming more aware of differences in fat composition, production, and their effects on human health. Grain-fed cattle, because of their high corn and soybean diets, have a higher omega-6 and lower omega-3 fat profile than their counterparts that are grass-fed. The latter typically have 7 percent of omega-3; wild animals can reach a level of about 4 percent. However, saturated fats have a purpose. They aid in meats retaining their quality because they are less subject to oxidation. Highly unsaturated fats are soft and oily and may lower the quality of pork and poultry carcasses because they are more readily oxidized and may reduce shelf life. Oxidation produces off-flavors.

A result of these differences can be seen in the appearance of the cuts. Those from a high fat diet, such as corn and soybeans, will typically have more fat in the body of the carcass as well as in the muscling, commonly referred to as marbling. The white streaks interlaced in different cuts will change the texture of the muscle.

Grass-fed beef has a higher antioxidant capacity than feedlot beef. This means grass-fed meat cuts retain their red color longer without artificial manipulation.

What does this mean for you? If you are purchasing an animal to butcher yourself, it

 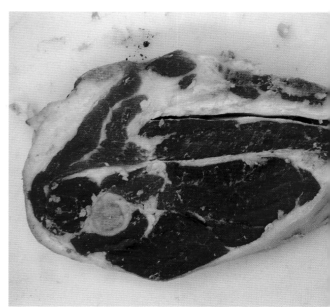

Above left: Oxidation, coupled with surface drying (dehydration of the proteins), causes a change in meat color because of the interaction between oxygen and myoglobin. Myoglobin is a meat color pigment that gives the meat its red color. When it binds with oxygen molecules, the color deepens. The longer muscles are exposed to air during the aging process, the more likely a change in surface color. You can cover exposed muscle with plastic wrapping to minimize its effects, or you can slice off affected portions. **Above right:** Well-grown lambs have a good layer of fat covering many of their prime cuts and in areas between the muscles. Most of the portions of fat around the exterior part of the cuts should be trimmed.

may provide further information to make a more informed choice and alert you to what you may encounter in cutting up a carcass.

Muscle Structure and Function

In its basic sense, the term *muscle* refers to numerous bundles of cells and fibers that can be contracted and expanded to produce bodily movements. There are three major types: skeletal, cardiac, and smooth muscles. Skeletal muscles are linked to bone by the bundles of collagen fibers known as tendons.

Skeletal muscles have several components known as muscle fibers that bundle together in various configurations to give them a striated appearance. These fibers form the basic mechanism that controls muscle contraction.

In meat, skeletal muscles are the most important of the three types because of quantity and economic value. These muscles support the body and initiate movement. Smooth muscles are commonly found in organs or the tubular system, such as the digestive tract, reproductive organs, circulatory system, and urinary tract. The cardiac muscle is found in the heart.

Skeletal muscles are the only voluntary muscles in the body, meaning they are actively controlled by the animal's intentions. Smooth and cardiac muscles are involuntary, meaning their movements are controlled by their own imprinted genetic nature rather than intentional.

A dense connective tissue sheath called the epimysium covers the skeletal muscles.

Feedlot cattle are raised in close confinement to utilize labor and facilities to the maximum advantage. The animal's diet is formulated to provide rapid growth in the minimum amount of time to reach target market weights.

Some producers raise animals on pasture. They may or may not include supplemental grain to their diets with the grasses. It generally takes more time to raise animals to market weight if exclusively raised on grass, but this will have some effect on their fat profile when compared to grain-fed animals.

Each of these muscles is divided into sections, called bundles, by a thick connective tissue layer called the perimysium. Clusters of fat cells, small blood vessels, and nerve bundles are found in this layer. The fat cells appear white (called marbling). These fat deposits give the muscle flavor and moisture when cooked.

The purpose and reflex action of different muscle groups attached in different areas of the skeletal system ultimately determines their texture as well as their economic value. Knowing their location and value will give you a better understanding of why some meat cuts are easier to cook or have more flavor than others.

Not all the muscles are the same. This means that their basic makeup—the muscle fibers—is different too. Some muscles contract rapidly while others contract more slowly. Typically, the muscles closest to the bones have higher proportions of red or slow fibers, giving them a darker red appearance, such as seen in the cut face of a fresh ham.

Within the muscle cells are pigment proteins. The differences in these proteins are responsible for variations in color between beef and pork, where beef is darker, or between a chicken leg and chicken breast.

Older animals typically yield meat cuts that tend to be less tender and will not be cut or chewed easily as younger animals. It is referred to as being "tough." One major factor affecting this condition is collagen, the single most abundant protein found in mammals. It is present in all tissues, with the highest concentrations in bone, skin, tendons, cartilage, and muscle.

Collagen primarily functions to provide strength and support to muscles and acts in the case of skin as a barrier to keep foreign materials out. Collagen also changes with age, leading to less tender cuts in older animals. Muscles whose primary purpose is to support structures, such as front and rear legs, typically have high connective tissue contents, while the loin and back areas have less, making these cuts the more desirable and higher in economic value. The best way to break down collagen is with moist-heat cooking methods.

There is also yellow-colored connective tissue that is found in carcasses called

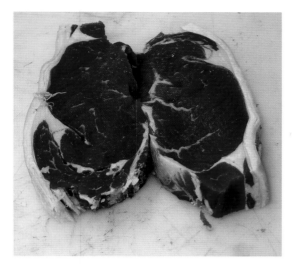

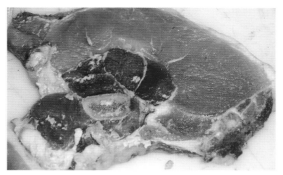

The amount and type of meat pigments in proteins differ between species. Beef, having more meat color pigment, is darker in color than meat from pigs. Both are darker in color than meat from chickens, ducks, and other fowl. Different muscles within the same cut can also have different amounts of pigment, resulting in color variation.

backstrap. This is a large collective strip of elastin, which is also found in arterial walls and gives elasticity to those tissues. Strips of elastin or backstrap cannot be broken apart or altered in form with moist-heat cooking and is usually discarded. Muscle tissue contains only very small amounts of elastin, making it highly consumable.

Converting Muscle to Meat

Changes happen within the muscles of an animal after it is slaughtered or harvested. Some life processes stop almost immediately. Other life processes gradually cease over a slightly longer, but finite, time period.

Although other dramatic changes occur initially, such as the loss of brain activity, heart action, lung function, blood transport, digestive action, and mobility, the changes occurring within the muscles can ultimately affect the eating quality of the meat.

Initially, when an animal is killed or dies in other circumstances, the muscle pH gradually drops. This results because the animal's glycogen reserves within the muscle are depleted and they are converted to lactic acid.

Oxygen is no longer available to the muscle cells after the animal is bled, causing a lactic acid buildup and a subsequent drop in pH.

With the loss of certain muscle reserves such as creatine phosphates, which help in muscle movements, the muscle filaments can no longer slide over one another and the muscle becomes still and rigid, resulting in a condition known as rigor mortis.

Several factors influence the amount of time for the muscle to reach its final pH level. These include the species, cooling rate, and the extent of the animal's struggle at the time of death. Beef and lamb muscles take longer to reach their final pH than those of a pig. Cooling affects the time because metabolism is slowed when the carcass is subjected to lower temperatures. Finally, the animals' activity level immediately prior to the killing will affect the pH; less activity will prolong the period of pH decline.

During the period after the slaughter or harvest, changes also occur in the muscle proteins as they begin to break down. This generally occurs during the cool storage period and is referred to as "aging" and results in increased meat tenderness. This process of protein fracturing will continue for one to two weeks, after which there is little appreciable increase in tenderness.

Meat Quality Challenges

For generations, people butchering animals have known the importance of harvesting healthy animals that have not been made excitable or stressed immediately prior to slaughter. If an animal undergoes vigorous stress or exercise before harvest, the glycogen content within the muscles may drop dramatically. This can result in a higher pH remaining in the muscles, causing the meat to become dark, firm, and dry—effectively reducing the tenderness and quality.

High pH meat typically is dark in color, believed to be the result of a greater water-holding capacity, which causes muscle fibers to swell. The meat from such animals generally has a reduced shelf life because a higher pH is more likely to accommodate bacterial growth.

A second quality problem can result because of the rate of pH decline. If the muscle pH drops too rapidly after killing, due to the muscle temperature being too high, it can become pale and soft. This results in a soft, mushy texture, a pale color, and the muscle lacking the ability to hold moisture. This condition typically results from high stress situations but also, in the case of some pigs, can be a hereditary stress condition resulting from porcine stress syndrome (PSS). The muscle temperature can be affected by animal excitement initiating a "fright or flight" response, further stimulating nervousness and sweating.

While there are meat quality issues associated with harvest and post-harvest handling of carcasses, quality and food safety issues can affect animals at pre-harvest. These include animal health, pregnancy, injury and bruising, and genetic influences. Anyone performing a harvest for home use or for sale should be aware of these factors. Recognizing unhealthy or unthrifty animals can help avoid subsequent meat quality problems. Common ailments can affect the quality, value, and wholesomeness of a carcass. If you are unsure about the health of an animal to be harvested for your own use, ask someone who is knowledgeable or consult a veterinarian.

Animals that have received therapeutic protocols, such as injections of antibiotics or

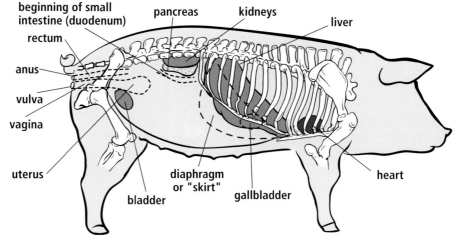

Studing the pig's anatomy before slaughter and butchering will help you understand the internal organ placement within the body cavity. This will be useful, particularly when butchering a pig for the first time.

beginning of small intestine (duodenum)
rectum
anus
vulva
vagina
uterus
bladder
pancreas
kidneys
liver
diaphragm or "skirt"
gallbladder
heart

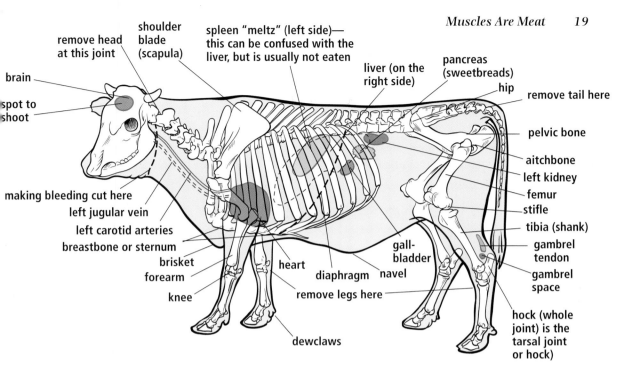

brain

spot to shoot

remove head at this joint

shoulder blade (scapula)

spleen "meltz" (left side)— this can be confused with the liver, but is usually not eaten

liver (on the right side)

pancreas (sweetbreads)

hip

remove tail here

pelvic bone

aitchbone

left kidney

femur

stifle

tibia (shank)

making bleeding cut here

left jugular vein

left carotid arteries

breastbone or sternum

brisket

forearm

knee

heart

diaphragm

navel

remove legs here

dewclaws

gall-bladder

gambrel tendon

gambrel space

hock (whole joint) is the tarsal joint or hock)

A beef animal has a much larger body structure than a pig, lamb, or most wild game animals. This drawing identifies areas for helping handle the carcass after it has been put down and the location of the internal organs in relation to the skeletal structure.

hormones, are required to be withheld from the human food chain for a specific period of time, depending on what is administered. It is extremely important to understand and abide by any withdrawal times associated with antibiotic use, and it is illegal to send any animal to market prior to the expiration of the specified withdrawal period.

Avoid harvesting a pregnant animal, particularly one in the last trimester. This period is characterized by an increase in the hormonal level, including oxytocin and estrogen. These may affect the entire animal and not simply specific parts. Also, the body temperature of a pregnant female may elevate slightly during this period prior to or after parturition. However, once her body temperature returns to normal and stabilizes at about 101 degrees Fahrenheit, in the case of a beef cow, you can proceed with a harvest. Similar conditions

are found in other species, so you will need to apply the same logic to whatever female animal you will be using for meat.

Animals that are healthy but have been injured because of an accident, such as a broken leg or pelvis, may be used for harvest but preferably as soon as possible. An injured animal easily becomes nervous or agitated, especially if it cannot move about as it was generally accustomed to doing. Pain from an injury may also influence its behavior. Although pain may influence the animal's movements or lack of them, it does not influence the quality of the meat by itself; it becomes a secondary contributor to meat quality. If an animal dies due to some non-viral condition such as bloat, where the gas formed in the digestive system has no way to escape and slowly builds pressure against the lungs to the point where they cease to function, or from a heart puncture, they can be used for meat, providing a knowledgeable person is present to immediately cut the throat and bleed the animal. Under no circumstances should a dead or diseased animal be used for human food.

Bruising is another condition that can affect meat quality. Bruises result from the hemorrhaging of blood vessels under the hide of the animal. You should not use any bruised meat for food. Most bruises occur during the loading and unloading of animals to transport them to the point of harvest. In cattle, the major sites for potential bruising are in the loin and sirloin area, ribs, and shoulders. In swine, the highest percentage of bruising occurs in the ham, shoulders, and loin. Sheep experience the highest percentage of bruising in the legs and loin due to grabbing them by the wool or catching them by the hind leg.

Factors Affecting Meat Safety

Other factors that can affect meat quality include toxins, bacteria, viruses, and temperature, time, and moisture. For many years, it was thought that the muscle of an animal was sterile if it had not been injured, cut into, or bruised. In recent years, however, researchers have found viable bacteria within muscle tissue. This means that when you harvest an animal, whether domestic or wild, extreme care must be taken to prevent the introduction of foreign bodies into the carcass through your actions. This care begins with the knives you use to sever the jugular vein at the beginning of the slaughtering process and continues until the cuts have been packaged, sealed, and stored—or the meat is immediately cooked for use. Sanitation is extremely important and is discussed in greater detail elsewhere in this book.

Preventing and retarding the development of harmful microorganisms should be your primary objective in harvesting your animal or in home processing any meat products. Consuming microorganisms that have grown and propagated in meat can cause illness or even death. This concern should not be taken lightly. When health problems arise related to eating meat, it is generally a result of intoxication or infection. Intoxication occurs when the microbe produces a toxin that is subsequently eaten by a human and sickness results. Infection occurs when an organism is eaten by a human, then grows and disrupts the normal functions of the body, such as salmonella and listeria.

There are several types of toxins, including exotoxins and endotoxins. Exotoxins are located outside the bacterial cell and are composed of proteins that can be destroyed by heat through cooking. Exotoxins are among the most poisonous substances known to humans. These include *Clostridium botulinum*, which causes tetanus and botulism poisoning.

Endotoxins attach to the outer membranes of cells but are not released unless the cell is disrupted. These are complex fat and carbohydrate molecules, such as *Staphylococcus aureus*, that are not destroyed by heat.

Bacteria are the most common and important microorganisms that can grow on meat. Not all bacteria are bad, however, as the human body may carry as many as 150 different kinds of bacteria on it.

Molds and yeasts are fungi that can affect meat quality, although their effect is far less significant or life threatening than toxins or bacteria. Molds typically cause spoilage in grains, cereals, flour, and nuts that have low moisture content and in fruits that have a low pH. Yeasts are generally involved where a food product contains high amounts of sugar. Yeasts that affect meat are generally not a problem because of the low sugar or carbohydrate content of muscle.

Viruses, while having the potential to cause food diseases, generally only affect raw or uncooked shellfish. Viruses are inert and unable to multiply outside a host cell.

There are a few parasites that you should be aware of that may cause problems in meat. A parasite infection will occur in the live animal before it occurs in a human. There are three parasites that are of major concern to humans: *Trichinella spiralis*, *Toxoplasma gondii*, and *Anisakis marina*. Trichinosis has long been identified as a parasite that can live in swine muscle and be transferred to humans through raw or uncooked pork. Toxoplasma is a small protozoan that occurs throughout the world and has been observed in a wide range of birds and mammals. Anisakis is a roundworm parasite found only in fish. Using and maintaining adequate or recommended cooking temperatures and time will destroy parasites.

Temperature and Time Effects on Meat Safety

Mismanagement of temperature is one of the most common reasons for outbreaks of food-borne diseases. This is closely followed by the time factor at a critical temperature where the correct temperature is either used too late or for too short a period.

Meat can generally be kept safe from harmful bacteria if stored under 40 degrees Fahrenheit. Cooking prevents most microorganisms from growing but does not kill them, although some parasites can be killed if kept in a frozen state for various lengths of time. However, most microorganisms are merely dormant and can revive when thawed. If meat is thawed from a frozen state, it should be used as soon as possible and not refrozen.

To kill microorganisms with heat, you must maintain a recommended temperature for a minimum period of time. You will damage or kill microorganisms more effectively by reaching a given temperature and holding it for a period of time rather than reaching a higher temperature but for a shorter period.

Meat can be kept safe when it is hot or cold, but not in between. If meat is being cooked, it should pass between the temperatures of 40 to 140 degrees Fahrenheit in four hours or less. If it is being cooled, it should pass from 140 to 40 degrees Fahrenheit within the same amount of time.

Most, but not all, microorganisms are killed at 140 degrees Fahrenheit. While the outside of a piece of meat may have become contaminated during your processing, the interior can be considered sterile, or nearly so, unless it has been cut into. When a piece of meat is cooked by conventional methods, except for by using a microwave oven, the outside cooks first and reaches a higher end temperature than the inside. Recent recommendations state that meat should be cooked to 160 degrees Fahrenheit because some microorganisms can still survive a 140-degree temperature. Poultry meat is more alkaline and should be cooked to 180 degrees Fahrenheit, and if red meat is to be reheated, it should reach 165 degrees for optimum safety. If you are grinding meat, be aware that it can become contaminated more easily than whole cuts because more of the meat particle surface areas are exposed and more processing and handling steps are involved.

Moisture in meat is essential for palatability but is also a medium for microbial growth.

Microbes Affecting Meat Quality

Microbe	Typical Cause	Effect	Control
Salmonella	Grows best in nonacid foods, transferred from farm animals and animal products to humans.	Insulation from 3 to 36 hours. Digestive upsets. Symptoms may last 1 to 7 days.	Killed by pasteurization. Avoid cross contamination from raw meat to cooked food or food eaten raw.
Escherichia coli (**E. coli**)	Improper harvest methods, unsanitary handling of meat, improper cooking, fecal contamination.	Severe abdominal illness; watery, bloody diarrhea; vomiting. Can affect kidney function and central nervous system.	Destroyed by internal temperatures of 160°F.
C. *jejuni*	Typically found in raw chicken because of high body temperature and pH.	Diarrhea, abdominal cramps, nausea symptoms last 2 to 3 days.	Avoid cross contamination between raw and cooked meat. Use good hygiene. Destroyed by pasteurization.
Listeria	Grows in damp areas, sewage, sludge; can survive freezing.	Most vulnerable are infants, chronically ill, elderly, and pregnant women. Can cause meningitis, encephalitis, or abscession.	Avoid raw milk products in meat recipes. Use good sanitation while processing meat. Avoid cross contamination of raw and cooked foods. Avoid postcooking contamination.

The level of moisture in fresh meat is high enough to provide spoilage organisms with an ideal environment to grow if unchecked. Research indicates that moisture levels in meat of at least 18 percent allows molds to grow. Drying meat through a smoking process typically eliminates moisture concerns.

Oxygen is needed for any living animal to survive but is not a welcome agent when processing meat. Oxygen is needed for aerobic microbes to grow. These include yeasts, molds, and many bacteria. Those that cannot grow when oxygen is present are called anaerobic. This group of microbes can be deadly because they include clostridium, which produces a toxin, and a group called putrifiers, which degrade proteins and produce foul-smelling gases. Preventing the growth of anaerobic microbes is essential if part of your food preservation plans includes canning.

Soon after an animal is harvested, the muscle undergoes a gradual change in pH, declining from about 7.0 to 5.5. This decline results from a loss of glycogen held within the muscle and its conversion to lactic acid. The degree of acidity or alkalinity (pH) will influence the growth of microorganisms. Most will thrive at a point that is nearly neutral—a pH of 7.0—than at any other level above or below. Although meat pH ranges from about 4.8 to 6.8, microorganisms generally grow slower at a pH of 5.0 or below. This acidity level helps preserve many sausages and acts as a flavor enhancer. Acidity levels are not a concern unless there is a long delay in processing the carcass at room temperatures.

A whole carcass has the minimum amount of exposed surface area. As large cuts are made, more area is exposed. When it is cut into smaller pieces, still more area is exposed. Finally, if the meat is ground, it exposes the most area for possible contamination. Simply put, the more meat is processed, the more it may be exposed to microorganisms. Using clean, sanitary equipment and clean table surfaces and keeping work area temperatures low while working as quickly as possible will help reduce microbial activity.

Increased Awareness for Food Safety

Understanding the factors affecting meat quality is not intended to discourage those who want to process their own meat. Rather, it is meant to increase your awareness to the potential for problems resulting from mishandling or inadequately processing your food products.

Humans have been safely processing meat for their families for generations because they understood the basic principles to preserve meat products properly. You can also learn these principles by studying and understanding where problems could occur and take the necessary precautions and steps to avoid them.

The Meat We Eat

A common vocabulary relating to the different cuts of meat is helpful to avoid confusion whether you are purchasing the cuts from market, offering cuts for sale, providing a butchering and cutting service for your customers, or simply eating at a restaurant that lists various cuts on their menu. Having this commonality of language greatly reduces mistakes and specifically identifies the exact location the cuts are derived from on the body of the animal.

A standardized system of naming wholesale or primal cuts for each species has been developed by the meat industry in the United States. This standardization provides for uniform sale and purchase of meat products as well as clarifies the terminology relating to them. Meat labeling practices adhere to these standards as a way to avoid misunderstanding and misrepresentation and to allow for the fair trade of meat cuts.

Wholesale Cuts

Wholesale cuts are large subdivisions of the carcass that are traded in volume. Wholesale cuts are sometimes referred to as primal cuts because they are the first large portion of the carcass to be fabricated. *Fabrication* is the industry term for cutting the whole carcass

Bone shapes in meat cuts can help identify where they are derived from in the carcass. The following drawings illustrate the bone structures for the seven retail meat cuts: arm, blade, rib, short loin, sirloin, leg or round, and breast or brisket. The shapes will be similar regardless of species.

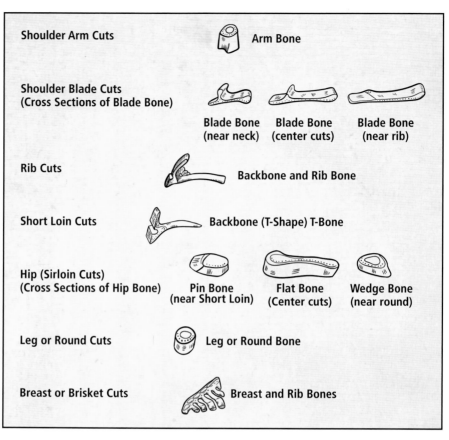

Shoulder Arm Cuts — Arm Bone

Shoulder Blade Cuts (Cross Sections of Blade Bone) — Blade Bone (near neck) | Blade Bone (center cuts) | Blade Bone (near rib)

Rib Cuts — Backbone and Rib Bone

Short Loin Cuts — Backbone (T-Shape) T-Bone

Hip (Sirloin Cuts) (Cross Sections of Hip Bone) — Pin Bone (near Short Loin) | Flat Bone (Center cuts) | Wedge Bone (near round)

Leg or Round Cuts — Leg or Round Bone

Breast or Brisket Cuts — Breast and Rib Bones

into smaller, more manageable, and precise pieces. This breaking down of large portions into smaller ones allows for the sale of the more valuable cuts separate from the rest of the carcass. The fabrication process transforms a heavy, unwieldy, oddly shaped carcass into pieces that can be packaged and neatly stacked in freezers. These terms typically are used referring to domestic animals that are slaughtered but can be used interchangeably with wild game of the same general species. For instance, terms used for beef cattle, pigs, sheep, and poultry can also be applied to bison, rabbits, pheasants, and others.

Wholesale or primal cuts separate the carcass into three general divisions: the legs that make up the large muscles used for locomotion; the back and loin, which are composed of large support muscle systems; and the thinner body walls.

From these sections, the subprimal cuts or subdivisions are made. These can be further broken down into smaller pieces called retail cuts. They are often sold to consumers in a form that is ready to cook or eat.

Seven Retail Cuts

If part of the bone is included in the cut, it is called a bone-in cut and can be classified into one of seven types based on the muscle or bone shape and the size relative to it. These seven primary retail cuts include the loin, rib, leg, arm, hip, blade, and belly or plate. Familiarizing yourself with them and understanding their location on the animal or carcass will help you do a better job of cutting up the carcass.

Loin and rib: Two of the seven retail cuts, the loin and rib, have an eye muscle that makes up part of the back's muscle structure. The loin lies in a length-wise direction on both sides of the spinal column and is a major muscle component. Although it has use in support and movement, its location makes it less used than other major muscle groups. Less use translates into a more tender muscle texture.

The ribs are designed for the protection of the internal organs and to provide sufficient room to allow them to expand and contract as the animal eats or fasts. Ribs are connected by small amounts of muscle and connective tissue. However, their large percentage of bone to meat makes ribs less valuable as cuts but very useful for specific, lower-value cuts and soup stock.

Legs and arm: The legs and arm cuts have a similar cross-section because of the round bones involved. However, there is a difference in the leg muscle configuration at the top, bottom, eye, and sirloin tip when compared to the arm cuts. Arm cuts are located in the front legs and contain more small muscles arranged in a different pattern.

Hip and blade: The hip and blade are two different cuts that have flat or irregularly shaped bones. The cuts from the hip are composed of a small number of fairly large, parallel muscles, while the blade cuts have numerous small, nonparallel muscles, much like those found in the foreleg.

Belly or plate: The seventh type of cut is the belly or plate. This is easily recognized by the alternating layers of fat, lean, and rib bones that make up the body wall and complete the enclosure of the internal organs. The meat taken from belly or plate cuts includes bacon, spare ribs, and beef brisket.

Bones: From a butchering standpoint, bones have little market value. Bones from home processing are often discarded or may be used as pet treats. However, from a culinary point of view, they can make remarkable soup stocks. The center part of the larger round bones is hollow and filled with the marrow. Bone marrow can have two different characteristics: either red or yellow. Yellow bone marrow is mostly fat, while red bone marrow is partly a fat but is interlaced with a network of blood vessels, connective tissue, and blood-forming cells. The proteins found in these cells can add to the nutritional value of sauces, soups, and other dishes.

Color identification and size: The color of the meat can be used for identification of species from which the cuts are derived. Beef cuts are typically large and have a cherry red color and a white, firm fat. Pork cuts are more intermediate in size and tend to have a grayish pink color. Their fat is also the softest, which makes it adaptable in making sausage and wild game cooking to prevent dryness. It is easy to understand why lamb cuts are small; they come from a much smaller animal than beef or pigs. In general, the larger the animal, the larger the cuts will be. The size of the cuts will decrease in relation to the decreasing size of the animal being butchered. Although there are cuts available in squirrels, rabbits, and other small domestic or game animals, there will only be very small pieces that can be used.

Left: Four different knives can accomplish most all tasks involved in slaughtering and fabrication of animals for home harvest. These include, from top to bottom, a 6-inch curved (flexible) knife, a 6-inch straight (stiff) knife, an 8-inch breaking (steak) knife, and a 10-inch breaking knife. Right: A skinning knife is slightly more curved than other knives and has a wider blade. It is used in making short, sweeping motions to separate the skin/hide from the carcass. A hook is used to pull the hide away from the carcass as it is being skinned to minimize contamination by foreign materials and dirty hands.

Meat saws are used to cut through bones or other areas of the carcass that may be less accessible for knife use. Most meat saws range from 12 to 25 inches in blade length.

Chapter 2

KNIVES AND OTHER EQUIPMENT

——◆——

You will achieve a more satisfactory result in your butchering process if you use equipment and knives that are sturdy, sharp, and appropriate for the task applied. The use of proper equipment and knives as well as the safety issues surrounding butchering need to be taken seriously. Injuries resulting from mishandling animals, using inappropriate equipment for the task, and not properly handling knives can be avoided by studying and understanding the importance of each.

Safety First

Personal safety for you and anyone working with you is of prime importance when handling live animals, slaughtering them, and cutting up the carcasses. Being injured by live animals can have devastating consequences. Similarly, you can be injured by unstable or inappropriate butchering equipment, whether it is being used for slaughter or for food processing. Knife injuries can occur quickly and unexpectedly and, in severe cases, may be life threatening. Common sense, caution, and alertness to potential dangers will help avoid serious injury.

The most simple knife rules include the following:

- Always use a sharp knife when cutting meat.
- Never hide the knife under your arm or under a piece of meat.
- Keep knives visible.
- Always keep the knife point down.
- Always cut down toward the cutting surface and away from you.

A large animal carcass, such as beef, has considerable weight, and the equipment you use to suspend it while working on it needs to be stable and strong enough so that it won't tip, buckle, or break while in use. Even smaller carcasses, such as deer and pigs, can have weights that challenge the equipment you might have.

Any carcass that falls to the floor or onto the ground, whether large or small, will be difficult to lift if no alternative method is available. Having to lift again a carcass that has fallen from its holding can cause delays in processing the meat, which can lead to spoilage. Also, there is potential damage from bruising of the muscles by the collapse or possible contamination of the carcass by dirt, manure, or any foreign substances it comes in contact with.

Knives will be needed from the start of the butchering process until your last cut is made. The number or style of knives you use may depend on the species or size of the carcass you are working with as well as what you deem necessary to complete the work safely and satisfactorily. This may range from a small hand knife to a large, sturdy butchering knife and a variety in between.

Different knives are available to make certain cuts easier and more precise while other, larger knives have many advantages for cutting up larger pieces of the carcass. One simple rule is that sharp knives always work best. However, they also carry safety concerns when using them.

Choosing Knives and Saws

An assortment of knives and saws used specifically for meat processing is available for home slaughtering and butchering. You can buy most, if not all, of the equipment used in commercial or local slaughterhouses. Purchase what you need at hardware stores, through companies on the Internet, or at stores specializing in such equipment.

When butchering, have a minimum of three types of knives available: one for sticking or cutting the throat, one for skinning, and one for eviscerating. The same holds true for cutting up the carcass and muscles. You should have a knife for larger cuts, one for boning or trimming, and one for breaking or cutting bones. You may also add to this list a saw specifically designed for use on meat.

You can purchase several knives for general use or even use knives you already have, depending on their size, condition, and intended purpose. For small animals, you may not need or want large knives or saws. You will need to use large knives and saws for big carcasses. You may want to have a separate knife for each task or you may consolidate these tasks by using only two or three different knives.

Gather together all the knives you will need before you begin butchering. Once you begin the process, you will need to work quickly and efficiently to get the animal from a live state to the freezer. Stopping to find a specific knife that is not on hand will delay this process. Take an inventory of the knives on hand and identify where they can be used during the butchering process.

Knives are typically available with wooden or plastic handles, have flexible or stiff blades, and come in many sizes and shapes. Some meat processors prefer wooden-handle knives, but these should not be cleaned in a dishwasher. Others prefer dishwasher-proof plastic handles. One disadvantage to these is that they can become slippery unless dried prior to use. This problem can be mitigated by using knives with handles that have a gritty finish, which allows increased safety when they become wet greasy.

Buy knives that are affordable, sharp, easy to maintain, and completely sanitary. Knives that are not sharp pose a safety hazard by not allowing you to complete the task at hand efficiently; they can slip, and more effort is required to pass the knife through the muscle or bone. If your knives are not easy to clean and kept sanitary, they may harbor harmful microorganisms that can affect the quality of the meat and possibly your health.

Identify the purposes of each knife before you begin butchering. Many knives can be

Fillet knives are long and flexible with thin blades. They are useful when trimming around bones. They are a preferred knife when skinning and cutting up fish. Fillet knives also can be used on small game animals.

interchangeable with different tasks. Always use the right size knife for the right task.

For slaughtering, a sticking knife is used for cutting an animal's throat and severing the jugular veins to obtain a good bleed before butchering the carcass. A sticking knife is generally long, thin, and has a double edge.

A boning knife has a long, straight edge for trimming and separating muscles from themselves and from the bones they are attached to. The tip of a boning knife may be ridged or flexible, allowing it to easily move around the bones. They usually range from 5 to 7 inches in length.

A trimming knife is a smaller, shorter version of a boning knife. It is useful for cleaning fat and tendon from small cuts and cleaning up steaks, chicken breasts, or cutting away small pieces of muscle in places that are difficult to reach.

A breaking knife is used to break down larger primal cuts into smaller pieces. It is essentially a longer version of a boning knife and is thin and curves gently up to a sharp point. A breaking knife is very useful for piercing and slicing and can be used to make primal and subprimal cuts on beef and deer.

Butcher knives are long and inflexible and are designed to allow piercing as well as cutting in a smooth linear direction. They may have either a tapered or rounded tip.

A skinning knife is generally short with a dramatic curve to the blade, and it has a bulbous tip to help the blade slide easily between meat and skin without damaging either when butchering. Those used for beef are slightly more curved than the ones used for lamb or other small animals.

Cleavers are the heaviest of all butcher knives. They have a thick square blade designed to crack and split bone.

Fillet knives are long, thin, and flexible. A good fillet knife bends easily to let you cut very thin slices of fish and meat with exact precision.

Meat saws are used to cut through bones or to sever portions of large carcasses into smaller, more manageable pieces. Most meat saws are between 12 to 25 inches in length with a serrated blade. Blades should be complete, and those that have developed rust spots or have chipped or missing teeth should not be used. Any meat saw should be thoroughly washed and sanitized before use, paying particular attention to the area where the handle attaches to the metal frame.

Folding Knives

Folding knives, as their name indicates, are those that have blades with joints that allow them to fold over, securing the edge in a protective cover—the handle. Jack knives, Swiss Army knives, and camping knives are some of the different folding knives available. They can have single or multiple blades.

Folding knives are often used during hunting because they have multiple uses,

are easy and safe to carry, and are sturdy enough to accomplish quick, precise cuts. Like larger knives, they also require special care. You should keep the blades sharp and the knife clean.

Folding knives will have a locking device that keeps the blade from opening on its own. They also have a pivot that is the rotation point that allows the blade to fold into the handle. Both the locking mechanism and the pivot need to be kept clean and free of debris to prevent contamination of the meat. Use a drop of light oil at the joint, or each joint in the case of multiple blades, to create a smooth blade action while opening and closing it. As with other knives used for butchering, your folding knives should be cleaned before and after each use.

Many folding knives come with leather pouches or sheaths. When not in use, you should store the knife and leather sheath separately because leather will absorb moisture and can rust the blades. Also, there are tanning salts and acids in leather that can rust or tarnish the steel. You can protect the leather sheaths and keep them limber by using a leather preservative or mink oil.

Electric Knives

Electric knives can be used in place of standard knives. If using an electric knife, be sure it has the appropriate blade attached for the task at hand. Electric knives may be easier to use to carve or fillet different cuts of meat, particularly if handling heavy portions is a concern. Electric knives and blades will need care and maintenance like other electric equipment and should be kept away from water sources.

Blade Considerations

Regardless of the different kinds of knives you use, you will want ones that have

Hunting knives include general-purpose types, such as a folding drop-point (top left) and a folding clip-point (at bottom). The tip of a clip-point is more acute and curves up higher than that of a drop-point. Special-purpose types include a folding bird knife (top right), with a hook for field-dressing birds. *Creative Publishing international*

A folding combination knife (top) with a blunt-tip blade used for slitting abdomens without puncturing intestines, a clip-point blade, and a saw for cutting through breastbones and pelvic bones of big game is another special-purpose knife. A big-game skinning knife (bottom) whose blade has a blunt tip to avoid punching holes in the hide is also useful in the field. *Creative Publishing international*

high-carbon steel blades; usually most reliable ones are at about 0.5 percent carbon. If the blade is made of too little carbon, it will be soft and the edge of the knife may bend over. If it is too high in carbon, it will generally be too hard and will be more difficult to sharpen.

Many knives sold through commercial outlets today are made to hold their edge or their sharpness for long periods of time and

A quick steeling of your knife with a steel sharpener will keep the blade edge perfectly straight and in top condition for cutting. During a butchering session steel your knife frequently. Hold the base of the blade against the steel at the angle at which it was originally sharpened. Draw the knife toward you in an arc from base to tip. Repeat on other side. Alternate sides until the blade is sharp.

use. Older knives may not have those characteristics but may be very usable if correctly sharpened. Even high quality knives will dull after a period of use and need sharpening. You may have them sharpened by someone specializing in blades or you may sharpen them yourself.

Sharpening Knives

There are three basic steps in sharpening knives: grinding, honing, and steeling. Each is a different technique, although they may seem the same to most beginners, and each can be used depending on the condition of the knife.

Grinding

Grinding gives the blade the thinness and will remove part of the blade. Because of this, you will need to be cautious with any grinding so that you do not lose more of the blade than intended. Some knives need to be ground before they can be honed or sharpened. Purchased knives will come with a properly beveled blade.

Keeping a round steel close at hand during the slaughter and fabrication will allow you to maintain the edge on your knife for easier cutting. It can be suspended from your waist by a chain.

Safety First: Steps for Grinding a Knife Blade
- Wet the grind wheel with oil.
- Hold the knife in one hand with blade at a 20-degree angle to the wheel; turn the wheel with the other hand, or pedal with feet; draw the knife slowly across the moving wheel.
- Avoid grinding the blade farther back than the ¼-inch bevel.

Sharpening your knife before each use will make cutting up a carcass much easier. A sharpening and honing stone can be part of one unit, and the process for each can be changed by turning the stone over.

too much heat from the friction of the wheel, causing it to burn the temper on the blade. However, if sharpened slowly in steps, you can avoid most problems with heat generated from wheels.

The purpose of the grinding process is to make one side of the blade meet the other side while pushing up a small curl of metal called a burr. If you stop grinding before the burr is formed, your knife will not be as sharp as it could be. If you grind too much, you lose any burr. As you are grinding, always check both sides of the blade all along its length. The burr tends to form quickly at the base of the blade but takes a little longer at the tip. To have fully ground one side, you must feel a burr running all the way from the heel of the blade near the handle to the tip.

Honing

Honing sharpens the beveled edge. You will need a stone with a finer surface than a grinding stone. In honing, the stone remains stationary. It is important to keep the honing stone from moving while applying the blade pressure. Putting it in a wood base or attaching the stone to a table with clamps will help.

Grinding produces a beveled or angled edge on the blade. In most cases, grinding is not used for sharpening, only for creating a proper angle that can then be honed to sharpen it. One of the easiest ways to grind an edge is to use a round stone that spins to grind the blade. These can be hand-turned, foot-pedaled, or electric-driven while the knife is held stationary against the stone.

Some professional knife sharpeners advise against using a power-driven grinding wheel because of the potential of creating

Steps to Hone a Knife Blade

- Wet the stone with oil or water and place securely on a flat surface.
- Hold the knife handle. Place the end of the knife blade nearest the handle near the edge of the stone closest to you.
- Tilt the blade so the bevel lies flat on the surface, making a 20-degree angle.
- Place your fingertips on the flat side of the blade near the back, unsharpened edge.
- Use your fingertips to apply the pressure on the blade.
- With a sweeping motion, draw the knife across the stone in one direction, then turn it and draw it in the opposite direction.

Steeling

After honing, you will need to steel the blade. Steeling makes the edge perfectly straight by removing any burrs so that they do not roll over on themselves, which can cause tearing of meat when cutting. A steel will realign the edge of the knife, forcing any rolled over spots back into line and making it useable again.

Knife steels come in a variety of sizes and shapes including round steels, oval steels, grooved steels, and several others not typically used in homes. A coarse steel texture will create more tiny points of contact with the edge of the blade, causing a more aggressive abrasion. You will need to be careful in not applying too much pressure so that an uneven surface is created.

A round steel is generally 10 to 12 inches long and can be held in one hand or placed in a vertical position with the handle up and the tip resting on a folded towel to keep it from slipping. By using this position, you will be able to place the knife edge against the steel with the blade held perpendicular at a 90-degree angle. Rotate your wrist to reduce the angle by half—45 degrees—and then rotate it again by half to about 22.5 degrees and then slightly more to a desired point at approximately 20 degrees. In general, you want to steel at a slightly steeper angle than the edge bevel of the knife.

The best result of your steeling action occurs when you lock your wrist and stroke the knife from heel to tip by moving your shoulder and slowly dropping your forearm. By locking your wrist and elbow, you will keep a stable angle from top to bottom. This is the key to maintaining a consistent angle all the way through the stroke. Standard steels do not remove metal, but only realign the cutting edge. One advantage of this method is that you won't have to apply much pressure to realign the edge. Steeling keeps the edge straight and honing sharpens it.

With a properly sharpened knife you "cut" through the carcass rather than "push" through the meat, which is often the case with dull knives. If you learn to sharpen knives correctly, it will save wear on them later. If you are unsure of your ability to sharpen knives or prefer not to, there are professional sharpening businesses that may be able to help you.

Keep your knives sharp, clean, and dry, and avoid storing them in places where they can get nicked and damaged by other objects. Even small nicks or scratches can dull the sharpest knives.

Testing a sharpened knife should be done with paper rather than your fingers. Avoid running your finger across a newly sharpened edge to test it. A better and safer method is to cut a single piece of paper while holding it loosely between two fingers. A suitably sharp knife will allow you to cut through the paper with little motion.

Remember there is an inherent danger to handling, using, and sharpening knives. Knife safety, particularly during sharpening, is a matter of common sense. If you go slowly, pay attention, and stay focused, you should have little trouble. Always keep knives out of the reach of young children.

Knife and Saw Care

You should clean your knives before and after each use to keep them in the best condition and to promote food safety. Use mild soapy water and clean by hand. A dishwasher's hot temperatures may affect the temper of the blade so it will not hold its edge later when sharpened. Also, the water jets in the dishwasher can toss your knives about and cause nicks in the blades.

When cleaning knives, you should pay close attention to the area where the blade attaches to the handle. This is the most likely area where meat or blood residue will remain after cutting and is an ideal habitat for microorganisms to grow. A thorough washing before, after, and in between cutting will maintain cleanliness.

Washing meat saws will require more attention because of the teeth on the blade. They can be cleaned with mild soapy water like knives but should never be washed in a dishwasher. Pay close attention to cleaning the teeth and the connecting joints where the blade attaches to the frame. Most meat saws have the ability to be dismantled for washing.

Storing Knives

Knives can be useful for years if stored properly. Keep knives or meat saws in an area that is cool with low humidity. Avoid storage

areas with a high relative humidity or that have a great shift in temperature, such as attics or basements that are not insulated or heated. Large variations in temperature and humidity can cause condensation and moisture to come in contact with knives that are left exposed.

Using a silica gel or other drying agent will help keep knives dry if you live in a humid area. Although tarnishing or oxidation is a normal part of high carbon steel knives and cannot be entirely avoided, using a gel or drying agent helps protect the knife from rust. Its residue will appear as a blue-gray hue rather than red rust tones. You can protect the blades by applying drops of any quality oil or silicon treatment with a soft cotton cloth or by removing moisture with the cloth.

If your butchering knives are to be stored for long periods between use, you should check them periodically for reddish spots that may show early signs of tarnish or oxidation—the initial rust stages. If this is present, you should clean the blades. Stainless-steel blades are not rustproof, although most are rust and stain resistant. You can remove any stains or tarnish by using a standard metal cleaner or polish.

Cutting Surfaces

The cutting surface will have a major impact on knife blades. Always use a cutting surface that will allow you to get the most out of the knives' sharpness. Cutting surfaces or cutting boards should be made of material that is easy to clean and fairly soft. Natural wood or synthetic materials, such as soft polyethylene, are good cutting surfaces. Avoid using glass, ceramic, metal, marble, or any other hard surface material for cutting meat because these can have a damaging effect on knife blades and edges.

A heavy mesh butcher's cutting glove is worn on the off-knife-holding hand and is designed to protect your hands against cuts, slashes, and punctures from your knives. Always wash and disinfect the glove before and after use and dry properly. Gloves of this type are sold in different sizes and can be used on either hand.

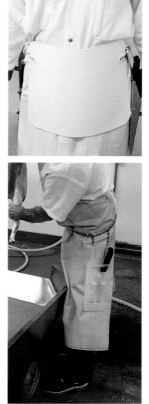

An abdominal apron is an essential barrier against accidental slippage of your knife. Their effectiveness in providing safety will outweigh any inconvenience in wearing one. Fully outfitted, you will be ready for cutting up the carcass.

A rubber apron is easy to wash and will protect your clothing from splattering of blood and keep you dry when rinsing the carcass with water.

Using a barrel to catch the blood draining from the carcass will keep your work area clean. It will also help in disposing or composting the blood. If you plan to keep the blood for sausage making, be sure the catch barrel or tub is thoroughly washed and sanitized, and free of any rust or foreign matter, before being used.

Cutting surfaces can provide an ideal area for cross contamination of food products, which is a major food safety concern. Bacteria transferred from knives to cutting surfaces or cutting boards to other foods can lead to food poisoning. Always clean and sanitize the surface you use for cutting meat before and after each use.

Gloves and Aprons

Other items you should have include protective gloves and aprons. Gloves are one of the best protective items you can use. A butcher glove is designed to be worn on the free hand from which you hold a knife. They come in several sizes and are easy to wash. Some are made of thousands of braided stainless-steel threads woven into the glove that resist cuts and are difficult to puncture. A heavy mesh glove is made of solid stainless-steel rings that protect hands against cuts, slashes, and laceration hazards but may not entirely stop punctures. Both types of gloves serve to reduce the chances for injury to hands and fingers. Before and after each use, you should thoroughly clean, sanitize, and dry them.

Aprons made from leather, naugahyde, heavy canvas, or rubber can be a protection from injury or keep your clothes from becoming soiled or bloody during the slaughtering process of large animals. An apron will also keep you dry.

A heavy apron or abdominal protection made of material impenetrable from sharp knives is a good safeguard. While they may restrict some leg movement, such aprons are an insurance against injury should your knife slip or you accidentally draw it toward your body.

According to a 2005 USDA report, worldwide consumption of beef, bison, and veal accounts for about 23 percent of the total meat products consumed. *Shutterstock/Joe Mercier*

Chapter 3

BEEF, BISON, AND VEAL

Beef has been a diet staple and popular meat for millennia because of its availability, nutrition, and the volume derived from one carcass. Its versatility allows it to be included in a wide array of dishes made from whole cuts, ground meat, and strips. Also, beef adapts well to different curing methods such as smoking, canning, and pickling.

Concerns about dietary fats have directed attention to bison meat because of its leanness, or higher ratio of muscle to fat when compared to conventionally raised, domesticated beef animals. This lower fat level within the carcass and muscles is perceived as a more healthful alternative.

Veal is immature beef produced from calves weighing about 200 pounds. They are raised on diets, often indirectly dictated by consumer tastes and expectations, to produce a specific color and texture. In recent years, concern about their housing and

Select a healthy animal for home butchering, whether you raise or purchase it. Well-grown, healthy animals will yield the best carcasses both in quality and quantity of meat.

feeding protocols has increased consumer awareness of humane veal production. As a result, growing procedures have often been altered or changed to address these concerns and minimize animal stress.

A 2005 United States Department of Agriculture (USDA) report noted that world-wide consumption of beef, bison, and veal accounts for about 23 percent of the total meat products consumed.

Handling a Live Animal

While the process for handling a carcass is very much the same in each case for beef and dairy cattle or bison (buffalo), it is the live animal that may pose a challenge. A 1,000-

pound live animal can vary in attitude and temperament. If it must be transported, it will need time to adjust to your surround-ings before you plan to butcher it.

Although a beef animal and a dairy cow may be more docile to work with, it is good to remember that bison, no matter how domes-ticated they may be perceived to be, are still only one step from being in the wild, and their attitude may demonstrate that. Any animal sensing a threat will react in unex-pected ways. If you choose to work with a live animal, be sure you have sturdy gating and pens, a plan to quickly and safely dis-patch it, and proper and safe equipment that is ready to use. Preparation for your harvest should include a thorough knowledge of the carcass, sharp and clean knives, and meat cutting saws. You must have adequate help available when needed.

You can eliminate the concerns about handling live animals by arranging the purchase of an animal and have it killed at a local meat locker. Then you can retrieve the carcass to cut it up yourself if you have a safe, sanitary, and refrigerated means to transport it.

Choosing an Animal

If you raise livestock, you will be aware of the care they need to reach a sufficient weight for harvest and which animal appears to be the healthiest for your use. If you choose to purchase a live animal from a livestock producer, make sure it is healthy in appearance. If you choose to dispatch it yourself, you will need a place to keep it until you are ready.

You should withhold any feed from your animal for at least 24 hours before you choose to harvest it. However, make certain it has full access to water so that it does not dehydrate. Cattle will lose about 3 to 4 percent of their weight if kept off feed for this period. This is called shrinkage, but it will eliminate much of the rumen contents and intestinal fecal material so that you will not have to work with it later. During this fasting period, it is very important to eliminate any excitement for the animal or unnecessary handling. Rough handling or excitement causes the blood to be forced to the outermost capillaries from which it will not drain as thoroughly as it would under normal heart action. This retained blood will lower the quality of the meat.

Putting the Animal Down

If working with a live animal, you will be faced with the decision of how to put the animal down so that you can begin the first of the harvesting processes: the sticking of the jugular vein to facilitate a bleeding of the carcass. There are several ways to dispatch an animal, and none of them are for the faint

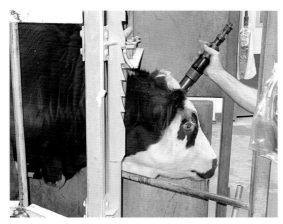

Restraining large animals is the best way to assure a clean kill and allows you to properly place the compression gun or rifle used. A stunning gun renders the animal unconsciousness so that it feels no further pain but allows for a more complete bleed because the heart is still pumping.

Stun or shoot the animal in the forehead, at a point where imaginary lines from each eye to the opposite horn root, or pole, crosses. If the animal does not have horns, imagine where they would be if they did.

of heart. A misapplied stun or gunshot will result in a frantic animal that will be harder to approach for a second attempt and also increase its heart rate, causing the capillary effect on the muscle and lowering the quality of your carcass.

It is best if you decide prior to harvest how you will put the animal down. A gunshot to the middle of the forehead is used by some, but it is not an effective method to create a complete bleed as possible because it causes the heart to stop beating. That makes for a slower and incomplete bleed.

You can use a power-activated compression gun if you have properly restrained the animal. They have either long or short handles and can be a penetrating or non-penetrating type. One advantage is that they are portable and can be moved from one farm to another and from one position in your facility to another. These advantages make them comfortable to use. However, if you are inexperienced in their use, you may want to have someone who is skilled provide the service. The advantage of stunning the animal is that while it loses consciousness, its heart keeps beating, aiding in the desired blood loss after sticking.

A major consideration about where you down the animal is how you will raise it off the floor or platform where it is standing. The weight of the animal should be a consideration in how you approach this procedure as well as the height of any ceiling present. You can use a shed or even lift the animal to an open area if you have the machine to handle it properly. Remember that once the animal is stunned or shot, you need to begin work to bleed it quickly after raising it in the air.

Your work should proceed in an area that is clean and free from dust, dirt, insects, and anything that might contaminate the carcass once it's opened. Dripping blood will quickly attract insects and flies that can lay eggs in a very short period of time. For these reasons, it is best if the sticking and evisceration is done in an enclosed area.

How you lift the animal depends on where you work. An electric winch that is firmly attached to a ceiling will work in enclosed rooms. If you choose an outdoor area, you can use a tractor with a front end lift or a skid loader that allows you to move it into place and has enough reach to keep the head from touching the ground. A 1,000-pound animal carcass will increase in length—as much as 7 to 8 feet—as the muscles relax and stretch as it is suspended.

Equipment Needed

Prior to stunning the animal, you should have all of your equipment, knives, and saws ready for immediate use. The list can be extensive as you wish, but you should have several knives available, two meat saws, a catch pan for the blood, a metal or plastic tub for the entrails, a pan for the liver, and any other items you deem necessary. A metal rod with a spiral-looped end will help with separating the trachea and esophagus. All of these items should be thoroughly washed and sanitized before they are used. A pail with soapy water and one with clean warm water should be available to wash your hands, and towels and cloths should also be handy.

Starting the Process

Once the animal is unconscious, you can wrap a chain around the end of the canon bone above each ankle. These bones are strong and will allow you to raise the carcass. The standard method for sticking is to make an incision, through the hide only, between

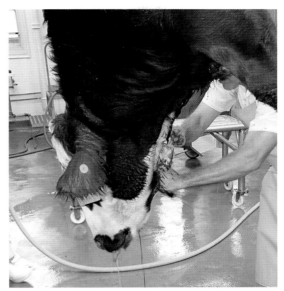

After the animal is raised, sever the carotid arteries and jugular vein to begin the bleeding. Make a deep incision just in front of the brisket and then down to the jaw. While you are waiting for the blood to completely drain, you can begin other steps.

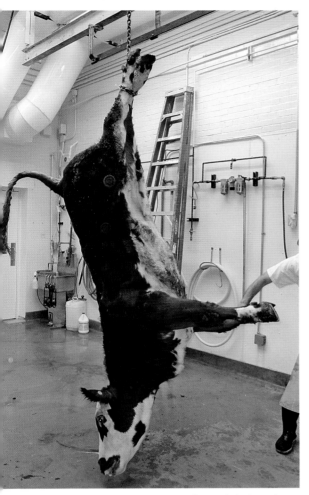

To raise the animal off the ground or floor, tightly chain the hind legs together between the hock and feet and lift it with a winch or loader. Be careful to avoid injury to yourself because once an animal is stunned, you may only have about 15 to 20 seconds to set the chains before the involuntary body reflexes react to the stunning and the legs begin to kick and thrash. However, they will subside within the next few minutes.

the brisket and jaw. Peel the skin apart to expose the carotid arteries and jugular vein and sever them with your knife. Catch the blood in a large tub, vat, or barrel. The blood volume may vary between animals but will generally be between 6 to 8 percent of the live weight. For a 1,000-pound animal, this will amount to about 60 to 80 pounds. A good stick will remove about 50 percent of the total blood in the carcass, or in this case about 30 to 40 pounds will fall into your catch pan, tub, or barrel.

The evisceration will be easier later if you separate the esophagus from the trachea while the carcass is suspended. If they are still attached when you try to remove the entrails, they will not come free from the thoracic cavity. It is easier to separate them at this point and makes your work less difficult later. After the bleeding is completed, you can use a metal rod that has a handle on one end and several spiral loops at the other. These loops should be threaded onto the esophagus just behind the Adam's apple and forced toward the rumen. An alternative method is used if the animal is laid on its back in a skinning cradle. Then after the brisket is

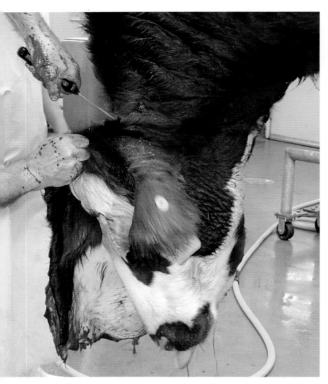

It will be easier to remove the head if you make a cut at the atlas joint just behind the poll or top of the head. Skin the head before you finish removing it. The atlas joint is the first neck bone and is connected to the axis joint (connected to the skull).

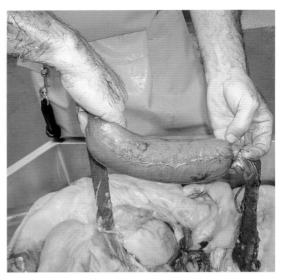

Tie the esophagus shut tightly with a string before cutting through it when removing the head. Cut below the string to keep all the stomach contents in the gastrointestinal tract. Without tying the esophagus closed, fecal material will spill throughout the inside body cavity and contaminate it.

split, the esophagus is tied with string to seal it off and prevent any rumen contents from spilling out into the carcass cavity.

Removing the Head

The head should be one of the first parts removed because of its weight, to aid in bleeding, and to provide easier access to the carcass. Begin by making a cut from the poll at the top of the head down the center of the nose and down to the jaw. You can skin out one side of the face, peeling the skin back as you go, before skinning out the other side. Grasp the bottom jaw with your free hand,

pulling upwards so the poll bends back and cut through the Adam's apple and the atlas joint at the base of the skull. Be careful when removing the head because a 1,000-pound animal will have a head that weighs about 25 pounds. However, it is not all waste product because you can utilize the cheek meat and the tongue.

In the past, some families made use of the brain. However, because of the development of links between bovine spongiform encephalopathy (BSE) found in infected cattle and variant Creutzfeldt-Jakob disease (CJD) in humans, you are strongly advised **not** to eat any part of the brain, spinal column, and other parts of the nervous system. Discarding the head, except for the cheek meat and tongue, and any remnants of the spinal cord is the safest route. Also, you should not feed the brain, spinal cord, blood, or other nervous system parts to other

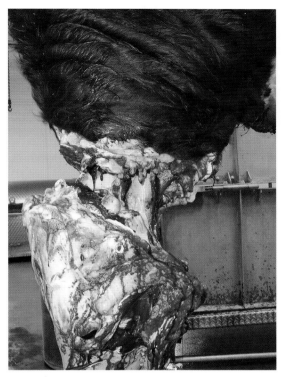

With the head skinned, finish cutting through the atlas joint with a breaking knife or saw. The face (cheek) muscles can be trimmed for sausage and the tongue cut out to cook as a specialty dish.

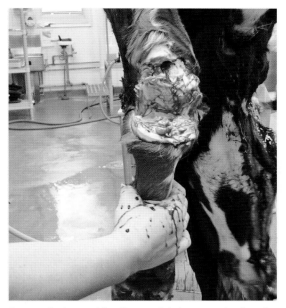

Remove the legs and feet first to minimize contamination of the carcass by manure or dirt attached to them. The front feet can be removed while the animal is still suspended. Make your cut about 1 inch below the knee joint, which should allow you to break it once the tendons are severed.

livestock or chickens. This will reduce the potential for any transference of infective agents from one animal to another.

Removing Legs

Your next step is to remove the legs to prevent possible contamination of the carcass with manure and dirt dropped from the hooves. Depending on your harvesting facility configuration, you can do this while the animal is suspended, or if you have a skinning cradle, you can lay the carcass out on its back and remove the legs.

Use the tip of your knife to open the skin, starting with a circle cut around the backside of the front leg near the dewclaw. Cut a line

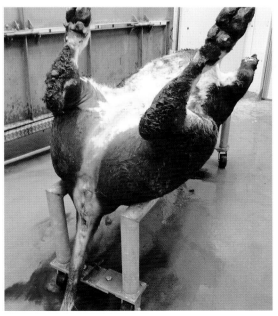

After the bleeding is finished and the head and front legs are removed, lower the carcass onto a sturdy trolley or platform called a cradle to begin removing the hide and the hind legs.

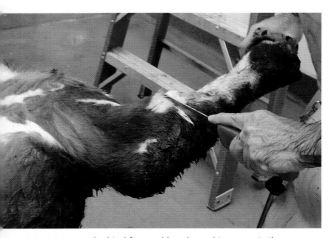

Remove the hind feet and legs by making cuts similar to those made in the front legs, except you will need to avoid cutting the tendons so they can be used to lift the carcass for evisceration. Make a cut at the joint located just below the hock. This will allow you to break the leg in half to finish severing it. Then finish the other hind leg. A handsaw can also be used to remove the leg.

up the foreshank until you reach the elbow and then continue across to the midline of the brisket. Peel back the skin to expose the entire leg bone.

To remove the foreleg, cut across the shank to sever the tendon, which will release the tension on the lower part of the leg. Next, cut through the flat joint, which is about 1 inch below the knee joint. If it is too difficult to cut with your knife, use your meat saw. Then make the same cuts on the other foreshank.

The procedure for removing the hind legs is almost identical, except you will be making your initial cut up the inside of the hind leg and across to a midline point directly below the anus. In removing the hindshank, be sure to make your cut below the point where the tendon anchors itself to the joint. This will allow you to hang the carcass by the tendons, which are strong enough to hold the weight. However, to do this, the tendons must still be attached and intact.

Removing the Hide and Lifting the Carcass

To open the hide, you can start at either end, and this is easier if the carcass is on its back. Pull the hide upward as you make a cut from the throat to the anus, following an imaginary midline of the carcass. Pulling the hide toward you will prevent cutting into the carcass or through the abdominal wall. Next, firmly grasp the hide and use your skinning knife to make long, smooth strokes to separate and peel the skin from the carcass. Avoid unnecessary cuts in the hide if you plan to use it later for tanning.

After removing both sides of the hide as far as possible while the carcass is lying on its back, you can open the brisket. To do this, use your knife to cut through the fat and muscle covering it. When the brisket bone is exposed, you can use a saw to open it. You can separate the esophagus and trachea now unless you did it earlier when the carcass was suspended.

To lift the carcass, attach hooks to the hind leg tendons and lift so that the legs spread apart when suspended. Raise the carcass to a level that is comfortable to work with and is clear of the floor space. You can use clean chains or cables wrapped around the hind leg, but these will need to be tightly attached so they do not slip off because of the carcass's weight.

Because of the carcass's length, it will be easier to split the pelvic bone, or the aitchbone, before it is fully suspended and while still at a convenient height. It will also be easier to cut the anus loose, remove the tail, and the hide from the rump and rear quarters before lifting it. If it is a male carcass, remove the pizzle by cutting it loose from the belly and back to the pelvic junction where it originates.

Cut through the muscles and membranes at a center point in the pelvis to expose the aitchbone, using your saw to cut it in half. Loosen the anus by cutting completely around it, severing all connecting tissue. Be careful not to cut into the intestine. When the anus is loose, tightly tie the end shut with a clean cord or clean heavy string, and let it slide into the body where it can be reached from the belly cavity later. You can remove the pizzle with the anus. Remove the tail by severing the two joints where it attaches adjacent the body and cut the skin completely around its base. You should now be able to pull out the tail.

If you prefer, you can begin to split the carcass while it is in this position by using a saw to cut part way down the backbone; again, be careful not to cut into the intestines. Or you can raise the carcass until it is fully suspended and begin removing the remaining hide and start the evisceration process.

Remove the remaining hide by starting at the top and running your skinning knife down along the carcass. The weight of the hide will help separate it from the carcass. When finished, you can discard the hide or save it for tanning.

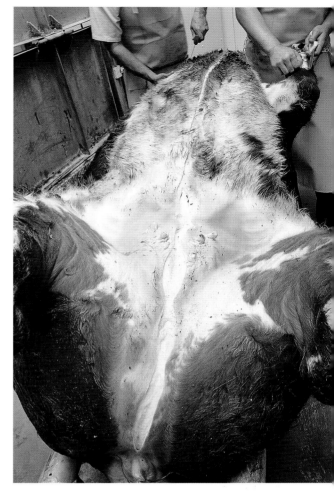

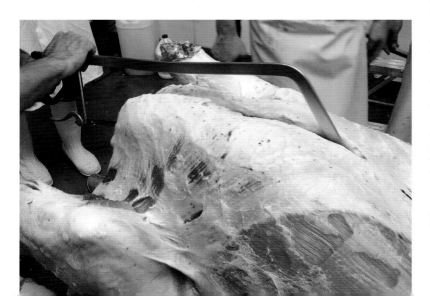

Above: Begin removing the hide by making a small midline incision from the brisket to the anus. Pull the skin up and away from the body to prevent cutting into the muscle or through the abdominal wall. Rinse your knife several times to minimize contamination.

Left: After removing as much of the hide as you can while the carcass is still on its back, open the brisket by cutting through the fat and muscle with a butchering knife. When the brisket bone (sternum) is exposed, use a saw to open it and expose the thoracic cavity.

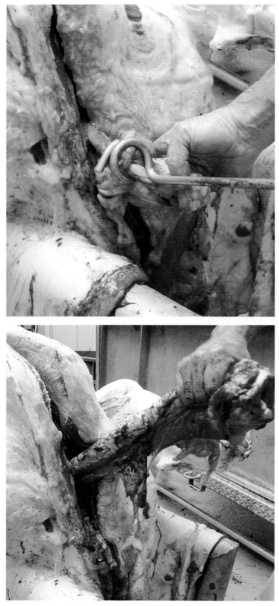

The carcass can be lifted by inserting the points of the gambrel between the rear shank bone and the tendon attached to it. Before lifting it, you can remove the tail by cutting through the joint closest to the last sacral vertebrae. The oxtail is often used for soup stock.

Evisceration

Place a tub beneath the carcass to catch the viscera after it is cut loose and to collect any blood still draining from the carcass. To open the body cavity, start at the point where you cut through to the aitch bone. Slice an opening large enough to insert your knife, handle first, into the cavity and position the blade upward and outward. This allows you to protect the intestines and rumen with your fist. You do not want the blade to cut into the intestine or rumen, as it will contaminate the carcass with fecal and rumen materials. Since you've already opened the brisket, you should make one continuous cut from the top down to the brisket opening.

As you slice down the belly, part of the viscera will spill outward but will still be held

Top and above: Once the brisket is opened, pull the esophagus and trachea out. Use a weasand rod, which is placed over the windpipe and pulled through the looped rod. This separates the esophagus, which goes to the stomach, from the trachea, which connects to the lungs. You can also strip these two apart using your hands. This separation is done so that the stomach will not be attached to the thoracic cavity during evisceration, potentially causing the esophagus to tear and result in stomach content spillage.

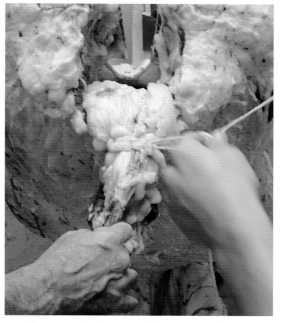

Several steps need to be taken before evisceration. First, make a circular cut around the anus to loosen the muscles from the pelvic bone. When free, tightly tie it shut with a heavy string or cord so fecal content will not contaminate the interior of the body cavity.

by membranes that hold the anus, intestines, liver, and bladder to the inside body cavity.

With the belly completely open, sever the fat and membranes that hold the viscera. Start at the top and cut the ureters that hold the kidneys. These can be removed later. You can loosen the liver with your hands and then sever it from the backbone with your knife. Set it in a separate pan for later inspection.

As you loosen more connective membranes, the weight of the viscera will cause it to drop outward. As it does, pull the loosened esophagus up through the diaphragm. This should allow everything to fall freely into your collecting tub.

The diaphragm separates the abdomen from the lungs, heart, and esophagus. Some

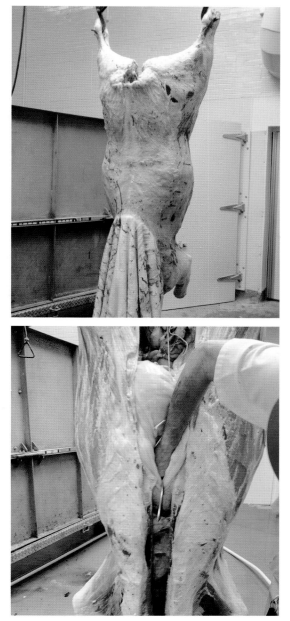

Top: The aitchbone can be split with a saw either before loosening the anus or after lifting the carcass. Once the carcass is suspended, you can finish removing the hide.
Above: Begin evisceration with a slow and careful cut below the aitchbone and down the midline to the brisket. Avoid cutting the intestines, stomach, or internal organs with your blade. The weight of the viscera will draw it down and outward, and it can be placed in a tub once removed.

With the viscera removed, the diaphragm can be opened to remove the lungs, heart, and trachea. By separating the esophagus and trachea, the esophagus was removed when the viscera fell out. Once the thoracic cavity is cleaned, you can split the carcass.

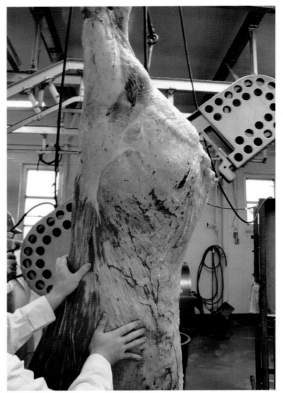

Above: You can split a carcass using a handsaw or an electric meat saw. Start at the aitch bone and carefully cut down the middle of the spine and down the center of the spinal column. If done correctly, the backbone will be split in half, and the loin eye muscles will not be scored or cut into.
Opposite: After the carcass is split in halves, wash the interior and outside with cold water. Carefully inspect the carcass and remove any remaining hair, skin, dirt, feces, blood, or other materials attached to the carcass before cooling and cutting it up. The carcass needs to be as clean as possible to minimize microbial growth on its surface.

people like to leave the diaphragm muscle intact and use it as hanging tenderloin. To remove the heart, lungs, and esophagus, sever the membrane and pull them out and drop them into your tub.

Splitting

With all the internal organs and intestines removed, you can now split the carcass in half. You can use your handsaw or an electric meat saw. Begin at the top and slowly make your cut in the exact center of the spine. Continue down until each half is free. Wash the carcass inside and out with cold or lukewarm water to remove any remaining blood, tissue, or foreign material. It is now ready for chilling. When you have finished with the carcass, inspect the liver and

temperatures of 40 to 60 degrees Fahrenheit. It is important to chill the carcass for at least 24 hours to prevent the meat from spoiling. Letting it remain in temperatures of 34 to 38 degrees Fahrenheit will make the process of cutting up the carcass much easier as well.

Chilling a large carcass may not be feasible for a single animal, and you may have to make arrangements with a local meat service with adequate cooling facilities. You may be able to convert a large chest freezer into a cooler by setting its thermostat to a temperature just above freezing. This will approximate or mimic a still air cooler at some meat services. Depending on the size of the carcass and the cooling activity used, it may take up to 48 hours for the carcass to reach an internal temperature of 40 degrees Fahrenheit or lower. If you use a chest freezer to chill the carcass, make certain that there is space between the two sides of the freezer so that the air will completely circulate around it for even cooling. You can expect about a 2 to 3 percent loss in carcass weight during the chilling of a hot carcass immediately after slaughter. Most of this is due to loss of water.

Aging

Aging is the process that allows the enzymes in meat to change structure in the collagen and muscle fibers that will enhance the beef flavor and increase its tenderness. Seven to eleven days is typically required to reach maximum flavor. Aging is useful for meats to be frozen but tends to decrease the shelf life of fresh meat products. There will typically be some weight loss during the aging process due to dehydration of the lean and fat. The length of time to age beef is mainly a personal preference. If unsure, it is probably better to age it for a minimum of seven days as is typically done.

other internal organs to assess their health. A healthy-looking liver that is pink- or salmon-colored and free of lesions or dark spots will suggest a healthy animal. The liver and heart may be cooled and used later in sausage making. Generally, the intestines from cattle are too large to be very useful as casings in making sausages.

Chilling

Prior to any harvest, you should decide how you are going to chill the carcass to keep it from spoiling. After the butchering process, internal temperatures of animal carcasses will generally range between 85 to 102 degrees Fahrenheit. This body heat must be removed during the initial chilling. Meat is a perishable product and can spoil at

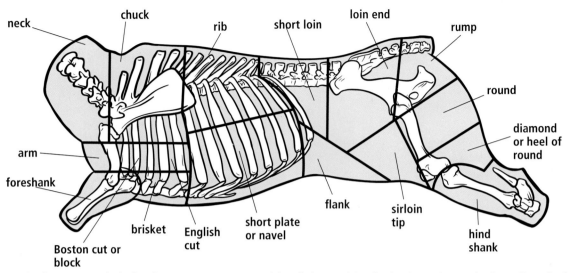

neck · chuck · rib · short loin · loin end · rump · round · diamond or heel of round · arm · foreshank · brisket · English cut · short plate or navel · flank · sirloin tip · hind shank · Boston cut or block

A beef anatomy can be broken down into imaginary cuts while still alive. Studying the drawing and comparing it to a live animal will lead to better understanding of the structure when the slaughter process begins.

There are several considerations if you decide to age beef on your own. First, it should be done in sanitary surroundings. Air should be allowed to circulate around the carcass sides completely, and avoid freezing the carcass, as that will temporarily stop the aging process. Remember that as the length of the aging time increases, so does the aged beef flavor, the tenderness, and the weight loss.

Cutting the Carcass

After the carcass has been aged, you can begin to break it down into smaller parts and pieces, which is called fabrication. Each carcass can be divided into quarters: the two forequarters and two hindquarters. Each forequarter consists of five major cuts: chuck, rib, brisket, plate, and shank. The hindquarter contains the most valuable retail cuts, including the round, loin, and flank.

Begin by dividing the forequarter and hindquarter between the twelfth and thirteenth ribs. These can be easily found by counting the exposed vertebrae rather than the individual ribs. From the rear, count off seven and a half vertebrae, reaching a point midway between the twelfth and thirteenth rib. Use a saw to cut through the vertebrae and a knife to cut through the rest.

Forequarter

After splitting one side in half, separate the rib and plate from the chuck, brisket, and shank of the forequarter by making a cut between the fifth and sixth ribs, again using your saw to sever the vertebrae. Separate the plate, which is the bottom portion of the ribs, by making a horizontal cut across them starting about 10 inches below the rib eye muscle. There are two ends to this piece, one called the blade end (nearest the scapula), and the other is the loin end because it is next to the loin in the hindquarter.

The next cut should be made about 3 inches from the loin eye so that it severs the bottom portion of the ribs. Those rib ends may be made into short ribs. Next, with a saw remove the chine bones, which are located at the top of the ribs. There is very little usable meat on this cut, but it can be used for soup stock.

There is a strip of flexible but solid connective tissue called the backstrap that is still attached to the bottom portion of the ribs. This needs to be removed because it is not palatable, even with cooking.

Next, remove the blade bone and any cartilage with it. Finally, trim any outside fat off that is more than ¼-inch thick. What is left is called a standing rib roast. The blade end will be larger than the loin end. If you slice the rib roast into separate pieces, those from the loin end are called rib steaks, small end. Rib steaks removed from the blade end are called rib steaks, large end. However, these will have more accessory muscles and won't be as palatable if used strictly as steaks. Another option is to remove the ribs to make a boneless rib roast or boneless rib steaks.

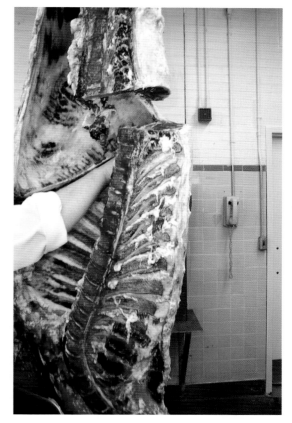

Above: The carcass side is divided into a forequarter and hindquarter by making a cut between the twelfth and thirteenth ribs, counting from the anterior (front) end. Use a saw to cut through the bone, and finish the cut with a knife, splitting the side in half.

Left: To separate the forequarter from the ribs, make a perpendicular cut to the shoulder between the fifth and sixth ribs. The shoulder, foreshank, and brisket can be set aside until needed.

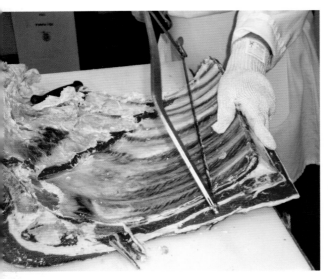

Trim fat from the bottom of the ribs and make lateral saw cuts about 1½ half inches from the previous cut. These will be short ribs that can be used for soup stock or boned out for ground beef or meat trimmings for sausages.

Expect to trim and remove discolored and dried parts of the carcass, such as this piece of diaphragm attached to the plate. The longer a carcass is held in a cooler before cutting, the more that will have to be removed and discarded.

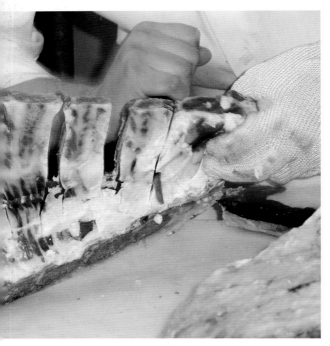

The ribs can be trimmed and the trim used for ground beef. It generally contains too much fat to be used in sausage making or soup stock.

The ribeye roll is a valuable cut and can be sliced into 1 or 2-inch portions for grilling or braising. It can also be left intact to make boneless ribeye roasts for prime rib.

Chuck

After the rib and plate have been removed, the chuck, brisket, and shank remain. The chuck is the largest cut on the beef animal, and the two (right and left) will account for about 25 percent of the carcass weight. Although the chuck contains much connective tissue and is often made into roasts, there is a considerable amount of lean trim, which can be used, and several minor cuts that can be used in various dishes.

One subprimal cut called the ribeye roll can be made when the ribs are cut out. If the rib bones are left on, bone-in rib roasts or rib steaks can be made. By removing the bones, boneless ribeye roasts or steaks can be made. You should remove any parts of the shoulder blade that remain if making boneless cuts.

To separate the chuck from the brisket and shank, use your knife to make a cut parallel to the top side of the chuck to sever the upper part of the shoulder. Then use your saw to cut through the rest of the shoulder bone.

As its name suggests, the square-cut chuck will have the shape of a square when you saw parallel to the arm 3 to 5 inches on the lower side of the brisket. Arm and blade roasts and steaks are made from this cut. The square-cut chuck will have fat seams even after trimming. It should be slowly cooked with moist heat for best results.

The chuck will contain some neck and rib bones that can be trimmed out by sawing across the ribs near the spine.

There is a piece of connective tissue called the backstrap that was responsible for holding the animal's head erect when it was alive. It is located on the top part of the chuck and is readily recognizable by its firm, white texture, which is impossible to make palatable. It

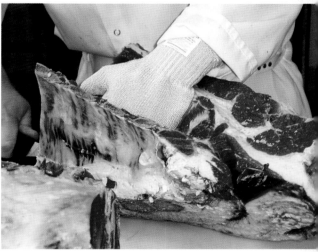

There is a natural seam you can cut through to remove the portion called the clod. This is typically made into roasts because it contains much connective tissue and some neck and rib bones, which can be trimmed. Practice your cutting skills on the less-valued cuts, such as the plate and brisket, before cutting the more valuable ones.

is very similar to the backstrap you cut from the ribs, and this can also be discarded.

The chuck can be cut into several pieces. First, make two or three blade roasts by sawing across the section that had attached to the ribs. You will be cutting through

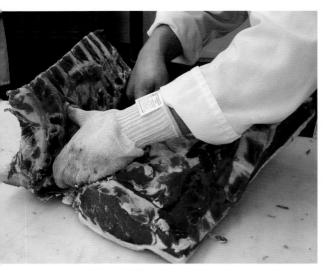

A strip of solid, flexible, yellowish-colored connective tissue is found in two prominent places in the carcass: the neck and the top of the back or rib section. This is called backstrap and is shown here as a yellowish strip running above the ribs. It is inedible and unpalatable, and it should be discarded. Trim these portions out of the rib section now and later when cutting up the neck.

Top: The chuck roll is located anterior to the ribeye roll. It can be cut into steaks, roasts, or trimmings. Typically, roasts are greater than 1½ in thickness when cut and steaks are less than 1½ inches in thickness. A band saw can quicky cut the chuck into arm and blade roasts.
Above: Animals with less finish will have less seam fat and fat between and over the outside of the muscles. Cuts with more connective tissue in the meat, such as shoulder roasts, will make them less palatable. A high degree of finish on the animal will also yield more kidney and pelvic fat.

the scapula or blade bone, which gives the roasts their name. A small portion of the rib eye will be in these cuts. Cut them about 1½-inch thick. Then turn the chuck 90 degrees to make several cuts across the arm bone. These are called arm roasts. They will be made of fewer, but larger, muscles than the blade roasts.

After removing two or three arm roasts, you can remove several more blade roasts. As you remove these, the spine of the scapula becomes evident with the shape of a number seven. When you arrive at the neck, this can be left as a seven-bone roast, but remove the lymph node and surrounding fat deposits in it. The neck roast can be trimmed and used for ground beef because it is a low-quality cut. It can also be cut and used for soup stock.

The chuck roasts are fairly large pieces. To make them easier to work with and cook,

cut them in half before packaging. You may want to trim excess fat from all these cuts prior to packaging. There are alternative methods for breaking down the chuck that you may want to study and become familiar with before beginning. Books describing different methods typically may be obtained through universities or agriculture extension offices.

Foreshank and Brisket

The foreshank and brisket are considered rough cuts but make up about one-quarter of the total carcass weight, about half of which can be utilized. The plate of the forequarter is the lowest part of the ribs but does not include part of the brisket. This will contain the diaphragm membrane, which should be trimmed. The plate can be used for ground beef or cut for stew meat.

Separate the foreshank from the brisket by making a cut through the natural seam that separates them. The brisket can be trimmed of all bone and used as a boneless brisket roast. Removing all the hard fat and muscles on the inside of this cut will allow you to use it for making corned beef. You can crosscut the foreshank or trim out the bone and use the lean meat for ground beef. Retain the bones for soup stock if desired.

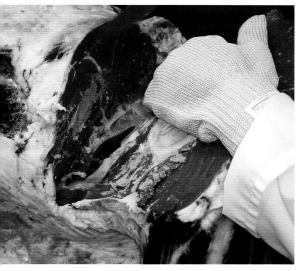

Above: To remove the foreshank, make a parallel cut to it from the point of elbow 4 to 5 inches toward the ribs. Then cut through the arm bone and look for the natural seam under the armpit that attaches to the foreshank and elbow, and cut off the elbow with your knife.

Above and Right: After the elbow is removed, there will be a choice to make. You can bore all the meat out or you can cut to make crosscut shank or soup bones. These can be cut with a knife and meat saw, or with a band saw if available. The rest can be cut into a roast.

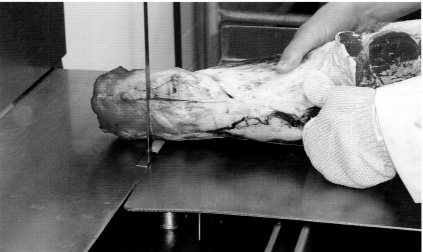

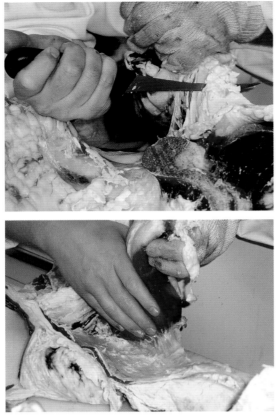

Remove the kidneys and kidney fat, but be careful not to damage the tenderloin area with your knife. You can leave the kidney fat intact after slaughter to reduce the dehydration of the meat, which can cause browning or brown spots on the loin, lowering its sale value and appearance. If you remove the kidney fat before cooling, don't age the carcass as long as you normally would if it was left intact.

Top: Four major cuts can be made from the hindquarter. These are the flank, round, shortloin, and sirloin. There are twelve ribs on the forequarter but only one on the hindquarter, the thirteenth rib. Begin by removing the flank, as there is only one per side. The tough membrane covering it can be pulled off and discarded. **Above:** The flank can be easily peeled out by hand. It should then be trimmed with a knife to remove any excess fat or connective tissue.

Hindquarter

The hindquarter contains three cuts that compose about half of the carcass weight: the round, loin, and flank. As with other parts of the carcass, there are several different ways to break down the hindquarter into cuts for your home use. The following is one method you can use.

One of the earliest cuts you should make is to remove the flank, which may be the easiest while the carcass is still suspended. Begin your cut by following the contour of the round—the large muscle above the hind leg, cutting toward the ribs but getting no closer than 6 inches to the loin. Use a saw to cut through the thirteenth rib. After this cut, you can finish the separation of the flank with a knife.

The flank is used mainly for trim and can be made into ground beef or used for sausage. Flank steak can be cut from each side. Because of the fat and connective tissue attached to it, you may as easily pull it from the interior surface as to trim it out. The flank steak can be broiled, marinated, or cubed.

You will not need to remove the kidneys or pelvic fat if you did this earlier during harvest. If the kidneys are still intact, you will need to remove them. They can be pulled free or trimmed but be careful with a knife so that the tenderloin muscle that lies under the fat is not cut.

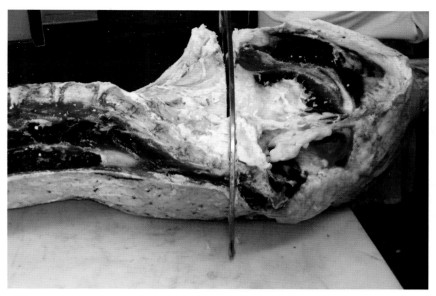

Left: Remove the round by making an angle saw cut from the point immediately next to the aitchbone and through the fifth sacral vertebrae. Use your knife to finish the cut to eliminate jagged edges on the round.

Below: There is a natural seam that separates the knuckle from the top and bottom rounds. Use a knife to make this separate. You should be able to feel the femur bone as you cut along this seam.

Round

To separate the round from the rest of the hindquarter, use a saw to begin your first cut at the rear of the aitchbone or pelvic bone. Cut just behind it and parallel to it, then saw through the large bone in the thigh called the femur. Removing the rump from the loin in this manner will provide you with two pieces without having split the sirloin tip, which may happen with other cutting options.

The round is fairly easy to cut up. The name of each cut is derived from their position when the round is laid out on a table. The top round is also called the inside round because in its natural position; it would be on the interior side of the live animal. The outside round is also called the bottom round because that is its position when it is placed on the table for cutting; it is on the bottom. The eye is located between the bottom round and the top round. The sirloin tip is that portion that is in front of the femur, or thigh bone, in the standing animal and is composed of four muscles. The top round

and sirloin tip are more tender than the bottom round and the eye.

If the round has been trimmed correctly, you will see the large round thigh bone (femur) positioned in about the middle. Begin by turning the round over so that the natural seam that separates the round tip from the top round is facing upward. Use your knife to cut along this seam until the end. Then sever the bottom round by cutting along the seam between it and the eye.

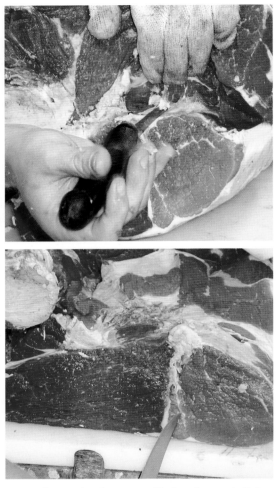

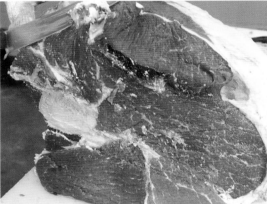

Top: From the cut just made, you can trim out the round sirloin tip, which is located at the junction of the sirloin and the round. This can be cut into 1-inch-thick steaks or left as a roast. **Above:** After the knuckle has been removed, the top and bottom rounds will be left. These will be large slices because this area of the round includes several muscle groups with different striations. You can cut round steaks or separate the top and bottom portion into boneless top round steaks/roasts and boneless bottom round steaks/roasts.

Top: Begin removing the top round by inserting your knife in the natural seam between the top round (top of picture) and the bottom round.
Above: After removing the top round, the remaining portion of the rump is composed mainly of the bottom round (on left) and the eye of round (on right). Connective tissue and fat should be trimmed off with your knife.

From this cut, you can trim out the round tip, which is located at the junction of the sirloin and the round. This makes an excellent roast and may be cut into steaks. The round tip cuts can be identified by the oval- or horseshoe-shaped connective line in the center of each cut.

Cut the round steaks to a width of about 1 inch after you have removed the round tip by cutting across the face of the round. These will be large pieces and can be folded over to be packaged or cut in half.

Next, remove the hind shank bone. Cut the Achilles tendon, which had held the weight of the carcass as it was suspended. Strong connective tissues in the shank anchor the muscles in the lower round. These must be severed to remove the shank bone. Tip your knife up and cut along this bone up into the round to the stifle joint. You can sever this joint with a knife and trim any remaining connective tissues; then remove the shank bone.

Turn the round over and trim out the rest of the stifle joint, making sure to cut close to the bone. The bottom round then can be separated from the top round by following the natural seam between them. You can cut steaks from the top round as they are considered more tender than other parts of the round. Steaks can also be cut from the bottom round if desired, or the meat can be used as cube steaks.

Rump

The rump is considered as part of the round and can make up about 4 percent of the

The eye of the round is a boneless cut made by separating it from the outside rounds, following the natural seams. On this view, the eye of the round is located as the bottom right triangular piece and can be separated from the other muscles by natural seams.

carcass weight. To separate the rump from the loin, make your cut along a line that would connect a point on the backbone between the fifth and first vertebra of the tail and the front tip of the inside end of the femur.

Begin trimming by cutting closely on both sides of the aitchbone until it is free. The remaining cut is the boneless rump that will tend to spread because it is not connected to any bone. It can be wrapped with netting to hold its shape.

Loin

The whole loin is composed of two parts: the sirloin and shortloin. The steak yields from the sirloin are about 5 percent of the carcass weight while the shortloin will be about 7 percent.

For the loin, make your cuts between the vertebrae. If you are cutting the entire loin into steaks, there will be different sizes and shapes as you move from front to back. The round bone steak contains the most meat of all the steaks of the sirloin because it has the smallest amount of bone and few fat seams.

Porterhouse steaks come from the end of the sirloin nearest the shortloin. They are easily identified by the large size of the tenderloin. The porterhouse also has an extra muscle attached to it, which decreases in size and disappears when you arrive at the shortloin. From this point on, the steaks become T-bone steaks, identified by their characteristic letter-shaped configuration.

You can trim the tenderloin as one cut if you desire. It can then be trimmed of accessory muscles and fat. Tenderloin fillet steaks come from trimmed tenderloin. It is the most palatable meat in the beef carcass.

When you have completed the last cut on this beef side, you can begin the same process with the second side of the carcass.

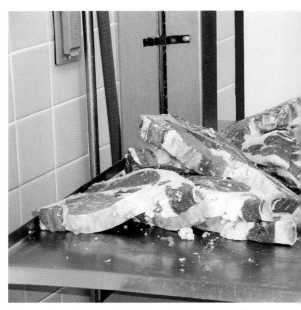

The whole loin is made up of two cuts, the sirloin and shortloin. The sizes and shapes will vary as you move from the front of the loin to the rear. They can be cut into porterhouse and T-bone steaks. The difference between them is the size of the loin eye. The porterhouse has a larger tenderloin than the T-bone.

When cutting T-bone steaks, don't stack them on top of each other for very long or you will get brown spots due to oxidation or muscle exposure to air. This can be avoided by putting plastic wrapping over each piece.

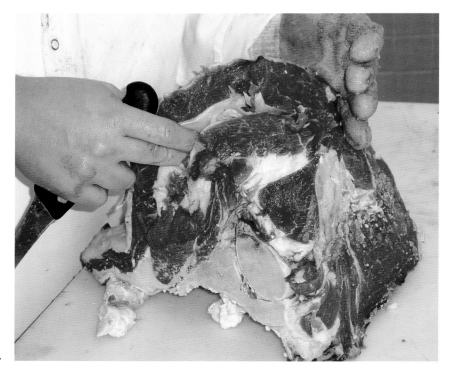

A cut called the tri-tip, or angular roast, is located below the bottom sirloin. To trim it out, follow the natural seams because it has muscle groups running in three different directions.

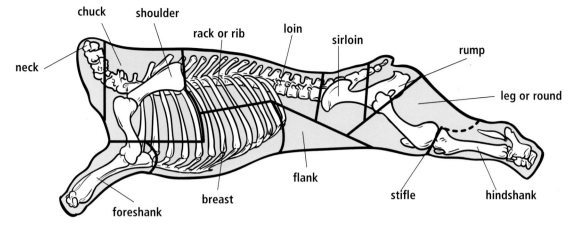

The anatomy of a veal calf is similar to a large beef animal. This drawing shows the skeletal structure in relation to some of the wholesale cuts.

Bison (Buffalo) Meat

American bison can be considered domesticated if they are raised on specialized farms or as big game in states that allow them to be hunted. Arrangements must be made for the transport and care of the carcass if it is hunted. The hunter may be given the head and hide, but the cost of the meat may be many times higher than beef due to various fees and licenses.

Buffalo may be difficult to handle and transport, and raising them in conventional ways or facilities may not be feasible. It may be difficult to find a local meat processor who is willing to harvest any buffalo you raise because of their size, difficulty in handling, and ability to damage equipment. However, harvested buffalo carcasses are broken down in a similar manner to beef. The head and hide are considered two of the most valuable trophies to be taken from them, and care must be used at the time of harvest so that they are not damaged.

Veal

The harvest of a veal calf is very similar to that of mature cattle, except the obvious difference in animal size and subsequent carcass weight and the amount of meat procured.

Veal is identified as meat from calves of all ages and weights, from birth to 20 weeks of age. There are four classifications of veal recognized by the meat industry: (1) baby, or bob veal, that includes calves 2 to 3 days to 1 month of age; (2) vealers, 4 to 12 weeks old, 80 to 120 pounds; (3) calves up to 20 weeks, 125 to 300 pounds; and (4) nature or special-fed veal, about 20 weeks of age, 180 to 240 pounds.

There are several important differences to recognize in harvesting a veal calf. First, there is very little fat cover on the body, and the carcass and muscles will have a higher moisture content than older animals. Second, the size of the cuts will be smaller, and some may be treated in a similar way to lamb cuts. For example, you may leave the sirloin on the leg instead removing it as a separate cut.

The meat of a veal calf will be pinkish white to grayish, or light pink in color. Veal has a mild, delicate flavor and is often served with sauces and/or spices.

Brisket of Beef

3 lbs. beef brisket
½ c. sliced onions
½ c. sliced carrots

½ c. diced celery with leaves
1½ tsp. salt

Cover beef with hot water, add vegetables, and simmer, covered, until meat is tender, about 2½ to 3 hours. Do not boil. Add salt when half done and more water if necessary. Remove meat from broth, slice, and serve with a sauce, if preferred. Allow ½ pound per serving.

Corned Beef

6 lbs. beef brisket
1½ lbs. fine salt

½ lb. brown sugar
½ oz. commercial cure

Scrub a plastic barrel thoroughly. Put as much fresh beef as desired to be corned in barrel and cover with cold water. Fill with enough water so that it is 2 inches above meat. Let stand for 48 hours. Drain off the water and measure the amount of water before discarding. Measure the same amount of cold water (hard water if possible) to every gallon of water formerly used, add the above proportions of salt, sugar, and cure. Boil for 15 minutes and skim the surface. When cold, pour over the beef. Keep meat under the brine. Store at a cool temperature. The corned beef will be ready for use after 10 days.

Boiled Corned Beef

6 lbs. corned beef   **Vinegar**
1 carrot   **Butter**
1 onion

Cover meat with cold water and let stand 1 hour. Drain and put into kettle with carrot and onion and enough cold water to cover. Add 1 teaspoon vinegar for each quart of water. Simmer until tender, 30 to 40 minutes for each pound. Let stand in the liquid 20 minutes, then drain and rub butter over the meat just before serving, if desired. Serves 12.

Baked Corned Beef Hash

2 c. diced cold boiled potatoes   **3 tbsp. butter**
1½ c. chopped corned beef   **Salt, pepper, and paprika**
1 small onion, minced   **6 eggs**
⅜ c. cream

Combine potatoes, corned beef, and onion. Add ¼ cup cream and 1 tablespoon melted butter. Season and mix well. Place mixture in buttered oblong baking dish. With the bottom of a custard cup, make 6 indentations in the hash and dot each with bits of butter, using 1 tablespoon in all. Bake at 450°F for 15 minutes. Remove from oven and break one egg into each indentation. Season and cover each egg with 1 teaspoon of cream and dot with remaining butter. Bake at 350°F until the eggs are set, 15 to 20 minutes. Serves 6.

Braised Oxtail

1 oxtail, about 2 lbs.
2 tbsp. fat
2 small onions, sliced
1 carrot, chopped
1 tbsp. chopped celery
2 tbsp. flour

1 c. hot water
1 c. tomatoes
3 bay leaves
3 whole cloves
Salt and pepper

Cut meat into 2-inch pieces and brown in fat. Add onion, carrot, and celery, and cook until brown. Sprinkle with browned flour. Add hot water, tomatoes, bay leaves, cloves, and salt and pepper. Place in casserole and cook 3 hours at 350°F until very tender. Serves 5 or 6.

Variation: Use beef stock instead of tomatoes and water, and omit cloves and garlic. Serve with noodles.

Braised Short Ribs

3 lbs. short ribs of beef
Flour

Salt and pepper
1 c. water

Cut meat into serving portions. Coat the meat with flour and brown in a hot kettle or oven. Season with salt and pepper, add water, cover and cook in kettle at simmering temperature or in oven at 300°F until tender, 1½ to 2 hours. Allow ½ pound per serving.

Oxtail Soup

1 oxtail
1 tbsp. fat
1 large onion, chopped
3 pints stock
1 carrot, cut in thin slices
1 stalk celery, cut in thin slices
½ c. chopped tomatoes

1 sprig thyme
2 springs parsley
1 bay leaf
1 tbsp. Worcestershire sauce
6 peppercorns
Salt

Wash oxtail well, split in small joints, and brown in fat with the chopped onion. Add stock, carrot, celery, tomatoes, and thyme, parsley, and bay leaf tied in cheesecloth sack. Season with Worcestershire sauce, crushed peppercorns, and salt, and heat to boiling. Simmer over low heat for 3 hours or until meat is tender. Remove herbs. Separate meat of oxtail from the bones, reheat, and serve meat with soup. Serves 6.

Beef Pot Roast

4 lbs. chuck, round, or rump of
   beef
¼ c. flour

3 tbsp. fat
Salt and pepper
½ c. water

Coat the meat with flour and heat fat in a Dutch oven. Brown meat on all sides, seasoning with salt and pepper. Add water, cover, and cook slowly over a low heat until tender, 3 to 4 hours. As the liquid cooks away, add more, as needed. Serve with gravy and vegetables. Serves 8.

Sauerbraten

4 lbs. beef (chuck, rump, or round)
Salt and pepper
1 pint vinegar
4 bay leaves
12 peppercorns

4 cloves
1 bunch carrots, cut into strips
6 onions, sliced
1 tbsp. sugar
12 gingersnaps

Wipe meat with damp cloth, and sprinkle thoroughly with salt and pepper. Place in an earthen dish and add vinegar and enough water to cover. Add bay leaves, peppercorns, and cloves, and let stand tightly covered in a cool place for 5 days. Drain meat, place in a Dutch oven, and brown well on all sides. Add carrots, onions, and 1 cup of spiced vinegar mixture. Cover tightly and cook over low heat about 3 hours or until meat is tender. When meat is cooked, add the sugar and crumbled gingersnaps and cook for 10 minutes. This makes gravy. If necessary, more of the spiced vinegar may be added for cooking meat or making gravy. Serves 8.

Swiss Steak

½ c. flour
Salt and pepper
2 lbs. steak, cut 2½ inches thick
     from shoulder, rump, or round
2 tbsp. fat

A few slices of onion
½ green pepper, chopped fine
1 c. boiling water
1 c. strained tomatoes

Season flour with salt and pepper, and pound the seasonings into the meat with a wooden meat mallet. Brown the meat. Add onions, green pepper, boiling water, and tomatoes. Cover closely. Simmer for 2 hours. This may be cooked in casserole at 350°F for about 1 to 1½ hours. Vegetables may be added as desired. Serves 6.

Roast Beef with Yorkshire Pudding

4 lbs. boned or boneless beef roast (chuck or round)
Salt and pepper

Onion or garlic (optional)
Bacon

Wipe the roast with damp cloth but do not wash. Rub with salt in proportion of 1 teaspoon per pound of meat. Rub with pepper, onion, or garlic if desired. Place meat, fat side up, on rack of pan. If the roast has little or no fat, place strips of bacon over it. This will baste the roast, and no other basting is needed. Do not add water, and do not cover pan. If meat thermometer is to be used, insert into center of thickest part of cut, being sure bulb of thermometer does not touch bone or fat. Roast at 300°F for 30 to 45 minutes. Allow about ½ pound per serving.

Beef Stew with Dumplings

1½ lbs. shank, neck, plate, flank, rump, or brisket
¼ c. flour
1½ tsp. salt

¼ tsp. pepper
1 small onion
⅓ c. carrots, cubed
4 c. potatoes, cut into quarters

Wipe meat, remove from bone, and cut into 1½-inch cubes. Mix flour with salt and pepper and coat meat with it. Cut some of the fat from meat and heat. When part of fat has fried out, brown the meat in it, stirring constantly. Add enough boiling water to cover the meat or add a pint of stewed and strained tomatoes and simmer until meat is tender, about 3 hours. Add onion and carrots during the last hour of cooking and the potatoes 20 minutes before serving. Add dumplings to stew, 15 minutes before serving. Cover kettle closely, and do not remove for at least 12 minutes. Serves 5.

Yorkshire Pudding

1 c. sifted flour	2 eggs
½ tsp. salt	Drippings from roast beef
1 c. milk	

Mix flour and salt. Combine milk and eggs, add to flour, and beat well until smooth. Pour hot drippings into hot shallow pan to depth of 1 inch. Pour in mixture quickly, and bake at 400°F for 30 minutes. The pudding may then be placed under the rack holding the roast beef and left for 15 minutes to catch the juices from the roast. If a rack is not used, cut pudding into squares and arrange in pan around roast. Serve with the meat.

Veal Birds

2 lbs. veal steak, cut ¼-inch thick	Flour
1 c. bread stuffing	Fat
Salt	1 c. milk or water

Cut veal into 2x4 inch pieces. Place a mound of stuffing on each piece, fold veal over stuffing, and fasten with toothpick. Season, roll in flour, brown in fat, and add milk. Cover and simmer or bake at 350°F for 1 hour. Serves 6.

Variation: Wrap veal around sausages, cooked whole carrots, pickles, or olives instead of stuffing.

Fillet Mignon

3 lbs. beef fillet
Salt pork
Butter

Salt and pepper
Flour

The fillet is the underside of the loin of beef, the tenderloin. Remove skin, fat, and ligament. Rub the entire surface with butter. Coat well with salt, pepper, and flour, and place the fillet, without water, in a small pan. Bake at 550°F for about 10 minutes. You can also cut the tenderloin into steaks and broil. Serves 8.

Wiener Schnitzel

6 veal chops or steaks
Salt and pepper
2 eggs, slightly beaten
Flour

3 tbsp. bacon drippings
Juice of 1 lemon
1 tbsp. flour
1 c. thick sour cream

Sprinkle veal with salt and pepper. Dip into eggs, then into flour. Brown on both sides in hot bacon drippings. Cover and cook slowly until chops are tender, about 1 hour. Sprinkle with lemon juice and arrange on hot platter. Blend flour with fat in pan, add sour cream, and cook 3 minutes, stirring constantly. Season with salt and pepper and serve with chops. Garnish with lemon slices. Serves 6.

Veal Cutlets with Cream Gravy

2 lbs. veal cutlets
Salt and pepper
2 eggs, beaten
Bread or cracker crumbs

Drippings
1 c. milk or cream
1 tbsp. flour

Wipe cutlets and sprinkle with salt and pepper. Dip into beaten eggs, then into fine bread or cracker crumbs. Brown the cutlets in the drippings. Place on platter, add cream to liquid in pan, and thicken slightly with mixture of flour and water. Serves 6.

Smoked Beef Tongue

1 smoked beef tongue
1 c. Spanish sauce (see next page)

10 chopped, cooked mushrooms

Scrub tongue and let stand overnight in cold water. Cover with fresh cold water and simmer for 4 hours or until tender. Drain, place in cold water 2 or 3 minutes, remove skin and roots, and place in hot water for a few minutes. Drain. Place on serving dish. Add mushrooms to Spanish sauce and pour over tongue. Serves 6.

Spanish Sauce

1 green chili pepper
2 cloves garlic
2 jalapeno peppers
3 green peppers

3 red tomatoes
½ c. chopped onion
⅛ tsp. soda

Chop tomatoes and sauté with onion. Mix garlic and peppers in blender and add to pan. Simmer 1 hour or until well cooked and thick. Stir in soda at very end. Pour over tongue.

Bison Meatloaf

1 pound fresh ground bison
   burger meat
½ c. oats
¼ c. chopped onion
1 tsp. salt

⅔ c. ketchup
½ c. packed brown sugar
1½ tsp. prepared mustard
1 egg
¾ c. milk

Beat the egg and milk together. Stir in oats, onion, and salt. Add ground bison and mix together well. Shape into eight loaves and place in a well-greased 13x9 baking dish. Combine ketchup, brown sugar, and mustard; spoon over loaves. Bake, uncovered, at 350°F for 35 minutes or until meat is no longer pink. Serve with baked potato slices and mixed vegetables.

With restaurants, grocery stores, and ethnic food outlets offering more and more options, meat from sheep, particularly lambs under one year of age, and goats is increasingly becoming a part of the American diet. *Shutterstock/Joe Mercier*

Chapter 4

SHEEP, LAMBS, AND GOATS

———◆———

Meat from sheep, particularly lambs under one year of age, and goats is increasingly popular in restaurants, grocery stores, ethnic food outlets, and the everyday family food table. The meat is high in protein and conjugated linoleic acid (CLA), a unique and potent antioxidant naturally produced through pasture grazing.

The meat from sheep up to one year of age is referred to as lamb and is usually taken from an animal that weighs between 90 and 140 pounds. Lamb is typically sold as whole or half carcasses if you decide to purchase one for cutting up yourself.

Whether you are harvesting sheep, lambs, or goats, make certain the animal is healthy and that you have the proper equipment and an appropriate place to butcher that is clean and free of dust, dirt, insects, flies, and rodents. Also have sufficient help on hand and the physical ability to carry out the work.

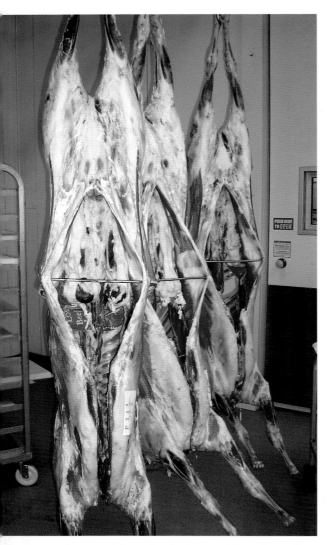

Lambs are typically marketed at between 90 to 140 pounds and sold as half or whole carcasses.

Chops

The term *chop* originally referred to any piece of meat that was chopped off with a cleaver. These were usually only small cuts because of the difficulty of chopping huge pieces of meat off at one time. If a saw was used, the pieces were called steaks. This is why lamb cuts, except for the leg slices that are steaked, are called chops.

First Considerations

A well-devised butchering plan will help achieve good results. It starts a day before you plan on slaughtering the sheep, lamb, or goat. Sheep and goats have a digestive tract that has a higher percentage of the live weight than other livestock, such as cattle and pigs. This makes it important to withhold all feed for between 18 to 24 hours. Fasting your animal will allow it to empty the stomach and intestinal tract of fecal material that has the potential to contaminate the carcass during evisceration. You will still need to provide full access to water. Providing water will avoid dehydration, which can result in tissue shrinkage and difficulty in removing the pelt.

Choosing an Animal

If you raised your own sheep or goats, you should be able to determine the healthiest one in your flock as a good candidate for butchering. It should also be one with the most muscling and least fat.

If you are purchasing a live sheep, goat, or a lamb, be sure to examine it first. The eyes, nose, and mouth should be clean with no watering or discharge. It should move about easily without exhibiting any lameness or limping. The presence of either may indicate an injury or other physical illness that will lower the carcass and muscle quality. Observe the animal's breathing pattern. If it is labored or fast, it may indicate lung problems or a fever. Refuse to purchase any animal if the physical signs you see do not appear as normal or you sense something might be wrong.

You may want to consider purchasing a female for butchering to avoid removing the male sex organs. Some believe there is a distinct difference in meat flavor between a female and intact male.

Lambs are typically marketed when they reach between 90 to 140 pounds live weight. After slaughter, the resulting carcass will weigh roughly 50 percent of this amount. Depending on your storage capacity, you may be able to purchase a whole or half carcass for butchering.

Handling

Proper handling of sheep and goats at all times is good husbandry and minimizes damage or injury to the live animal. It is particularly important during the time leading up to slaughter to reduce the chances of damaging or bruising the muscles. Bruised muscles yield a lower quality carcass and, if severe enough, may require the bruises to be cut out of the meat, lowering your total yield. To prevent bruising, provide sufficient room for the sheep to move about and still be caught without injury. Avoid lifting it by its fleece or hair, as this will also cause bruises to the carcass. When moving your animal to the confinement area, place one hand under its jaw and the other at the dock (tail) and lead it.

Be careful of the sheep or goat if it has horns, which can be used in defense if they perceive to be in imminent danger. Sheep or goat horns have pointed tips, which can cause serious injury to anyone handling them.

The process to harvest a sheep or goat is essentially identical, so the following descriptions apply to each.

Equipment and Tools

The minimum equipment you should have available include a sharp skinning knife for

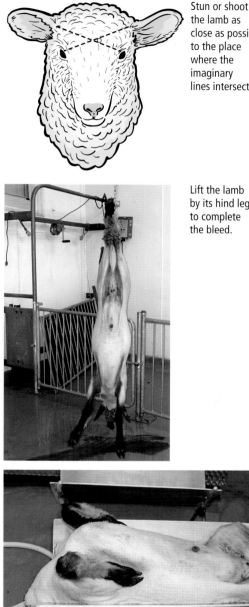

Stun or shoot the lamb as close as possible to the place where the imaginary lines intersect.

Lift the lamb by its hind legs to complete the bleed.

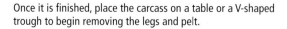

Once it is finished, place the carcass on a table or a V-shaped trough to begin removing the legs and pelt.

removing the pelt, a table or platform on which to lay the eviscerated carcass, or a hoist to lift the sheep by the hind legs to eye or chest level. If available, you can use a cradle, which is a trough about 6 inches wide at the bottom with sloping sides 6 inches high to be used for skinning. A dripping pan to catch the blood after sticking will keep the area below the carcass from becoming messy. Using a chain-mail glove on your free hand will prevent accidental cuts.

Stunning and Sticking

Several methods can be used to either stun or quickly dispatch a sheep. Inexpensive electrical stunners can be used for only one or two animals. These use an electric current to initiate cardiac arrest to kill the sheep. The animal can then be placed on a table, cradle, or hoist to begin the butchering process.

The simplest method to kill the sheep is to stick the jugular vein with your knife to create blood flow. This can be done by placing the sheep on its side, wrapping the front feet and rear feet together so that the hooves cannot cause you injury, and then placing it on a table or platform with its head draped over the edge.

If you choose to hoist the sheep by its hind legs, tie its front feet together with a rope or cord and then pull it tight toward its hind legs. This will hold the front legs steady, restrain the sheep, and allow you to make a swift, clean kill.

To cut the jugular veins, grasp the jaw or ear with one hand and insert the knife behind the jaw while drawing it blade edge outward and out through the pelt. This will sever the jugular veins and carotid arteries.

One advantage of sticking a sheep versus stunning it is that you achieve a more complete bleed from the body because the heart

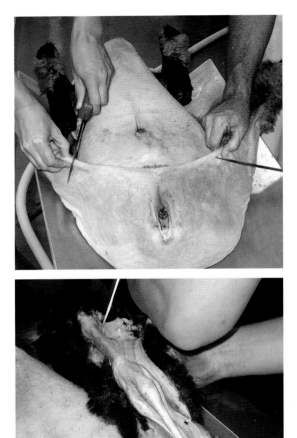

Begin removing the pelt by slicing down the rear legs from the hock to the midline of the pelvis and down the forelegs to the brisket. Peel the pelt back to expose the leg bones. Then remove them by making cuts at the break joint, which is located just above the foot.

is still beating. If the sheep is suspended by its hind legs, the flow of blood is downward and will continue while the heart works. Gravity will assist in making as complete a bleed as possible. For lambs, the blood yield may be as much as 3 percent of their live weight.

Skinning

When the blood has finished flowing from the carcass, you can place the sheep on its back in the cradle or on a table. To begin skinning the carcass, grasp a foreleg and slice the skin open with the point of your knife down toward the chest. Do the same with the other foreleg, having the two cuts meet at the front of the breastbone. Then finish skinning out both front legs.

Next, skin the hind legs. Begin by holding one leg and open it down the backside from the hoof to the rectum by holding your knife fairly flat as you slice down. Holding it in this way will help avoid cutting the tendon and the colorless connective tissue membrane just under the skin that separates it from the meat in the carcass. All four legs should now be skinless. You can start removing the feet at either the front or rear.

Remove the front feet by cutting through either the break joint or spool joint, depending on the age of the animal. In young lambs,

the break joint will be a swelling in the long canon bone just above the foot. Break joints in yearlings and older sheep are denser and harder to cut. For these, you should remove the foot at the first joint above the hoof.

To remove the hind feet, begin by removing the foot at the joint closest to the hoof. By not cutting it higher, you will leave the backside tendon anchored, which you can use to suspend the carcass. Carefully slice along the leg bone for about 3 inches, separating tissue holding the tendon to the leg bone. These slits will allow you to insert hooks that will hold the carcass for evisceration. Do the same with the opposite hind leg.

To separate the skin and fleece from the body, grasp the pelt at the cut, make a fist with your free hand, and slide it forward separating the skin from the body. Push your fist against the pelt and not the carcass as you are loosening it. By repeating this motion, you will loosen the skin without needing to use a knife. This will eliminate cuts and

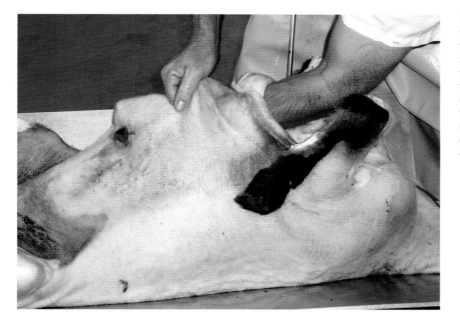

Place your fist between the pelt and muscles in the opening at the brisket and push inward to loosen the skin. This is called fisting and is the most effective way to separate the pelt from the body. Continue this motion down both sides while the carcass is still horizontal.

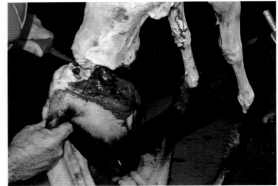

The pelt will still be attached to the front feet and head. Next remove the head by severing it at the atlas joint and finish removing the front feet at the break joints.

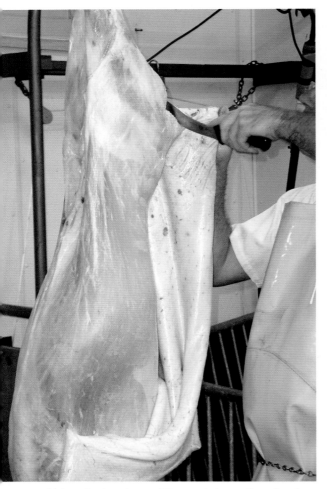

Make a circular cut around the anus to loosen the pelt and then pull downwards to strip it from the carcass.

bruises to the body of the carcass. Always have clean hands when loosening the pelt to avoid contaminating the carcass with wool and dirt from the fleece.

With most of the skin now loosened from the body, you can attach hooks to the hind leg tendons and raise the sheep to a level that allows you to comfortably work with the carcass. Once suspended, you can remove the head by cutting behind the jaw and separating it at the base of the skull.

The trachea and esophagus are still attached to the internal organs and must now be separated so that you can remove those organs during evisceration. You will then be able to pull them out when you remove the internal organs. If this separation is not done, you will need to split the brisket prior to evisceration to remove the abdominal and thoracic organs at the same time.

With the carcass suspended, cut open the center of the loosened pelt. Pull the fleece toward you as you slice down the belly being careful not to cut into the abdomen. Loosen all the skin by moving your fist around the entire carcass and up the legs. Avoid pulling or stripping the pelt off the carcass as this may damage the connective tissue membrane by tearing and exposing the muscle.

Sever the anus by cutting across it where it is attached to the pelt. Then use your fist to loosen it. Finish loosening the pelt at the shoulders. Once the pelt is completely loose, it should easily slide off the carcass.

Rinse the carcass with clean, lukewarm water before opening the body cavity. This will remove any dirt, wool, or other foreign materials that may have attached to it.

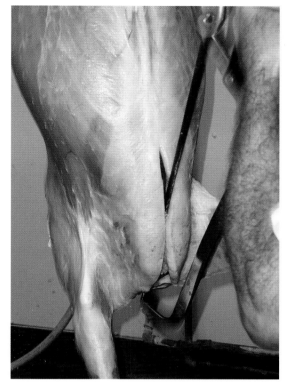

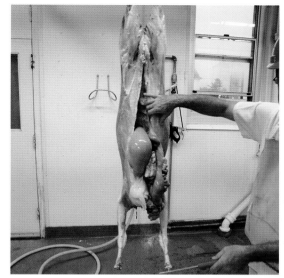

The visceral and thoracic cavities can be cleared in one step and placed in a tub for disposal or inspection. The carcass is now ready for trimming, followed by washing with clean, cold water.

To open the thoracic cavity, make a cut through the muscles to the brisket and saw through the sternum bone. Unlike beef, the esophagus and trachea do not need to be separated if the brisket is opened before both are removed.

Evisceration

Evisceration of sheep is very much like that of cattle and pigs, except they are smaller. Avoid cutting into the intestinal and digestive tract while opening the body cavity so that it is not contaminated by fecal material.

Place a bucket under the carcass to catch the intestines and blood. Begin by cutting around the anus, loosening it from the pelvis. Cut as close around the pelvic and tail bones as you can until it is free to pull out. You should tie the anus shut with string or a light cord so that any fecal contents do not spill out. Once securely tied, you can let it slide down into the body cavity.

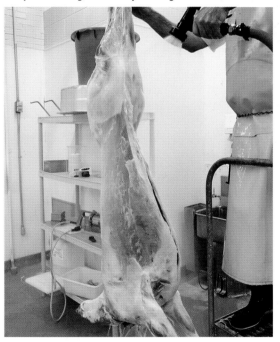

Inspect the carcass and remove any hair, fecal, or foreign matter attached to it. These are the main causes of lamb carcass contamination, which most often occurs during removal of the pelt. Once the carcass is clean, it is ready for washing, cooling, and later fabrication.

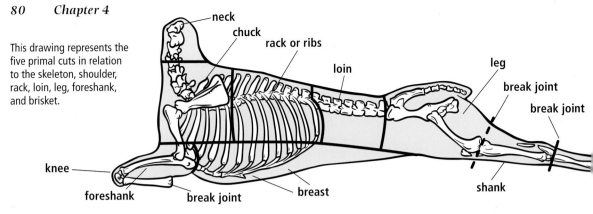

This drawing represents the five primal cuts in relation to the skeleton, shoulder, rack, loin, leg, foreshank, and brisket.

To open the belly, start your knife tip at a point just below the junction where the outer skin of the two hind legs intersects. Pull the skin toward you as you make a cut long enough to insert your first and second fingers to help guide the knife point. Or you can insert the handle into the abdomen cavity the same way as in cattle or pigs to open it.

After the body cavity is open, grasp the tied end of the anus that you let slide into the cavity earlier with your free hand and slowly pull the intestines and organs toward you. Gravity will help pull these from the body, and the bladder and kidneys will also drop as you sever the ureters.

When all the viscera have been removed, split the breastbone with a saw or sturdy knife. Wash both the inside and outside of the carcass with cool water and remove any traces of blood, dirt, tissue, and other foreign matter. You can also trim any scraggly ends or pieces from around the neck or other areas. The carcass is now ready to cool. Chilling the carcass makes it easier to cut up the various parts as the fat within the meat and the muscles become firm.

Lamb Cuts

With an average bone-out of about 30 percent meat for a market lamb, you can expect a yield of about 15 pounds from a lamb from a 100-pound carcass.

If cooled, lamb carcasses typically are left whole and not split in half before fabrication begins. If splitting the carcass, use a heavy knife or meat saw and slice down the backbone to separate the two sides. If not splitting the carcass lengthwise, you can begin with a lateral cut.

Five primal cuts begin the process of deconstructing the chilled carcass: leg, loin, rack (ribs), shoulder, and foreshank. These can be further broken down into the more valued cuts.

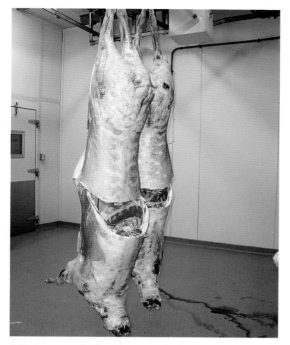

Split the carcass by first separating the foresaddle and hindsaddle between the twelfth and thirteenth ribs. The two carcasses shown here have been split but are still hanging in a cooler. Once they are placed on a cutting table, begin by cutting off the legs at the rear hocks and front knees.

Live Animal Lamb Cuts

12 percent from legs
4 percent from loin
4 percent from rack
10 percent from shoulder
30 percent total meat

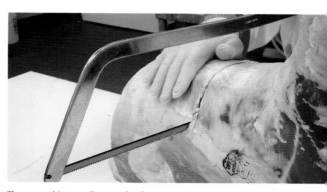

There are thirteen ribs on a lamb carcass. To separate the rack from the shoulder, count eight ribs from the posterior end and cut through the muscle with a knife; finish cutting through the backbone with a saw. There will be four ribs remaining in the shoulder.

The lamb carcass is not split longitudinally, from rump to shoulder. Rather it is cut laterally, across the body. For home use, this is not necessary because you are cutting the carcass to suit your needs rather than a specific market or other customer.

To split the carcass in half, you will need a meat saw or a heavy, sturdy knife to slice down the backbone. This is most easily done by suspending the carcass by the hind legs. Begin at the aitchbone of the pelvis and saw a straight line down and through the end of the neck.

If you are going to process the carcass during the same session, you can leave one half suspended while you cut up the other. Lay one half on a clean, sanitized table,

making sure that the equipment you use has been thoroughly cleaned and sanitized. The process of cutting up a lamb carcass allows you to break down large sections into smaller pieces for further cutting. Try to cut it up in a room with a cool temperature to keep the meat from becoming too warm.

Begin by dividing the half into two parts: the foresaddle and the hindsaddle. This roughly cuts it in half. The foresaddle consists of the shoulder, rack, foreshank, and breast and makes up about 51 percent of the carcass. The hindsaddle composes the loin, leg, and flank and represents about 49 percent. To separate them, make a lateral cut across the carcass between the twelfth and thirteenth ribs.

One very useful tool is a plastic bone scraper. This helps scrape away bone dust caused by the blade sawing through bone. Bone is a good medium for microorganisms to grow and reduces the shelf life of meat. Scraping away this bone dust will minimize those effects.

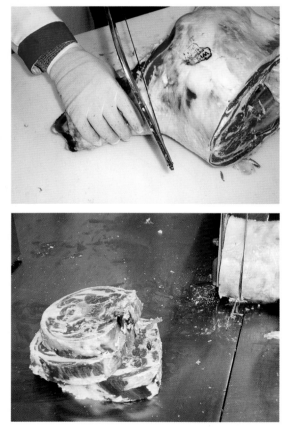

Remove the neck with a lateral cut just in front of the shoulder. It can then be cut into neck slices for roasting or braising, or trimmed and used as stew meat, ground lamb, or for sausage.

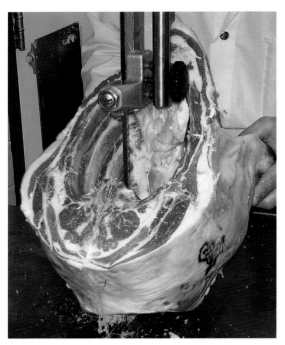

Split the shoulder in half and trim away the fat. Cut off the breast where cartilage appears and then remove the remaining portion of the foreshank. This should expose the brisket bone, which can be pulled out by hand.

Foresaddle

Slightly larger than the rear of the carcass, the foresaddle contains four major portions that can be further reduced. Begin by dividing it into two pieces that contain the shoulder and rack (ribs). This cut is made between the fourth and fifth ribs and will leave you with an eight-rib rack for later. At this point, the breast and foreshank are still attached. They should be separated from the shoulder and rack. Remove them by sawing across the arm bone at a point slightly above the junction of the arm bone and the foreshank bone.

The shoulder is the largest cut in the foresaddle and contains a number of bones that make it more difficult to carve and slice. However, if properly cooked, shoulders provide a delightful meal.

Remove the neck from the shoulder by cutting across it laterally, leaving about 1 inch of neck on the shoulder. The neck then can be sliced into small pieces.

The shoulder is often called a square-cut because it fits the dimensions of a square. It includes the blade face, which has a surface mostly of bone and lacks muscle, with part of the blade cartilage. Any chops removed from the shoulder are called blade chops because of the presence of the scapula, or shoulder blade. The most forward portion of the ribeye will extend through this area.

The arm chops come from the arm face that is positioned at a right angle to the blade face. This is the muscular part of the shoulder, but it is less tender because these muscles do a lot of work in providing locomotion for the live animal. Typically, muscles that have more use are less palatable and also contain a considerable amount of connective tissue to other less-used muscles.

Instead of making chops, you can cut out the rib cage and then the ribeye by following the natural seam. This is the boneless blade roll that can be held together with skewers. You can also cut out the shoulder bone and use it as a boneless roast. The rest of the shoulder pieces can be diced for stew meat or kabobs after the bones have been removed.

Hindsaddle

The hindsaddle contains the most valuable cuts of the sheep or lamb. These include the loin, leg, and flank. Start your cuts by removing as much of the flank as possible. Do this by making a cut about 2 inches away from the loin eye. The flank is a large, flat, straight muscle that, in beef, is cut into flank steaks. Because of its size, texture, and flavor, it is best used for ground meat with sheep and lambs, or it can be rolled to be roasted.

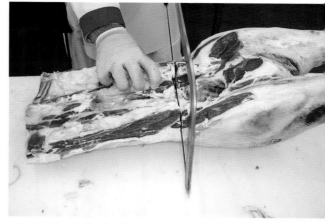

Before cutting the hindsaddle, remove as much of the flank as possible by making a cut 2 inches from the edge of the loin through the thirteenth rib and following the cut parallel to the loin and along the leg. These can be cut later into flank steaks or ground meat. Remove the leg by making a cut through the last lumbar vertebrae. Use your knife for your initial cut and finish with your saw.

Split the leg portion of the hindquarters into halves by sawing through the aitchbone.

You can remove the leg (shank portion) first if using a band saw. Otherwise, it can remain and be used to hold the lamb leg as you remove leg sirloin chops. There are two to three sirloin chops per leg per side. They are recognizable because part of the pelvic bone will be in them.

The leg is the largest cut and represents about one-third of the lamb carcass. When you cut the leg from the loin, the sirloin will be included with it. Although typically referred to as a leg of lamb, this term also implies that it is the whole leg with the sirloin still intact.

To separate this primal cut from the loin, sever it at the seventh, or last, vertebra. Use a saw to make your cut, as this will result in a flat face surface on the loin. To remove the tailbone with your knife, make the cut so that it leaves three tail vertebrae on the leg.

You can trim off any outside fat, but avoid removing the thin membrane that separates the pelt from the muscle. This membrane holds the shape of the leg and helps retain moisture and juices during cooking.

To remove the leg, cut the Achilles tendon, the large tendon above the hock where it attaches at the base of the leg muscle, leaving the other end attached to the hock. Cut through either the hock joint to remove the lower part of the leg or through the break joint that is located about 1½ inches above the hock. In lambs, you may be able to use your knife to break this soft area, but it will generally require the use of a saw for older sheep or goats.

The hindshank is composed of a large amount of connective tissue, which can be identified as white, silvery streaks. Because this is a less tender portion, it is best used as ground meat. You can remove the shank

Judas Goat

Sheep have a natural flocking instinct and will huddle together or follow the leader of the group, particularly if they perceive an outside threat. Because of this behavior, they can be manipulated in their movements by using a goat. At some packing houses, goats are usually reliable and will return time after time to lead lambs to slaughter. Any goat that fills this role is known as a Judas Goat for its deception and betrayal of the lambs.

The loin is the most valuable cut of the lamb carcass and will vary in size from end to end. It can be cut with the backbone attached for loin chops or completely cut out to make a boneless loin roast.

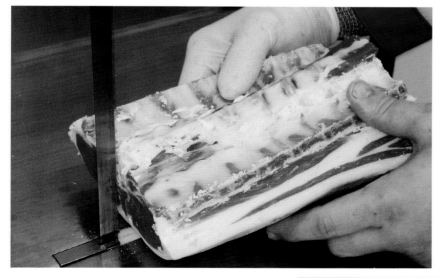

Left and Below: Split the loin down the spine into two separate halves being careful not to cut into the loin eye. You can make 2-inch lateral cuts to create chops. The bones can remain intact or removed as desired. Removing them creates boneless chops or a boneless loin roast.

muscle by cutting through at the stifle joint, which is the second joint above the foot. Once separated, you can trim the meat from the bone and set it aside for grinding, or it can be cut into smaller pieces for braising. The shank can also be roasted.

The sirloin may be removed from the leg with lateral cuts made into sirloin steaks. The

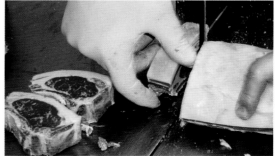

The ribs can be cut into four sections from the two carcass sides. Each of these can be grilled or roasted as a rack of ribs or riblets.

largest of these will be located at the top of the sirloin. You can saw the whole leg into chops and steaks. This will result in four to six sirloin chops, depending on how thick you wish to make them. These chops are similar to beef sirloin steaks in bone and muscle structure.

Because of the pelvic bone, the rump is not sliced or made into steaks. However, by trimming and removing this bone, the meat can be used for kabobs, stews, or ground into patties.

The lamb's legs may be separated into sirloin and shank halves, and these may be further broken down if desired. The leg can be either boned out or made into steaks. The boneless leg then can be roasted or tied into a rolled roast.

To remove the pelvic bone, cut around the ball where it joins the leg. You will be able to trim it out and then separate it from the leg bone at the ball joint. Remove the shank at the stifle joint, which will allow you to

cut around the end of the leg bone until it is loosened.

You should be able to remove the entire leg by pulling on it without cutting any of the muscles. There is a lymph node, usually surrounded by fat, located at the rear end of the boned leg between the bottom and the eye muscles. Carefully trim this node off without cutting into it. With the leg now finished, you can begin work on the loin.

Loin

The loin is the most valuable cut in the carcass because it contains the most tender muscles. The loin and rack (ribs) often compete for the higher price because there are so few of them from each animal. Only 4 percent of the live animal will end up being cut into loin chops.

From end to end, the loin will vary in size and shape. At the seventh lumbar vertebrae, the loin eye is oval-shaped and the tenderloin is at its maximum size. At the front end, the loin is larger and more symmetrically shaped.

You can cut the loin into chop widths of between 2 to 3 inches, leaving the bone, which looks like a T, and is similar to the T-bone steak in beef cuts. Or you can remove the vertebrae to produce a boneless loin chop, which can be rolled, netted, or tied. You can also leave the loin intact for a loin roast.

Rough Cuts

There are several pieces still left to cut, including the flank of the hindsaddle and the foreshank and breast of the foresaddle. These account for about 10 percent of the carcass weight but typically have more fat than muscle. Trim as much of the fat away as possible and use the meat pieces for grinding into patties.

The breast contains rib bones and the breastbone. You can cut each rib apart for riblets or you can cut them into sections of several ribs together for lamb spareribs. There is a thick muscle in the breast, which corresponds to the beef brisket, that can be trimmed and used for cubes.

The foreshank can be braised or trimmed and cubed for stew meat, or ground into patties. When finished with the first half of the carcass, you can begin with the opposite half to make the same cuts.

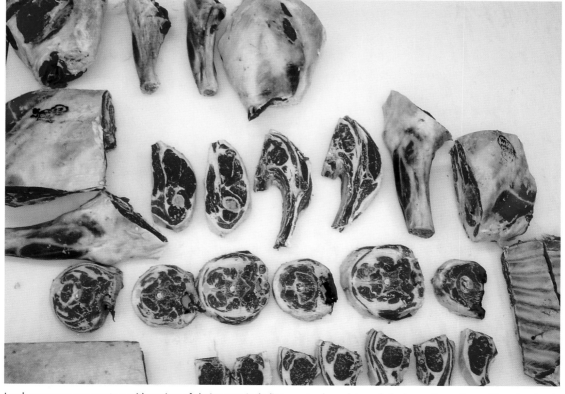

Lamb carcasses can create a wide variety of choice cuts, including roasts, chops, loin and rib chops, ribs, racks, and legs. Lamb cuts are increasing in popularity and provide an interesting alternative to beef and pork.

Broiled Lamb Patties

1½ lbs. ground lamb   1 tsp. salt
2 tbsp. grated onion   ½ tsp. pepper

Mix all ingredients thoroughly. Shape into thick patties. Place on a rack under preheated broiler, about 3 inches from source of heat so that by the time the patties are browned on the top they will be half done. Turn and brown on other side. Allow about 15 minutes to cook. Serves 6.

Roast Leg of Lamb

1 leg lamb, 5 to 6 pounds   ¼ tsp. pepper
1½ tbsp. salt

Remove shank bone. Rub meat with salt and pepper. Place fat side up on a rack in an uncovered roasting pan. Roast at 300° to 325°F for 30 to 35 minutes to the pound or until a meat thermometer registers 175° to 180°. Serve with a garnish. Variations: 1) Rub meat with the cut edge of a clove of garlic or place slivers of garlic into deep narrow gashes cut in meat. 2) Rub 1 teaspoon ginger over surface of meat. 3) Baste lamb with vinegar that has been seasoned with finely cut mint leaves. 4) Baste lamb with a mixture of ½ cup tomato ketchup and 2 tablespoons Worcestershire sauce. 5) Rub meat with finely chopped mint leaves. Baste meat frequently the last hour of roasting with ½ cup grape jelly melted in ½ cup water.

Shepherd's Pie

Leftover stew   **Mashed potatoes**

Use leftover stew. Line a baking dish with hot mashed potatoes. Fill the center with hot stew, cover with additional mashed potatoes, and place in hot oven at 425°F for 15 minutes or until potatoes are browned.

Braised Leg of Lamb or Mutton

1 leg of lamb or mutton, 5 to 6 pounds
½ c. each finely chopped celery, carrot, and onion
2 tbsp. drippings or other fat
3 cups vinegar
3 cups water
½ tsp. each of powdered thyme and marjoram

6 whole cloves
1 clove garlic
2 tbsp. chopped parsley
12 peppercorns
½ bay leaf
1 tbsp. salt
1 pint sour cream
½ pint stock

Sauté celery, carrot, and onion in drippings until light brown. Add vinegar and water, and cook until vegetables are tender. Cool. Place meat in a deep dish. Pour the first mixture over meat, being careful to have the meat entirely covered. Add seasonings. Marinate meat in this mixture for 24 hours. Drain and dry thoroughly. Place in a roasting pan and bake at 300°F for 30 minutes. Add sour cream and stock, cover and cook until tender, allowing 30 to 35 minutes per pound. Baste frequently. Boil the liquid in which the meat was marinated until only a small amount remains, strain, and pour over meat when serving.

Lamb Stew

2 pounds lamb cubes, shank,
   breast, neck, or shoulder
2 tbsp. flour
2 tbsp. fat
Salt and pepper
Hot water

6 potatoes
6 carrots
3 onions
1 c. fresh peas
3 tomatoes
Flour

Coat lamb with flour and brown in hot fat. Season with salt and pepper, cover with water, and simmer until nearly tender, about 1 to 1½ hours. Add peeled vegetables, except tomatoes, whole or cut in cubes and simmer 30 minutes longer or until tender. Add tomatoes and simmer 10 minutes longer. Mix a little flour with water to a smooth paste and add enough to the liquid to thicken slightly. Serves 6.

Barbecued Lamb

6-pound leg of lamb
2 tsp. salt
Flour
1 onion, sliced
1 c. water

½ c. ketchup
2 tbsp. steak sauce, such as A-1
2 tbsp. Worcestershire sauce
¼ tsp. cayenne powder

Wipe leg of lamb with damp cloth, rub with salt, and coat with flour. Place in a roasting pan and surround with onion. Combine remaining ingredients, mix well, and pour over meat. Roast at 350°F for 30 minutes for each pound. Baste every 20 minutes with the sauce. Serves 8.

Making Use of Leftovers

Coarse-grind meat trimmings. Add water and flavoring mixture. Regrind through ¼-inch plate. Using this formulation the following products can be made:

- Wieners—stuff in sheep casings; smoke and cook to 155°F internal temperature.

- Dinner franks—stuff in hog casings; smoke and cook to 155°F internal temperature.

- Ring bologna—stuff in 6-inch diameter fibrous casings; smoke and cook to 155°F internal temperature.

- Leona—add 10 pounds cooked, diced, and skinned hog jowls plus 5⅓ tablespoons garlic powder to the emulsion; stuff into 2-inch diameter fibrous casings; smoke and cook to 155°F internal temperature.

- Pickle and pimento loaf—add 2½ pounds sweet pickles and 2½ pounds pimentos. Stuff into parchment-lined metal molds or waterproof fibrous casing. Can be water-cooked or baked to internal temperature of 155°F.

- Macaroni and cheese loaf—add 2½ pounds cheese and 2½ pounds cooked macaroni. Proceed as with pickle and pimento loaf.

Source: North Dakota State University Agriculture and University Extension

A healthy, well-grown, 200-pound pig is a good choice for home butchering because it will yield about 100 to 110 pounds of eating meat. *Shutterstock/Adriano Castelli*

Chapter 5

PORK

Three eras stand out from a modern historical perspective in pork production that explain as much about society's taste patterns as they do about farming trends. These can be described as the eras of lard, meat and bacon, and lean white meat.

Lard once found many uses, such as in making candles, soaps, and cooking fats. As lard demand decreased with the advent of petroleum products, vegetable oils, electricity, and consumer dietary changes, the trend moved away from fat hogs to leaner ones with a higher ratio of muscle to fat. A period followed where the fat composition in pork meat dropped so dramatically that consumers found it lacking in flavor and moved more toward chicken consumption for their white meat. Today, a more tasteful pork product is produced because of a favorable balance between fat and lean.

A 200-pound pig with a typical 72 percent dressing weight will yield a carcass of about 145 pounds, or about 73 pounds per each half or side. This will include meat, bones, and fat. The cutting yield is the amount of meat you get from the total carcass. Using a typical cutout rate of 60 percent for pigs, this 145-pound carcass will yield about 110 pounds of meat for

You can raise the pigs yourself, purchase them live from a grower, or purchase a dressed carcass from a local butcher and fabricate the carcass yourself.

your use. The other 35 pounds will include fat trim, bones, and skin.

The largest part of the carcass is usually the ham, which can be about 23 percent of the live carcass, but 18 percent of a dressed one, or in this case about 27 pounds. The side or belly and the loin areas represent about 15 percent each, or about 40 pounds. The picnic and Boston butt are each about 10 percent or 16 to 20 pounds, and the miscellaneous portions—including the jowl, feet, neck bones, skin, fat, bone, and shrink—account for about 25 percent of the carcass weight. In our example, this would amount to about 38 pounds, which is well over a third of the entire carcass. There may be some variance between pigs; these percentages generally hold true for normal, well-developed pigs of that weight range.

Pork Cuts

The five major areas where cuts are derived can be further broken down into cuts often found in retail markets: the picnic shoulder, Boston butt, loin, ham, and belly or sides. One reason retailers or you, if you are marketing your meat to others, decide to charge higher price for certain cuts is because of supply, demand, taste, and ease of cooking. For example, pork chops typically are in demand and relatively easy to prepare. They sell quickly while other cuts may not move as fast.

The picnic shoulder includes the upper front leg above the knee. This cut lies just below the Boston butt and contains a higher level of fat than the other cuts, which makes it a flavorful and tender portion. The picnic shoulder can be smoked and cured to make the picnic ham, which is then ready to eat cold or hot. The arm and shank bones make up the shoulder and create a high ratio of bone to lean meat. When well-trimmed, this cut is used for lean ground pork and can be cubed or cut into strips to use for kabobs, stir-fry, or stews.

The Boston butt, also called the shoulder butt, is often a better cut than the picnic shoulder. It lies at the upper portion of the shoulder from the top to the plate to make the backbone. This cut is tender, full of flavor, and can be cut into roasts with the bone intact or cut out for boneless roasts. The roasts can be cut into blade steaks that can be broiled, grilled, or braised.

The pork loin cuts are located directly behind the Boston butt and include a portion of the shoulder blade bone. The loin includes most of the ribs and backbone all the way to the hipbone at the rear. There is a loin area on each side of the pig and together will account for about 20 percent of the carcass weight. Many retail cuts are derived from the loin, including top loin roasts, pork chops, baby back ribs, pork tenderloins, loin chops, rib chops, and blade chops.

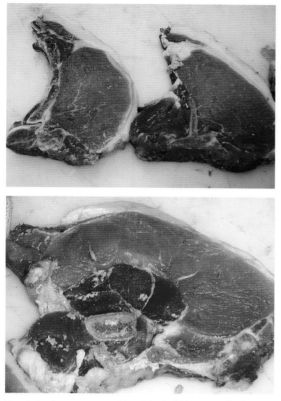

The meat and fat trimmings from pork can be used in several different ways, including mixing in sausage, particularly with wild game, to add texture and flavor.

Top: Loin chops are cut to ½ to 1 inch thicknesses. The loin chop has a portion of the loin on one side and tenderloin on the other, and it is located toward the junction of the leg and loin. The rib chop (on left) only contains the loin muscle.
Above: The sirloin chop can be identified by the round bone or flat bone shape. The rib chop, on the right, contains part of the rib bone the sirloin does not.

The loin constitutes a long strip that contains the top section of the ribs. When these are trimmed away, the result is a boneless pork loin. The section of the loin between the blade end and sirloin end is usually referred to as the center, as in center chops and center roasts. A boneless pork loin is smoked to produce Canadian bacon. Rib bones trimmed from the loin can be barbecued as pork back ribs. This is also the area where pork backfat is located. This is the thick layer of fat between the skin and the eye muscle, which may have some cooking uses but is used mostly to help determine carcass grades.

Hams make up about one-quarter of the carcass weight and come from the rear leg area of the pig and include the aitch, leg, and hindshank bones. This is a prime cut area of the pig because it contains little connective tissue, making it more flavorful whether it is cooked, cured, or smoked. Hams can be deboned, and the shank portion of the ham, called the ham hock, is used the same as the shoulder hock.

The pork belly or sides are where the bacon and spareribs are cut. They are located below the loin on each side and account for about 15 to 20 percent of the carcass weight. This area contains a lot of fat with streaks of lean meat. It also provides the spareribs, which are separated from the rest of the belly before cooking.

The miscellaneous portion of the carcass includes the jowl, pig's feet, tail, neck bones, skin, and fat. Some cooks highly prize these areas, but the parts are often dismissed by the general public as unusable.

Eating raw pork is strongly discouraged because of the presence of a parasite *Trichinella spiralis* that causes trichinosis in humans. These little roundworms migrate into pig muscles and mature into an infective stage. Unless destroyed by minimum cooking temperatures of 140 degrees Fahrenheit, they still will be viable parasites for infections. Most experts recommend a minimum of 150 degrees Fahrenheit for cooking because of the inaccuracy of many thermometers. Trichinosis infections in humans can cause nausea, diarrhea, muscle pains, and aching joints. It is a treatable infection but nevertheless is an uncomfortable experience.

Butchering at Home

Whether you are butchering at home or having a pig processed at a local meat slaughter plant, you will have to decide which pig to use if you have more than one to consider. Pork carcasses for home meat use should be the highest quality pig you produce and one that is from five to eight months of age. Pigs fed liberal amounts and quality feeds grow rapidly and will produce pork of proper size and finish.

Butchering at home requires some thought before, during, and after the entire process. Planning ahead for this event will minimize mistakes, reduce the chance of injury to helpers, and provide you with quality meat products for your family.

Develop a list of all the steps needed, from beginning to end, several days before butchering your pig. Planning ahead will reduce any surprises during the butchering process and help organize the event in a logical, efficient manner. Having a list of the equipment and

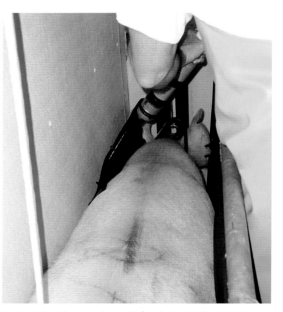

Begin with a clean work area before bringing the pig in to kill. The area used should be as free of dirt, dust, flies, and insects as possible. When everything is ready, you can use an electric stunner or a gun to immobilize the pig and to render it unconscious.

butchering tools required will ensure everything is at hand when needed. Attention must be paid to cleanliness at all times so the meat isn't contaminated during any part of the process. A review of the skeletal structure, digestive system, the placement of organs, and some understanding of the circulatory system will be useful when you are cutting the carcass. Knowing the precise location of the jugular veins with in the neck will help you make a clean, swift kill.

The location where you plan to carry out the kill should be properly equipped for the job. A shed or building that is free from dust or outside elements can provide a good place for the initial stages. If this is used, construct a small holding pen near the butchering table to reduce the distance the carcass has to be carried. If you decide to butcher the pig outside, a sheltered pen can be built near the area you will work to cut it up.

There are two ways to remove the skin and hair. One is by manually skinning the pig, which actually requires less effort, and the other is by using a scalding procedure. These will be detailed later in this chapter, but keep in mind that if you choose to use the scalding method, you will need a convenient heating arrangement, such as a scalding vat, and an efficient way of swinging the carcass into the boiling water with a block and tackle or some other apparatus.

A proper set of butchering tools includes sticking knives, skinning knives, boning knives, butcher knives, a steel sharpener, meat saws, and meat hooks. Other useful items include thermometers, a meat grinder, meat needles for sewing rolled cuts, hair scrapers, hand wash tubs, clean dry towels, soap, and vats with hot and cold water.

Providing a proper location and sharp tools will aid in more efficient slaughtering and less time spent looking for items at critical moments.

Care Before Butchering

Two to three days before butchering, confine the pig in a small solitary pen. Provide plenty of fresh water, but restrict feed 24 hours before butchering so the pig has less material in its stomach and intestines. Providing a cool and calm environment several days beforehand will keep the pig rested and quiet. Never attempt to butcher a pig that is overheated, excited, or fatigued. When the body temperature is above normal, the meat easily becomes feverish and is difficult to chill properly; poorly chilled meat cannot be properly cured. This increase in temperature can cause the meat to spoil or be tainted before it is cut up.

Some spoilage and low-quality meat can be directly attributed to natural forms of bacteria that have been allowed to develop and multiply. The bacteria that is found in the blood and tissues of a live pig must be held in check to prevent it from multiplying until the meat is cured. This is one reason butchering was historically done in the early spring or late fall of the year when the weather was cool. Think of it as a race between the bacterial action in the blood and tissues that want to multiply and the curing agents used, such as salt, cold water, and other factors, which depress bacterial growth. You need to win this race.

Dispatching Your Pig

When the butchering tools are laid out, the table is thoroughly washed with soap and dried, enough help is on hand, dripping pans are ready to catch blood, ice is in the cooling vat, and everything is in place, you can dispatch your pig.

This is perhaps the most critical time in the whole process, and if you feel uncomfortable sticking a knife into the throat of

Stun or shoot the hog at a point near the intersection of the two imaginary lines, just above the eyes and at the center of the forehead.

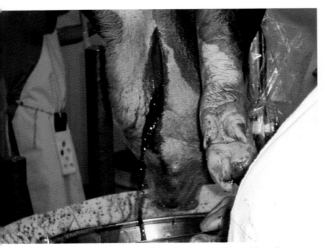

After the pig is unconscious, tie the rear feet with a chain or sturdy rope and raise it. Use your sticking knife positioned between the lower jaw and breastbone and press the blade deep into the center of the neck. Make a small vertical incision to sever the jugular vein. This will release a large quantity of blood, which can then be caught in a pan or tub.

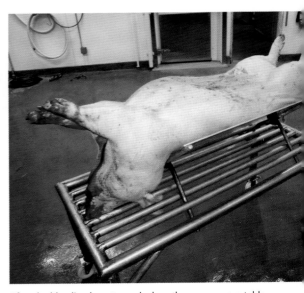

After the bleeding has stopped, place the carcass on a table or rack. The V-shaped trough shown here can be made for use with pigs, sheep, deer, goats, or veal calves.

a live pig, you may want to have someone else adept at the task handle this part of the process. This should be arranged prior to this day and not be a last-minute decision.

Butchering a pig by only sticking it with a knife is the most practical, efficient, and humane method of killing a pig. Other methods, such as shooting, are less reliable unless the pig is very agitated. A good bleed is difficult to obtain when the pig is shot because the heart stops and no longer pumps blood through the body. If you shoot the pig, you will need to rely on gravity to drain most of the blood from the carcass rather than being assisted by heart action.

You can stick the pig either in a raised or prone position, depending on whether or not you have equipment to raise it in the air. To hoist the pig in the air, a chain or straps can be looped between the hock and the hoof in order not to bruise the hams. The pig has less ability to free itself if hanging upside down than if it is rolled on its back and the feet are held by several people while one person sticks it. This upside down posture tends to immobilize the pig and makes the actions with your knife easier and safer for you. The most satisfactory bleed occurs when a pig's head hangs downward. Be aware that this position will be very uncomfortable for the pig and it will typically flail its feet that are free. The feet must be firmly immobilized, as they can be used by the pig to defend itself.

When the pig is safely immobilized, press the sharp blade edge of the sticking knife in front of the point of the breastbone and quickly slide it in to make a short vertical incision about 4 inches long in the center of the neck. This should sever the jugular veins and release large quantities of blood. Having tubs placed below to catch the blood will make cleaning up easier and allow you to work around the pig in dry conditions. The knife should not be inserted too far into the

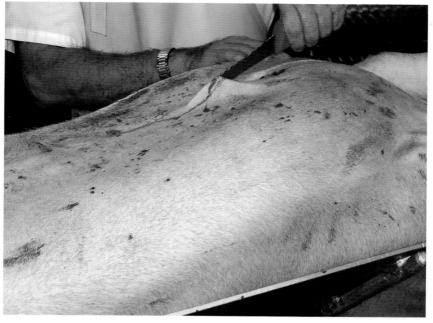

Skinning is the easiest way to remove the hair and hide if it is not used for tanning. Begin by making a vertical cut down the midline, knife blade out, of the carcass from the jowl to the pelvis, but avoid cutting through the abdominal wall.

neck so that it enters the chest cavity, as this will cause internal bleeding and blood clots.

Do not stick the heart, as it is needed to continue working properly to pump out the blood as rapidly as possible. Cutting the heart will cause internal bleeding and create lower quality meat. The key to this phase is to get a good bleed as quickly as possible. When the blood flow has stopped or slowed to a drip, your pig can be moved to a table where it can be skinned, which requires less time and effort than scalding it.

Skinning

Skinning is the removal of the hide from the pig and takes off the outside layer without using hot water or the extra effort of scraping the hair. Most home butchering will not require the use of the skin, which is generally discarded. In the past, the skin was left on the bacon and hams to protect them, but this is not required with modern refrigeration.

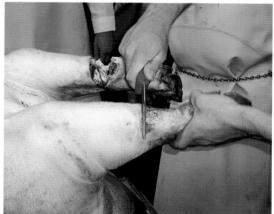

Remove the front feet by cutting at a point just below the back of the knee joint. Severing the tendons will allow you to break the joint forward. Then cut completely through the exposed joint to sever the foot. Do the same with the rear feet.

When skinning a pig it's important to remove the skin from the belly without puncturing the abdomen with your knife. This is best accomplished by laying the carcass on a table or trolley for suspending it at an appropriate work height.

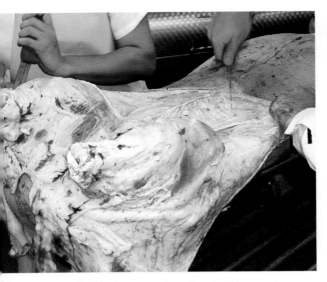

Begin the skinning process by pulling the skin up and away from the carcass, and make slow, sweeping motions between the skin and body with your skinning knife. Applying an outward pressure with you knife blade while skinning will help avoid cutting into the carcass.

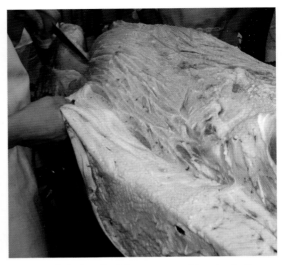

As you work the length of the carcass, avoid contaminating it with hair or dirt from the skin. Have clean water nearby to wash your free hand. Also, wash your knife frequently. If the carcass is on its back, you will need to turn it or raise it to finish removing the skin. Be sure the surface where you lay the partially skinned carcass is clean.

With a short skinning knife, begin your first cuts at the rear ankles and slice completely around them, but avoid cutting the tendons above the hocks. Cut down the inside center of each leg to a point below the pelvis and avoid deep cuts into the meat. Do the same with the front legs and cut to a center point at the base of the chest. Use your knife to score a line down the center of the belly, from the anus to the base of the chest, without penetrating the abdominal wall. Start at the chest and create tension on the skin by pulling it away with one hand as you slice with the other. This tension will help separate the skin from the body.

When finished with both front legs, start on the belly and slowly work to the rear, pulling the skin away from the center until you reach the base. Do the same with the other side. Start at the top of the rear legs by pulling the skin over the hams. At this point,

the skin should be loose from the belly and legs, and by pulling downward and slicing the skin, the weight of the skin will create tension to help with the rest of the process. Once the skin is completely removed, it can be set aside.

Scalding

If you do not want to use the skin for any further processes, such as tanning, you can dispense with scalding the pig. If you choose to scald the carcass, having the proper equipment makes the job easier, and you can use a tank or barrel for this step. The tank needs to be filled with water brought to a boil prior to immersing your pig. The water can be brought to a boil by using a pit fire underneath the tank, a gas or propane heater, or other means to safely raise the water temperature. This saves time in keeping the process moving because it is difficult to raise the water temperature once the pig is immersed in the water. The water should be kept at between 150 to 160 degrees Fahrenheit.

If you are using a long horizontal tank, rotate the carcass until the hair starts to slip. If using a barrel, first lower the head into the water while the feet and legs are dry. Then turn it around, placing the meat hooks in the lower jaw and lower the rear end into the boiling water. This is a more difficult method but will work if no other tank is available. Using an accurate thermometer will help you maintain the temperature, making the scalding easier and eliminating the chance of the hair setting tight against the skin. After lifting the carcass from the scalding water, wash it clean with hot water, scrape off any remaining scruff, and rinse it down again with cold water.

Be very careful when working with boiling water, as any spills can be harmful to you or anyone else helping. An accidental tipping of a barrel of boiling water can create hazardous conditions.

Scraping

Scraping the hair off the skin is the next step of the butchering process, and some of it can be done while the pig is still in the scalding vat when you are ready to lift the carcass out and place it out on the table. Using a scraper, start first at the head and feet, as these areas are the first to cool. Your scraping strokes should go in the direction the hair lays, as it will come off easier. After the hair has been removed, use your scraper in a circular motion to work out dirt or scruff that may be imbedded in the skin. A soft bristle brush is useful for cleaning up the carcass once the hair is removed. Any stray bristles of hair can be removed with a little hot water and a sharp knife.

Use a clean chain, rope, or gambrel to lift the carcass to allow easier removal of the remaining skin. To use a gambrel, make a slit in front of the rear leg bones without cutting the tendons. Place the gambrel points in the slits and raise the carcass. The tendons are strong enough to hold the heavy carcass while suspended if they haven't been cut.

Hanging

If the pig is laid out on the table, locate the area between the foot and the hock on the rear legs. Make deep cuts up the center of the bone on each leg to find three tendons. Use your fingers to pull the tendons out and slip the gambrel stick through one tendon and then the other. These tendons are strong enough to hold a hanging carcass while you open up the body cavity. Before you make any cuts and incisions to open the carcass, be sure all knives and butchering tools have been scalded and cleaned. Any knife or other tool to be used should be scalded again before use if they have been dropped on the floor. From here on, cleanliness is absolutely essential.

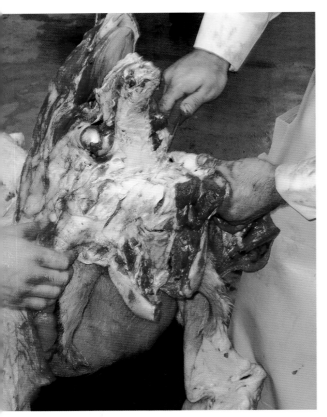

The head can be removed before skinning or after the carcass is raised. If left until skinning is finished, remove it by making a cut behind the ears between the axis and atlas joint and around the lower jaw to sever it. The axis joint is the first cervical vertebrae. Then remove the cheek muscles, tongue, and fat.

Removing the Head

Removing the head first accomplishes two things: It gets it out of the way and aids in quickly cooling the carcass. It also permits blood to completely drain from the carcass. Begin by cutting above the ears at the first joint of the backbone and then across the back of the neck. When you reach the windpipe and throat, cut through them and the head will drop, but don't slice the head completely off just yet. Pull down on the ears and continue your cut around the ears to the eyes and then toward the point of the

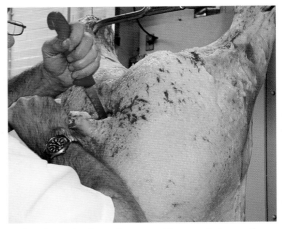

Begin evisceration by cutting around the anus to loosen the muscles holding it. Tie the anus shut.

jawbone. When you slice through the last part of the skin at the end of the jaw, the head will come free, but the jowls will still be attached. Wash the head quickly and trim it as soon as possible.

Splitting the Carcass

Splitting the carcass is easiest to accomplish when it is suspended. Cut a clean line down the center of the belly between the hams to the sticking point at the base of the chest, but do not cut through the belly wall. To split the breastbone, place the heel of your knife against the bone and cut outward. You may have to work the blade to split the breastbone and divide the first pair of ribs. If your knife will not cut through the breastbone, you may need to use a saw to cut it.

In either case, you should avoid cutting past the upper portion of the breastbone and into the stomach. This is a thin area, and you do not want to cut the stomach open. By cutting through the breastbone and first rib, you will open the chest cavity sufficiently to allow any blood that has accumulated to drain out.

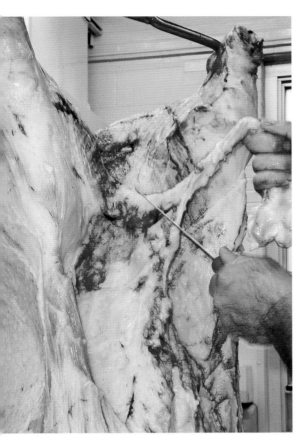

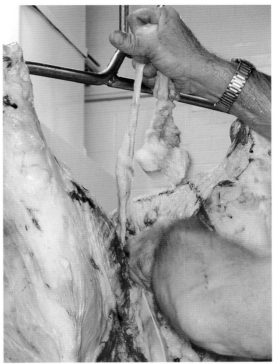

A castrated male pig, or barrow, will have the penis and sheath still intact. This should be removed like the skin by cutting upward toward the anus until it is severed. It can be finally removed where it is attached at the aitchbone.

After splitting the breastbone, make an incision near the top of the abdominal wall to pull the skin outward with your fingers. Gravity will pull the intestines down toward the bottom of the chest cavity and leave room for you to insert the knife and your free hand. Grip the handle of the knife with the blade turned toward you. You will slice downward and cut with the heel of the blade and push the intestines away from the knife as you slice down the belly. Keep the intestines away from the blade so that you don't cut them and spill their contents, which can contaminate the cavity. As you reach the parted breastbone, the intestines will fall forward and downward. They are still attached by muscle fiber and will not fall far. This is an easier method than drawing the knife upward to slice open the belly. Although it is a bit awkward, it minimizes the chance of puncturing the intestines.

The next step is to split the aitchbone. This will separate the hips and make the cut down the spine easier. A tub should be placed under the carcass to catch the viscera as you pull the kidneys, heart, liver, and stomach toward the opening. First, make a cut in the center between the two hams until you reach the aitchbone. This can be severed either with the heel of the blade or with a meat saw. At this point, the intestines are still suspended by the gut leading to the anus. Before

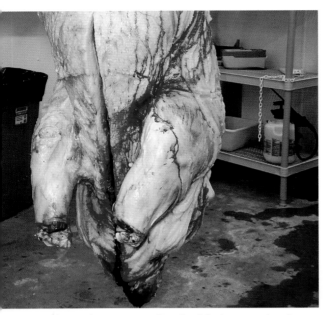

Above: The sternum can be split while the carcass is on its back or after it has been lifted. This will allow access to the thoracic cavity once the abdominal wall is opened.
Right: Open the abdomen by starting at a midline point at the pelvis. Once you carefully slice an opening large enough to insert your hand and knife, turn the blade outward while holding the heel with your hand on the inside. Use your hand to hold back the intestines as you slice down the midline in a smooth, continuous motion until reaching the opening of the thoracic cavity.

you make a cut around this, tie the end of the anus securely with a cord to keep any fecal contents from falling out. Start in front and cut completely around the anus until it is free. This should allow the viscera to fall outward and downward. The diaphragm will now be exposed, and you will see the gullet that leads to the stomach. When you sever the gullet, the entire mass of viscera should come free and drop into the tub.

You can place the viscera on a table to cut off the liver and wash it in clean, cold water. Trim out the gallbladder and remove the spleen. The stomach should be tied off with a cord and cut free. The heart and lungs

should still be inside the carcass cavity at this point, located in front of the diaphragm. Make an incision in the diaphragm where the red muscle joins the connective tissue. This will expose the heart and lungs, which should be pulled downward and cut free from the backbone. Trim any fat off the heart and lungs and wash them with cold water.

If you plan to use the intestines for sausage casing, they will have to be cleaned and rinsed with a salt solution several times. The easiest way to do this is to turn them inside out after cutting them into several lengths and scrape off the mucous coating. Generally, the small intestines are used for sausages, so

As you slice down, the viscera will fall down and out, but because they are held by connective tissue, they will not come out completely. Sever the connective tissues to allow the intestines and internal organs to fall free from the body cavity. Have a tub placed under the carcass before making this cut to catch the viscera.

tie off the large intestine and sever it from the small intestines and discard it. The heart and liver can be saved and ground in with meat for sausage.

Splitting the Backbone

The hanging carcass should be split apart while it is still warm. First, wash the inside of the carcass cavity and, using either a hand or electric meat saw, slice down the center of the backbone. Be sure to make a straight cut, or you may damage some of the loin areas. You can leave about 12 inches of skin uncut at the shoulders to keep the carcass from separating if you are concerned about

it slipping off the gambrel. If you are not concerned about it slipping, continue to separate the back.

If you choose, the hams can be partially filleted while the carcass is suspended. Start your cut at the flank and continue to follow the curvature of the ham until you reach the pelvis; do the same on the other side.

Chilling

Your carcass is now ready to be chilled. A cold carcass is easier to trim and cut up than a warm one. Cooling it quickly also minimizes bacterial growth and souring of the meat. It is easier to cool the carcass when it has been split apart, as the air circulates around more of the body.

To properly chill your carcass, have a separate tub or vat large enough to completely submerse both halves in ice water maintained at a temperature between 34 to 38 degrees Fahrenheit for a minimum period of 24 hours. If you are using a refrigerator, it is possible to maintain a temperature of 38 degrees Fahrenheit at the bone within 12 to 24 hours. Chilled carcasses should not be worked with until all the tissue heat is gone. When it is thoroughly chilled, you are ready to cut up the carcass.

Cutting the Carcass

Before you begin to cut up the carcass, make sure you have sharp knives and several tubs available with cold water mixed with salt to start the curing process. One cup salt for 2 gallons of water is a good mixture. There are many ways of creating salt brines for curing meat. Too little salt may result in spoilage, while too much salt creates hard, dry, over-salty meat.

If you use a meat saw to make the cuts, you should scrape the bone dust from the

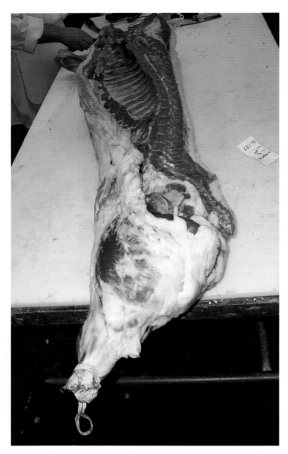

To begin fabrication, place one carcass side on a clean table. There are four major cuts to be made to separate the ham, shoulder, loin, and belly. To remove the ham, make a cut perpendicular to the leg bone from ½ to 2½ inches anterior to the aitchbone.

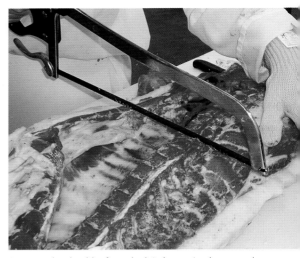

Separate the shoulder from the loin by sawing between the second and third rib, perpendicular to the back. This will separate the Boston butt and picnic shoulder from the belly and loin.

cuts after sawing. This mixture of small particles of meat and bone results from sawing. Cleaning off the saw blades or the cuts makes them less "crunchy" and reduces the chances of creating a bacterial haven.

Place one side of the carcass on a clean table, and start by removing the front and rear feet. Using the meat saw, cut off the legs at the hocks and the knees. The hind feet are generally not used because they contain a very high proportion of bone to edible meat. However,

the front feet have a larger percentage of muscle to bone and can be used as pickled pigs' feet or trimmed and used for sausage.

The next step is to remove the ham. Begin with a cut at a point about 2½ inches in front of the tip of the aitchbone and then cut through the fifth and sixth lumbar vertebrae. After the bone has been severed with a saw, use a knife to complete the cut through the rest of the tissue. Trim off most of the fat, but leave about ¼ inch on the whole ham. The pelvic bone will still be part of the ham and may be a problem in packaging or cooking because of its large size. You can trim out the bone and cut the ham into smaller pieces for easier cooking and packaging. You can also make bone-in roasts by cutting across the face of the ham to create ham steaks.

The next step is to saw off the shoulder at the third rib, counting from the neck. The shoulder has two major primal cuts—the Boston butt and the picnic shoulder—and three minor cuts—the neck bones, the jowl,

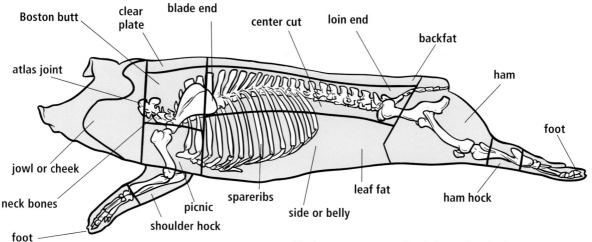

Boston butt
clear plate
blade end
center cut
loin end
backfat
atlas joint
ham
jowl or cheek
foot
neck bones
leaf fat
ham hock
spareribs
foot
picnic
side or belly
shoulder hock

The hog carcass anatomy in relation to the primal cuts.

and the clear plate. The shoulder can be kept whole, cured, smoked, or it can be divided into Boston butt and pork shoulder picnic.

The first step in cutting the shoulder is to remove the neck bones. There will be seven neck vertebrae, regardless of the length of neck. Trim these out as completely as possible. The neck bones can be used for soup stock or sauces, or may be barbequed.

To remove the jowl, cut at the fat immediately above the foreshank and continue across the top portion of the shoulder. Trim out as much of the muscle as possible. This piece can be smoked or used in sausage.

The clear plate is a fat cut, much like that of backfat. It is removed from the top part of the shoulder by trimming close to the Boston butt. This large fat piece can be trimmed of any lean and the rest discarded or rendered, if you choose.

Divide the shoulder into picnic and Boston butt by cutting about 1 inch below the shoulder blade and parallel with the breast. The most popular cut of the Boston butt is the pork shoulder blade steak, which contains only one blade bone. Square the

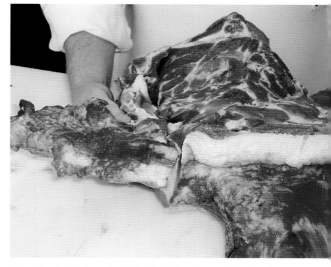

Removing the jowl begins at the fat collar immediately above the foreshank and continues straight across the top part of the shoulder. This should be trimmed of muscle and the fat set aside for sausage making.

picnic by sawing off the foreleg. Most bones in the shoulder are located in the picnic, including the foreshank bone and the arm bone. First remove the foreshank, which is high in connective tissue, before removing the arm bone.

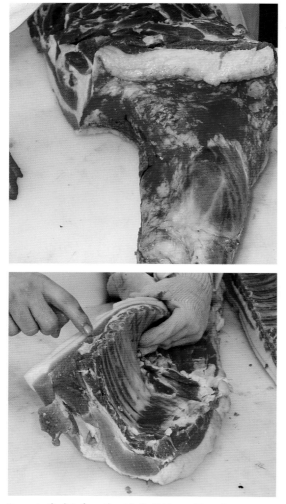

Left: After removing the jowl, remove the clear plate, a fat cut much like the backfat, from the shoulder. The shoulder is composed of two wholesale cuts, the Boston butt and the picnic shoulder. **Above:** Separate the Boston butt and picnic shoulder by cutting 1 inch below the shoulder blade toward the leg and parallel with the sternum. Make the first cut with a knife, and then with a saw to sever the blade bone. Continue to trim excess fat down to ¼ inch or less when making your cuts.

Separate the loin from the side (belly) by making a long, straight cut from the first rib (anterior) close to the backbone to the ham end, where the cut will be next to and closely follow the tenderloin, without cutting into or scoring the tenderloin.

The loin is usually the most valuable cut in the pork carcass and may be about 16 percent of the carcass weight. The pork loin is a longer area of the carcass than that of the beef or lamb loin. The loin is separated from the shoulder by sawing across the third rib.

To separate the loin from the ribs, make a straight cut from a point close to the lower edge of the backbone at the shoulder to a point just below the tenderloin muscle from which the ham was cut. The spareribs and belly are now separated from the loin. When trimming the loin, leave about ¼ inch of fat. The trimmed pork loin has a center that is higher valued than the two ends, which include muscles from the leg or ham and shoulder.

The whole pork loin is comprised of a blade section, a center section, and a sirloin section. The whole loin can be cut into bone-in pork chops or roasts. Or if preferred, the bones can be removed to make boneless pork chops or loin roasts.

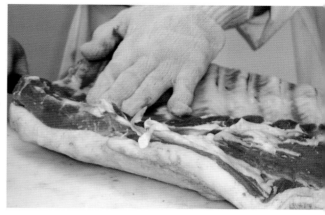

Bacon is made from the belly after the spare ribs have been removed. Square up the belly, trim the fat, and remove any rudimentary mammary glands and teat lines. It is then ready for smoking and curing.

Begin your cuts with the end of the loin that was nearest the shoulder. Make cuts between each rib bone and the attached cartilage to create blade chops until you reach the fifth rib. The loin from the fifth to the tenth ribs will yield the center-cut loin chops, which are very desirable because they contain the tenderloin. The cuts from the rear end of the loin are referred to as sirloin chops, which contain portions of the eye and tenderloin, the top sirloin muscle, and hipbone.

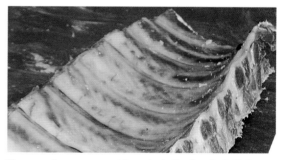

The spareribs are removed from the belly after the belly is separated from the loin. Be sure to trim out all bone and cartilage from the belly, as this is not desirable in bacon.

The portion left is the belly or side. This will contain parts of the ribs that must be trimmed. You can use a straight knife and cut between the backfat and the belly to remove the ribs. The length of the ribs and the width of the belly will be determined by the location of the cut you made to separate the loin. You should remove all remaining bones and cartilage with the spareribs, because these will make very unpalatable bacon.

Once the spareribs have been removed, you can slice the belly or side into strips for bacon. You should square up the belly by trimming the outside parts evenly. This will remove any rudimentary mammary glands and teat lines that remain. The most common use of the belly is to cure and smoke it for bacon. Some people enjoy fresh pork belly, also called side pork, which may also be sliced. Most bellies are skinned before being cured and smoked.

The spareribs may be cured and smoked but can also be used fresh and barbequed. Generally, spareribs are cut into portions containing between two to six ribs.

Roast Spareribs

2 lbs. spareribs
Salt and pepper
1 c. bread crumbs

¼ tsp. sage
¼ tsp. minced onion

Place spareribs in a shallow baking dish, and sprinkle with salt and pepper. Roast at 350°F, allowing 40 to 45 minutes per pound. Allow 1 pound per serving.

Cover spareribs and roast for ¾ hour, then roast uncovered for remaining time. Just before taking meat from oven, sprinkle with 1 cup bread crumbs seasoned with ¼ teaspoon each of sage and minced onion. Baste with drippings in pan and return to oven 5 minutes longer.

Variations: Stuffed spareribs—Use 2 matching sections of spareribs. Sew the edges together, except at one end. Fill with bread stuffing, celery stuffing, apple stuffing, or other desired. Sew or skewer the edges together. Bake at 325°F for 1½ hours.

Braised spareribs—Place spareribs in a baking dish and brown in hot oven at 450°F. Season with salt and pepper, add ½ cup water, cover pan, and return to oven. Reduce temperature to 325°F and continue cooking until tender, about 50 minutes longer.

With sauerkraut—Brown spareribs. Place sauerkraut in a greased baking dish. Sprinkle with brown sugar. Add ½ cup water and arrange spareribs on top. Cover dish and cook at 350°F for 1 hour.

Stuffed Pork Chops

6 double pork chops
2 c. bread crumbs
¾ tsp. salt
¼ tsp. pepper
1½ tbsp. minced parsley

1 tsp. sage
1 tbsp. grated onion
3 tbsp. milk
Fat

Cut a pocket on the bone side of each chop. Combine next 7 ingredients and mix well. Stuff each chop with mixture. Brown chops in fat, season, add a little water, and bake at 350°F about 1 hour or until tender. Serves 6.

Baked Ham

1 smoked ham
Glaze

Whole cloves

Have ham warmed to room temperature and bake, allowing 15 minutes per pound for hams 12 pounds or over. Allow 18 minutes per pound for hams under 12 pounds, and allow 22 minutes per pound for half hams. Or bake to an internal temperature of 150°F, being sure bulb of thermometer is inserted into center of thickest part of meat and does not touch bone. Bake at 300°F until within 45 minutes of total baking time. Spread with desired glaze. Bake uncovered at 325°F for remaining 45 minutes.

Pork Tenderloin

1 lb. tenderloin
Flour
3 tbsp. bacon drippings

Salt and pepper
¾ c. sour cream

Cut tenderloin crosswise into 2-inch pieces. Flatten out and dredge into flour. Place in hot pan or skillet containing drippings. Brown on both sides; season with salt and pepper. Reduce heat, add cream, cover, and simmer 30 minutes. Serves 6.

Boiled Pigs' Feet

6 pigs' feet

1½ tbsp. salt

Scrape feet, wash thoroughly, and tie each separately in a piece of cheesecloth. Cover with boiling water and add salt. Heat to boiling, reduce heat, and simmer 6 hours. Cool in the water. When cold, drain, but do not remove cloth. Chill. Use for broiling, frying, or pickling. Serves 6.

Pigs' Knuckles and Sauerkraut

4 pigs' knuckles
3 tsp. salt

2 qts. boiling water
1 qt. sauerkraut

Place whole knuckles in boiling salt water. Cover and simmer until meat is tender, about 2½ to 3 hours. Twenty minutes before serving, pour off most of the water and add sauerkraut. Heat thoroughly. Serve the meat on a bed of sauerkraut. Serves 4.

Headcheese

1 hog's head
1 hog's tongue

Salt and pepper
Sage or chili powder

Clean and scrape hog's head and wash thoroughly. Wash and trim tongue. Cover head and tongue with slightly salted water and simmer until meat falls from bone. Drain meat, shred, and season with sage or chili powder. Pack tightly in bowl, cover, and weight it down. Let stand 3 days in a cold place. Slice. Makes 6 to 8 pounds.

Glazes

- 1 c. brown sugar, juice, and grated rind of 1 orange
- 1 c. brown or white sugar and ½ c. maraschino cherry juice, cider, or sweet pickle juice from pickled fruit
- 1 c. honey
- 1 c. brown sugar, 1 tbsp. mustard
- 1 c. puréed apricots, rhubarb, or applesauce
- 1 glass currant jelly, melted

- ½ c. orange marmalade
- ¾ c. pineapple juice, ¾ c. strained honey, and ½ tsp. mustard cooked until thick
- ½ c. maple syrup, ½ c. cider or apple juice, and 2 tbsp. mustard
- Cook ½ pound fresh cranberries with 1 c. maple syrup until skins pop open. Press mixture through sieve and spread over ham.

Start with healthy chickens for home butchering, either by raising them yourself or purchasing them from other growers. Withhold feed for eight to twelve hours before butchering, but allow full access to water. A well-grown, 7-pound bird can have a dressing yield of 70 percent, giving you a 5-pound carcass.

Chapter 6

POULTRY AND OTHER FOWL

Butchering poultry and other fowl has been a human experience for thousands of years. Throughout the world, chickens are common livestock in agrarian cultures. The eggs and meat they provide are an important source of protein. As recently as 70 years ago, it was still very common on U.S. farms for chickens to be butchered at home. Providing meals for large gatherings, such as wedding dinners or for crews harvesting crops, meant chickens were butchered in the morning and served later that day. Today, refrigeration allows at-home butchering to be done anytime and the poultry or fowl are frozen for use throughout the year.

In the United States overall consumption of chicken has greatly increased in the last 10 years. Several reasons account for this increased consumption including lower fat content of the meat, lower store price, and the versatility of use in meat dishes.

Many cities and villages have adopted ordinances to allow raising backyard poultry. This is most often for egg production; however, once the hens reach the end of their productive egg-laying life, they are generally culled and can be butchered. Understanding the procedures for safely handling poultry and other fowl, allows you to harvest your own at a convenient time that fits your schedule with little or no special equipment.

Raising Poultry

Raising poultry and other domesticated fowl is relatively easy. You will need to provide the basics of food, shelter, and water, but, by and large, poultry are very self-sufficient.

Selecting Healthy Birds

Whether you are purchasing live birds for slaughter or raising them yourself, make sure you choose healthy birds. Considerations for selecting or raising healthy birds are:

- Purchase chicks from reputable companies or farmers.
- Consider available space for number of birds desired.
- Observe daily for any physical, respiratory, or digestive abnormalities.
- Select meat-type breeds for home butchering.
- Feed proper nutritional ration to reach target weights in about 7 weeks of age.

Many books and guides are available on how to raise poultry and other fowl (including Voyageur Press' *How to Raise Poultry*), and you should consult them.

If you raise poultry, some breeds are good for laying eggs, others for meat production, and some that are good for both. Some breeds are deep-sided and rangy, some have a thin meat, and others are thick-meated and full-breasted. Deciding which of these characteristics are most important to you will largely determine which breed you choose to raise. Laying hens can later be used for meat, and meat hens can be used for modest egg production. If your layers are finished producing eggs, you can place them on a special finishing ration to develop their muscles for butchering.

Home-grown poultry and fowl typically receive a varied diet when compared to their counterparts raised in confinement. A varied diet tends to allow their muscles to grow in a rhythm more in line with their natural body processes. While they may take a little longer to reach a desired body weight, the exercise they receive in open spaces will increase the muscle density, yielding a more substantial flavor when compared to commercial broiler production.

Purchasing Birds

If you don't wish to raise them yourself, you may be able to purchase birds for butchering from local farmers. This will reduce your feeding and housing needs, but not necessarily be less costly than raising them yourself. If its flavor and texture you're looking for, then the cost of raising them will seem minimal. If purchasing birds to butcher, make sure they are healthy and free of any physical defects, such as damaged limbs, wings, or skin tears. Breaks or bruises will have some impact on

Chickens may be kept in their coop until needed, or you can move them into a more confined area where they may be easier to catch. Depending on the number of people helping, you may want to divide the work into equal sessions. For example, start with four birds and complete all the steps from head removal to ice chest before beginning work on a second group.

the quality of muscle you will harvest as meat. Healthy birds will give you healthy meat; unhealthy birds will not.

You may be able to buy whole dressed birds and finish cutting up the birds yourself. If purchasing this way, keep the carcasses cold during transport and until you are ready to cut them up. Time and temperature will be your two biggest allies in processing your chickens, but they can also be your two biggest concerns in regard to food safety.

Butchering Basics

There is more than one way to butcher chickens, and you can make the process as elaborate as you wish, but a simple procedure is explained here. Processing poultry requires four basic steps, which should be done in separate areas to prevent contamination:

1. Slaughtering
2. Scalding and plucking feathers
3. Eviscerating (cutting open and removing the internal organs) and washing
4. Chilling and packaging

Assemble your equipment and lay it out before you begin. Use a sturdy table for cutting up the carcass. Supplies should include soap; pans for icing internal body parts, such as the heart, liver, and gizzard; clean water; towels; and any other item you may want handy.

Arrange your work area prior to starting to help move the process along swiftly and safely. If properly done, your processing can be a pleasant experience.

Equipment Needed

The tools, knives, and equipment needed for processing a few birds is often less than if you are handling many birds, although the processing principles are the same.

Use sharp knives for working with the carcasses. These can include a straight boning knife shown on the left, a meat shears for cutting cartilage and bone, a butchering knife, a steel for sharpening knives during use, and a small, folding knife. Other knives can be used as needed.

In the most basic operation, you will need knives for eviscerating and cutting, an axe and chopping block for removing the heads, several five-gallon pails, a scalding tub, heating coil, a propane tank, a canvas or tarpaulin, and a sturdy table. Your chopping block will work best if you pound two large nails into it at distance of about 1 or 2 inches apart, depending on the size of the birds. For ducks and geese, you may want to increase that width an inch.

The area you use for processing should be clean, have plenty of water available, and be as free from flies and insects as possible. Working early in the morning is often a good idea if you expect flies and insects to be a problem later in the day. Scrub tables with soap, water, and a diluted chlorine solution prior to use. If this is not possible, use a disposable plastic cover.

Sharpen and sanitize all knives before starting. Keep in a clean and accessible area.

You can use galvanized or plastic garbage cans or pails to hold the cooling water. Be sure these containers have been thoroughly washed, sanitized, and rinsed with clean water before they are refilled with carcasses to be chilled. Set up similar cans, pails, or plastic-lined boxes to use for feathers and unwanted body parts. While butchering, keep a water thermometer handy for checking the scalding water, which should be kept between 120 to 160 degrees Fahrenheit.

Keep your packing materials close by. Have plastic-lined boxes or portable coolers filled with ice where you can cool the eviscerated carcasses quickly.

Make a list of all things needing to be done. This will allow you to envision the process from beginning to end. It is better to make adjustments at this stage than when the processing begins. Identify areas where the potential for contamination may exist, and keep these in mind as you are working so you can avoid them. Once all your equipment is clean and set out, you are ready to begin.

Other equipment or supplies may include 5-gallon pails for bleeding the birds. Using a tarpaulin on which you can pluck feathers will make for easier cleaning later. The feathers can be composted or placed in a plastic-lined bin for disposal.

Handling and Slaughtering

The chickens or other fowl you choose for slaughter should be taken off feed between 8 to 12 hours beforehand. Always provide them access to water. The removal of feed allows time for the crop and digestive tract to empty, helping prevent contamination during butchering. Birds can be kept in the same area used for housing them and then moved into a smaller, more accessible enclosure when ready to begin.

The method you use to slaughter the bird may involve an axe, a killing cone, or suspending them by their feet with a shackle or cord. Using an axe will require some coordination with a heavy blade, wood block, and an agitated bird that may not wish to cooperate. Safety with a sharp axe blade is very important, and it may help to restrain or tie the feet and legs of the bird together. If you feel you can hold the feet and legs steady while chopping off the head, you may not need to use any other restraints. However, several other methods can be used, such as wrapping the body in a linen sack or cloth. This will hold the wings close to the body and immobilize them. Once the head is chopped off, you will need to hold the bird by the legs for a few moments until its reflexes stop.

A cone is a safe and effective aid in restraining the bird for butchering. It is a large funnel in which the bird is placed upside down with its head falling through the small opening at the bottom. This method accomplishes several objectives by restraining the bird safely, preventing damage to its body, and using the downward pressure of its weight to force the blood toward its head to aid in bleeding.

Shackles or cords can be used to hold the feet steady and keep the legs apart as the bird is suspended upside down. A clothesline

The butchering process proceeds quickly once the head is removed. Before you begin, make sure the water temperature in the scalding tank is between 120 to 160 degrees Fahrenheit. A simple method is to set up an open flame heater fueled by bottled propane that can be regulated. Plucking feathers will be easier if the water is maintained at a constant temperature during the entire butchering session.

You can use a wood block with two nails set 1 to 2 inches apart to chop off the heads of your chickens. A sharp hatchet will make a swift, efficient cut to remove the head.

or other sturdy design can be used to hold a bird off the ground and will allow you unencumbered movements around it. Suspending the bird at your eye level will help with the process. If using this method, allow time for the bird to settle down before beginning.

Whether using an axe, cone, or shackles, you want to have a clean and humane

Begin by grasping the chicken's feet and hold it upside down to immobilize it until you place its head on the block. Stretch the neck by pulling on the legs as the head is held between the nails. One swift chop should be sufficient to sever the head from the body. Be sure to keep your hand and fingers clear of the hatchet.

kill. With an axe, you can chop against a wood block with one quick motion. Hold the bird tightly by the feet and legs with your free hand. Place its head on the wood block between the nails and stretch out the neck by pulling back on the legs. One quick chop with the axe should be sufficient.

If using either a cone or shackles, you have ready access to the neck of the bird. There are several options for killing the animal. The simplest is to sever the head completely. Another option is to sever the jugular veins. This is done by making a cut just behind the jaw. This cut should sever the veins without cutting the esophagus or windpipe. Cutting only the neck vein, reduces the chance of carcass contamination by blood being drawn into the air sacs. This is a humane method because the bird is unconscious due to the loss of blood from the brain.

To do this, hold the beak with one hand and pull down slightly to steady the bird.

There are two veins in the neck leading to the head, and both pass near an ear lobe. Be sure to hold the front part of the head firmly to avoid cutting your hand. Press the point of the knife into the flesh, lift the handle upward, and cut downward with the blade severing the veins. This should result in a good bleed. If not, try again until there is free bleeding.

Bleeding the Bird

It will not take long to bleed the bird. However, it is still important that your bird is killed in a manner that allows as much of the blood to drain from the body as possible while preventing damage to the carcass. Only about 50 percent of the blood is actually removed from a bird. What remains does no harm if the carcass is to be cooked immediately. Since blood spoils more quickly than other parts, it is beneficial to remove as much blood as possible to lengthen the shelf life for either fresh or frozen poultry or fowl.

Once the head is removed, hold the bird upside down in a 5-gallon pail or similar container for 15 seconds to begin the bleed. The bird's reflexes will continue to flap the wings, but the confinement will eliminate or greatly reduce any damage to the bird. They can remain in the pail or container until you are ready to scald the carcass.

Be aware that any method that involves beheading or breaking the neck will accomplish the killing but will not produce the same type of bleeding as severing the jugular veins because the heart stops when the spinal cord is severed.

If you are removing the heads, you can bleed the birds by placing them upside down in a 5-gallon pail once the head is off. Hold them by their legs until their reflexes stop to prevent any damage to their body and leave them in the pail until you are ready to scald them.

If using a cone or shackles, you can let the blood drop into a container below for easier cleanup. When the bleeding is finished, you are ready to remove the feathers.

Scalding Carcasses

Birds must be properly bled and all body reflex movements stopped before any scalding should be done. Hot scalding, with water temperatures above 155 degrees Fahrenheit, is an easy, quick method to remove feathers. Start by holding the bird tightly by its legs and immerse it neck first into the scalding water. It is important to get enough water into the feathers. Move the bird up and down and from side to side to get an even and thorough scalding, which will make the feathers easier to remove. Repeated dips may be needed, but don't overdo it to prevent burning.

One simple rule to follow when scalding is that the higher the temperature of the water, the less time of immersion needed (although another method that involves immersing the carcass for longer periods at lower temperatures can be successfully used too). You can avoid over-scalding by following the temperature and time recommendation for the birds you are using. Over-scalding causes the skin to tear and discolor

To scald the carcass, hold the feet and gently dip it into the hot water. Hold for five seconds before pulling out. Then dip again while slowly moving it from side to side, completely submerging the feathers. Do not overscald the bird.

and gives the bird a cooked appearance; the carcass will lack bloom and turn brown rapidly, or bright red when frozen.

Water that is hot will cause the outer cuticle layer of the skin to slough off as the feathers are plucked from the carcass. This cuticle layer is the yellow pigment area commonly seen on dressed chickens. The use of high temperature for a shorter period of time, while it increases the ease of plucking, risks the loss of this yellow cuticle layer of the skin, which may result in the skin tearing more easily. If you choose not to keep the skin, this may not be a concern.

For young birds with tender skins, the scalding temperature should be between 125 to 130 degrees Fahrenheit for 30 to 75 seconds. It may reach between 155 to 160 degrees Fahrenheit for older birds for the same length of time. At this temperature, the cuticle covering the skin typically will be removed.

Feathers from waterfowl, ducks, and geese are more difficult to remove. Scald these birds at higher temperatures of between 160 to 170 degrees Fahrenheit for 1 to 2 minutes. Waterfowl have natural water repellant oils in their feathers. You can add detergent to the scalding water used on waterfowl to help the water penetrate through the feathers.

Fat birds will hold their color longer because the melted fat forms a film over the skin, reducing the effects of the air. You can increase the yellow coloring on fat birds of the yellow-skinned variety by dipping them into boiling water and then immediately plunging them into cold water. The hot water melts the fat and draws it and the yellow pigment to the surface of the skin. The cold water causes the fat to harden and the color to set in the fat.

Plucking Feathers

Picking off the feathers, or plucking feathers, is the next step. Birds should be plucked immediately after scalding. You can lay them on a canvas or tarpaulin, or suspend them by their legs to do this. There is no one correct way to remove the feathers, and all feathers need to be removed.

You can remove the tail and wing feathers first and then the rest of the body feathers. If properly scalded, the tail and wing feathers can be quickly and easily removed before you move on to the main body. Chickens and

Top: When scalding is complete, begin to remove the feathers by pulling on them. You can place the feathers on the tarpaulin for later disposal. The large feathers can be removed quickly. If needed, you can quickly dip the carcass again to loosen the rest.

Above: Some pin feathers may remain after plucking. There are several ways to remove them if you choose to keep the skin on, including singeing, removal with a small knife, or continued plucking by hand. Pin feathers can remain on the carcass through cooking with no effect upon the meat. Whether you keep the pin feathers completely intact is a matter of personal choice.

other domestic and wild fowl have pinfeathers, which are tiny, immature feathers lying below the surface of the larger feathers. They are more difficult to remove because of their size. Remove them by using a pinning knife or dull knife to gently scrape or pluck them off.

Plucking feathers is not hard but takes time and patience. Work quickly and dip the carcass again if needed to avoid it drying out. You can use a rolling or rocking motion to remove feathers or pull in the direction they grow to minimize skin tears. If you intend to show your carcass at an exhibition, tears in the skin need to be avoided because the skin needs to be completely intact.

Inspect the carcass to ensure all feathers have been removed. If some very fine "hairs" remain, you can remove them by a process called singeing. This is where a gas bottle torch or an open flame on a gas range can be used to burn them off. The potential for injury to you or your bird by using this method may not outweigh the advantages of removing every last one, particularly if you don't intend to eat the skin. Singeing is usually not necessary on young birds, but more mature chickens and turkeys may have hairs remaining after the feathers are removed.

Dry-plucking Feathers

Dry-plucking (also called dry-picking) is a process used to remove feathers from birds such as waterfowl. This involves removing the feathers without first immersing the carcass in water. However, this method requires a prior process called debraining, which relaxes the feather muscles, aiding in their removal. This process also requires the bird be suspended so that you can work more easily.

To begin, locate the slit in the roof of the mouth and insert a small-blade knife, blade edge up, into the cleft in the roof of the mouth at a slight angle. Force it toward the back of the brain with the handle about parallel to the upper beak. If properly debrained, the bird may give out a peculiar squawk. In contrast, a turkey will relax its wings and spread out its main tail feathers in the shape of a fan.

The puncturing of the brain relaxes the feather muscles, causing the feathers to become loose and more easily plucked. However, this condition generally only lasts about three minutes before the muscles begin to tighten up. You will need to quickly pluck the feathers with this method.

In dry-picking, it is easiest to remove the feathers in the order in which the parts of the bird bled out, beginning with the tail because it was bled upside down. Twist out the tail and the main wing feathers first, and then pluck the breast, neck, back, thighs, and legs. After the large feathers have been removed, you can begin removing the pinfeathers. Again, handle and pluck the bird so that the outside layer of skin is free from tears, bruise spots, or abrasions and cuts.

After you have completed plucking the feathers, rinse the carcass with clean water to remove any loose feathers, dirt, blood, or other foreign matter that may still adhere to it. You are now ready to dress the carcass.

Wax Picking

Wax picking works well to remove small feathers and down from ducks and geese after most feathers have been removed and the carcass has dried for a short time. Paraffin wax can be heated in a tub separate from the scalding water to about 135 to 160 degrees Fahrenheit to create a liquid bath. Dip the bird into the wax bath for 30 to 60 seconds, and then dip it into cold water to set the wax. The wax will adhere to the dry feathers, down, and stubs, which are very short broken feathers. You may need to dip the bird a second time if enough wax does not cover the bird.

While the wax is still flexible, you can begin to peel it off. This will remove any feathers, pinfeathers, hair, and down that has adhered to the wax. Finally, rinse or wash the carcass to remove any remaining particles and to moisten the carcass again.

Chilling the Carcass

Unless you immediately proceed to cut up the carcass, removing the body heat is important at this stage. Put the carcasses in a cold water bath with temperatures between 32 to 36 degrees Fahrenheit. Birds should never be frozen before being chilled down because the meat will be less tender later as the muscle fibers slide and lock together. Placing the birds in chopped ice will rapidly cool them.

Evisceration

To make your work easier, there is a proper order for evisceration, which is cutting open and removing the internal organs from the body cavity, plus the removal of the head and feet.

First, remove the head and neck. The head will have been removed if you used an axe and chopping block earlier. If the bird

was suspended by its feet and you simply cut its throat, you will now need to remove the head and neck.

To remove the head, cut between it and the first neck vertebra, giving it a little twist as you cut. Avoid cutting through the spine. As you cut through the back of the skin on the neck, peel down the skin and sever the skin close to the shoulders where it enters the body cavity. This will expose the crop, trachea (windpipe), and gullet (esophagus). These can be removed by hooking the short gullet with your index finger and peeling the crop loose from the skin by pulling it out without using a knife. Next, cut off the neck by cutting into the neck muscle at the shoulder and then twisting it off. You can wash it and set it in a chilling pan for later.

Next, remove the shanks. To remove the feet, place the bird breast up on a table or a

Begin cutting up the carcass by removing the feet. Make your cuts at the first joint. Feet can be discarded, or they can be used for soup stock.

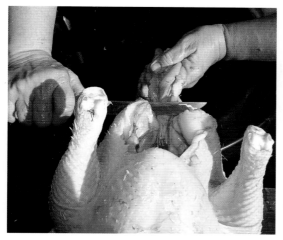

Next place the carcass breast side up and remove the oil gland in the tail by making a first cut in the anterior portion of the rectum. Cut along the sides as you pull back on the tail. Sever the oil gland by making a final cut where the tail vertebra joins the backbone.

The opening created by removing the oil gland should be large enough for you to reach your hand into the body cavity pull out the internal organs and intestines. Make a short cut with your meat shears if the opening needs to be larger. Draw out the viscera and organs, and place them on a clean surface.

stable cutting surface while holding a shank (leg) in one hand. Cut through the hock joint by drawing the bottom part toward you as you cut away.

With the bird breast down on the table, you can remove the oil gland near the tail. The oil gland can be seen at the base of the tail. Make a forward cut 1 inch from it and cut deep into the tail vertebra, then follow it to the end of the tail in a scooping motion to remove the gland.

The body cavity can be opened by making a small cut near the rectum. Be careful not to cut the intestines or contaminate the carcass with fecal material. Two types of cuts can be used to make this opening, depending how you will use the bird. A midline, vertical, or "J" cut is often used for broilers and other small poultry not to be trussed when cooked. The traverse or bar cut can be used for turkeys, capons, or other large fowl.

To make a vertical or midline cut, pull the abdominal skin forward and up away from

Open the body cavity using a meat shears, cutting the breastbone lengthwise to the neck if it is still intact. If not, the neck can be cut from the body now more easily than if done earlier. Then use the shears to cut the bottom half of the body.

the tail. Start just to the right of the breastbone with your knife point and cut through the skin and body wall. Extend the cut to the tail alongside the vent (rectum). Go slow so that you do not cut the intestine. Cut entirely around the rectum as you slowly pull it and the end of the intestine out and away from the opening of the body cavity.

The heart, liver, lungs, gizzard, and other organs and viscera should have a healthy look. Examine them. If they appear off-color or any lesions are noticeable, it may indicate an unhealthy bird, and you may want to consider disposing of it. A healthy bird will have bright-colored, vibrant organs and viscera.

The gizzard is highly prized by some people. Slice it in half and remove any feed contents that may remain. It should be nearly empty if feed was withheld for 12 hours prior to butchering. The lining on the inside should be removed before cooking and is easily peeled off.

To make a bar cut, cut a half circle around the rectum next to the tail. Insert your index finger as a guide to make a complete circle to free the rectum taking care not to cut the intestine.

Next, draw the intestinal tract, the heart, lungs, and liver through this opening. You may insert your hand to assist in extracting these parts. You can loosen the lungs from the entrance of the shoulder with your hand if these organs do not easily pull out. When the lungs are loose, you can use a scooping motion with your fingers to bring out the rest of the viscera (internal organs).

After the viscera have been removed and placed on a clean table, you can remove the green gallbladder from the liver. It can either be cut or pinched off. The gizzard, liver, and heart should also be removed. Cut the gizzard from the intestines and stomach. It can be split lengthwise and the contents washed away. The lining inside the gizzard should be peeled away and can be easily removed by using your fingers.

Remove the heart and trim off the sac and heavy vessels around its top. Squeeze it to force out any remaining blood. Rinse the giblets (heart, gizzard) well and place all the parts in a pan of cool water.

Next, wash the inside of the carcass thoroughly with clean, cold water after you have finished removing the insides. The carcass is now ready for cooling.

Cooling

After evisceration is complete, cool the carcass as soon as possible by placing it in a cold bath of clean water at a temperature of 35 to 40 degrees Fahrenheit. Once cool, it is ready for cooking, freezing, or cutting it up.

If birds are to be frozen, the gizzard, heart, and liver can be wrapped in waxed paper and

You may decide not to cut up the carcasses until all of the butchering, feather plucking, and viscera removal is completed for all the birds. If you wait to cut up the birds until later, you need to place the whole eviscerated carcasses in cold water to remove the body heat of each bird as quickly as possible.

placed inside the body cavity. The birds can then be placed in a moisture and vaporproof bag and frozen. Birds can be shaped to give them a plump, attractive appearance. Birds for roasting should be trussed by using cord or wire that is drawn over the fore part of the breast, over the wings, and then crossed over the back. Then bring the wire over the ends of the drumsticks and tie it tightly at the back of the rump.

Chilling and Packaging

Before packaging a poultry carcass, it should be cooled to below 40 degrees Fahrenheit within two to six hours after cutting it up to maintain high quality meat and minimize bacterial growth. Small birds can be chilled in a couple of hours while turkeys, large capons, and roasting birds may require several hours to reach this temperature. If using a container with ice water, you may need to change the water several times. Always make sure that the water is clean and your container is large enough to submerge the entire carcass. For this you can use an ice

water bath in an insulated chest, bucket, or other clean container.

Skinning

If you do not wish to use the skin later, you can remove it along with the feathers, saving you the scalding and feather plucking steps. The birds are killed and bled in the same way as those which have their feathers plucked.

To skin your bird, begin with a cut into the skin at the bottom of the breastbone with the carcass on its back and its head away from you. Lift the skin and cut it forward to the front of the neck. Peel the skin and feathers back with your hands and expose the breast muscles. Use your hands to work the skin loose from the thighs. Push back the skin to expose the hock joint and then cut through the joint. Remove the skin from this area on each foot. Next, loosen the skin to the joint between the first and second section of the wing. Then remove the last two sections of the wing along with the skin.

Loosen the skin at the base of the neck and cut the meat around the base of the neck near the shoulders. Twist the neck off the carcass. The final cut is the removal of the tail and the attached skin with feathers. The carcass is now skinless, neckless, tailless, and only has the upper section of the wing left. Remove the skin with feathers and place the carcass in a pan of clean water while you clean and sanitize your table or cutting surface before eviscerating the bird.

Cutting Up Birds

Unless you decide to roast the entire bird, you will likely want to cut the carcass into various pieces. Most of these pieces are made by cuts at certain joints. Breaking down the bird into parts is a simple procedure using a sharp knife. Typically, the edible yield for

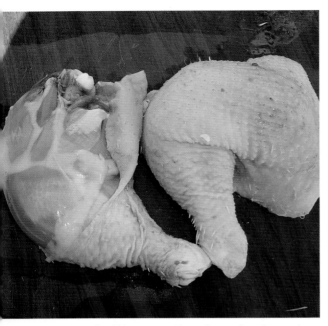

Your cuts should leave you with two legs and two breast pieces, as well as assorted internal parts. The heart and liver can be ground up to be used in sausage or dressing. After your cuts are finished, place those in cold water until you package them.

fryers and broilers is about 65 percent with the rest lost as bones and viscera.

Legs, Thighs, and Drumsticks
It is easier to cut up the carcass if you remove the wings and legs first. A leg includes the thigh and drumstick and is removed by making a first cut at the hip joint. The skin on the back or on the pelvic bone is not included with this cut.

Start by laying the carcass on its back. Cut the skin between the thighs and the body. Then lift the carcass by holding a leg in each hand. Bend the legs back until the hip joints snap free. This will allow you to cut each leg off at the joint as close as possible to the backbone.

Next, cut through the knee joint to separate the thigh from the drumstick. If

you are unsure of its location, you can find it by squeezing the thigh and drumstick together. The joint that moves is the one you are seeking.

Wings
Wings include the entire wing with all muscle and skin intact. You can remove the wing tips, which can be used for soup stock. Cut through the joint closest to the body to remove them.

Tail
The tail can be removed by cutting along each side and through the joint at the end of the backbone.

Breasts
A breast is separated from the back of the bird at the shoulder. Start by placing the carcass on the neck end. Cut along the side of the backbone, starting from the tail and continuing through the rib joints to the neck. Then bend the carcass back to find the joint before cutting through the meat and skin. The ribs may or may not be removed.

You can split the breast lengthwise by first placing it skin side down. Then cut through the white cartilage at the V of the neck. You can bend each side back as you push up on the breast from the bottom to snap the breastbone free. The wishbone is the clavicle and can be removed by severing it from the breast. Make your cut halfway between the front of the backbone to a point where the clavicle joins the shoulder.

Turkeys
Domestic turkeys differ from wild turkeys, but they can be cut up in similar ways to chickens, only larger portions are involved. Butchering wild turkeys is discussed in a

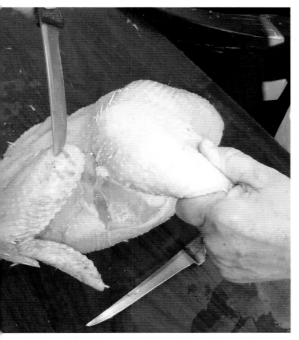

The wings should be removed by cutting as close to the shoulder as possible, severing them at the joints. Some prefer to remove the outermost tip of the wing while retaining the two inner shanks.

following chapter. A domestic turkey will yield a greater volume of meat than a chicken because it is a much larger and denser bird. A typical turkey will yield about 71 percent edible meat with about 29 percent of the carcass lost to bones and viscera.

Because of a turkey's large size, the containers used for scalding it need to be larger if you decide to keep the skin on. This also requires more water and a greater physical effort to handle a large, heavy bird.

Ducks and Geese

Waterfowl are difficult to scald because they are very tight-feathered. This allows them to stay dry and warm in their natural habitat by keeping the water and cold away from their bodies. But it presents challenges in butchering because you need to use a much higher water temperature or steam to help remove the feathers. To do this, wrap the bird in a burlap cloth and then immerse it in water that is near the boiling point. You can use a lower temperature to 160 degrees Fahrenheit, but the scalding time will be much longer—up to two or three minutes.

You can dry-pick properly bled and debrained waterfowl, but you will need to remove the fine down feathers by scalding or waxing if you want to retain the skin.

Geese present a special challenge in removing all the pinfeathers. Typically, geese can be raised and ready for market within 10 weeks or less. To produce geese with minimal pinfeathers, they will require 20 weeks or more for them to mature.

Guinea Fowl and Pheasants

You can dry-pick or semi-scald most guinea fowl as you do chickens, and they can be processed in a similar manner. Pheasants can be skinned or semi-scalded before you pick and eviscerate them.

Ostriches and Emus

Ostriches and emus are flightless birds referred to as ratites and are distantly related. Both have the same genetic base as the turkey but reach a larger mature size with the ostrich and emu weighing up to 300 pounds and standing 6 feet tall at the shoulder.

At one time ostrich and emu meat was a byproduct, as the birds were traditionally used for the production of feathers, high-quality leather, and fat. The feathers were used for making hats and long, fluffy scarves known as boas, while the hides were processed into expensive leather for shoes, boots, purses, and other accessories. Their 4-pound eggs could be sold to painters and collectors.

In recent years, their intense red-colored meat has appeared on gourmet menus in upscale restaurants and in home processing. Their meat can be made into steaks, ground meat patties, sausages, and jerky. It is low in fat and cholesterol, and the best cuts come from the thigh and the larger muscles of the drum and lower leg.

If butchering one of these large birds, you should use good restraint methods for the feet and head, both of which can be used as weapons by a frightened bird.

Because of their large size, skinning the ostrich or emu would be the easiest method instead of trying to scald them. The feathers can be saved for other uses. Cutting up the ostrich or emu is roughly similar to cutting up a large turkey.

Game Birds

The major game birds taken by hunters include pheasants, quail, grouse, partridges, wild turkeys, and mourning doves. With the possible exception of the wild turkey, game birds are generally cleaned by removing the skin with the feathers intact because it is much easier and faster than plucking.

Pheasants

Pheasants are popular game birds that are one of the meatiest for their size, commonly yielding a 1 to 2 pound carcass. The majority of their edible meat is located on the breast.

Pheasants grow in a number of states, and they are subject to a considerable variation of laws and regulations relating to the hunting season and the bag and the possession limits. Hen pheasants are off-limits for hunting in most states, and you should always check the regulations before hunting them. It is the hunter's obligation to know, understand, and abide by the state regulations. Because it is illegal to shoot a hen pheasant in most states, you are required to leave the head and feet on the bird while it is being transported.

You can clean pheasants using two different methods. The first is to skin the bird and process it in the same way as poultry. The second method is faster and neater and is preferred by hunters who do not like to handle the entrails. However, in states where the heads must be left on as they are transported across state lines, this procedure may not be legal.

In this second method, you skin the bird by making a small cut on the underside of the breast before pulling the skin and feathers off the carcass. Next, cut down both sides of the back, starting by the neck and cut through to the last rib. Pull the breast apart from the neck, back, and legs. This should leave the intestinal tract, heart, lungs, and liver attached to the back portion. Then remove the feet and lower legs at the joints below the drumsticks. To remove each leg, cut through the joint attached to the back.

You will produce three pieces by dressing pheasants as two thighs and a drumstick and one breast. You can discard the back and neck because they contain very little meat, although they may be used for soup stock.

Quail, Grouse, Partridges, and Doves

Small game birds such as quail, grouse, partridges, and doves have the majority of their edible meat in the breast. This portion is the most used as the rest of the carcass has limited food value. Removing the feathers and skin together is a favored way of dressing them because it eliminates the tedious task of picking them off small bodies. It is generally easier to dress these birds by removing the entrails from the whole carcass.

Roast Chicken

Roast uncovered at 325°F until tender. Season when half done. A chicken from 4 to 5 pounds requires 35 to 40 minutes per pound; for a smaller chicken, roast at 350°F for 40 to 45 minutes per pound.

Fried Chicken

2 broilers
Salt and pepper

Flour
¼ c. butter

Cut each chicken into four to six pieces, dip each piece quickly into cold water, drain, season with salt and pepper, and roll in flour to make a thick coating. Sauté the chicken in a little butter until each piece is tender and brown on both sides. Drain the pieces well and arrange on a warm platter. Set the dish in a warm oven to keep the meat from cooling while the gravy is made. Serves 4. For one variation, roll the pieces of chicken in whole cereal flakes instead of flour before frying.

Chicken and Dumplings

1 4-lb. chicken
Salt and pepper
1 whole onion, if desired
1 stalk celery, if desired

3 tbsp. flour
1 c. milk
1 recipe egg dumplings (below)

Cut the chicken into serving portions. Place in a pot, season, and nearly cover with water. Cover the pot and simmer gently for about 1½ hours. Remove the cover during the last half hour of cooking, reducing the broth to about 1½ pints. If desired, an onion and a stalk of celery may be cooked with the chicken before the dumplings are added.

About 20 minutes before serving time, add egg dumplings. When dumplings are cooked and ready to serve, remove to hot pan.

Egg Dumplings

1 egg, beaten
1 tsp. salt

½ c. milk
1½ c. sifted flour

Add salt and milk to beaten egg, and stir into flour to form a smooth batter. Drop by teaspoons into boiling salted water or soup, cover tightly, and cook 15 minutes. Makes 8 dumplings.

Roast Duck

1 5-lb. duck	Salt and pepper
Apples (optional)	Garlic
Celery (optional)	Currant or cranberry jelly
Onions (optional)	

Some consider that ducks have too strong a flavor, and to absorb this flavor, lay cored and quartered apples inside the body. These are removed before the duck is put on the table. Celery and onions also may be placed inside the duck to season it and improve the flavor. Use two tablespoons of chopped onion to every cup of chopped celery.

Wash and clean the duck; season with salt and pepper, rub with garlic, and fill with apples, if desired. Place in pan and roast uncovered at 325°F, allowing 20 to 30 minutes per pound. Baste every 10 minutes using 1 cup of orange juice, if the flavor is desired. Serve with currant or cranberry jelly. Serves 5.

Roast Goose

1 8-lb. goose	Flour
Salt and pepper	

Rinse goose with cold water and dry on outside. Roast at 325°F for 45 minutes on rack in uncovered roasting pan. Remove from the oven, pour off fat, season with salt and pepper, dredge with flour, and return to oven.

When the flour is browned, pour 1 cup hot water into pan and baste the goose often, dredging each time with a slight sifting of flour to absorb fat. Allow 20 minutes per pound for a young goose, and 25 minutes for older goose. Remove from pan and add 1 cup hot water to gravy and thicken, if necessary, with browned flour. Serves 5.

Salamis of Goose

Use leftover roast goose. To 4 cups sliced goose, add 2 tbsp. each of lemon juice and Worcestershire sauce, and 2 cups goose gravy; simmer 20 minutes. Add ½ cup sherry and 12 ripe, sliced olives, and reheat. Garnish with parsley and serve on hot buttered toast.

Roast Turkey

Place the fresh turkey breast up on rack of a shallow pan. Brush with melted butter and cover with aluminum foil, making sure the breast, wings, and legs are well covered. Roast uncovered at 300°F until tender. Allow 25 minutes per pound for birds under 12 pounds, or 20 minutes per pound for larger birds. Baste several times with melted butter or drippings in the pan. Season when half done. Allow ¾ to 1 pound per serving. Any frozen turkey must be properly thawed prior to baking. Thaw in cold water or in refrigerator overnight before use.

Roast Canadian Goose

1 5-lb. wild goose
Lemon juice
6 c. dressing

2 tbsp. melted butter
2 c. water

Prepare goose. Brush cavity with lemon juice. Insert stuffing (see recipe below) and sew the cavity shut. Mix salt and pepper in melted butter and brush on the outside of goose. Heat oven to 450°F. Pour water in roasting pan. Place goose on a rack in pan. Turn oven down to 350°F and cook 20 minutes per pound or until tender.

Dressing

2½ qts. dried bread, chopped
1 large onion, chopped
Giblets
Giblet stock
2 diced apples

Salt
Pepper
Sage
Garlic

Boil giblets until tender; reserve stock. Remove skin from giblets and chop fine. Combine bread, onion, and apples; mix well. Add salt, pepper, sage, and garlic to taste. Moisten with giblet stock.

Rub cavity of goose with ⅛ teaspoon salt per pound. Bake at 375°F for 15 to 20 minutes. Dip out fat and stuff the bird. Prick fat on back, around the tail, and the skin around the wings and legs. Cover and roast at 325°F for 4 hours for an 8-pound goose; 4½ hours for an 11-pound bird. If goose is very fat, remove excess fat from pan during roasting.

Braised Duck

1 4-lb. duck	Salt and pepper
4 slices bacon	4 c. boiling water
1 onion, minced	2 tbsp. melted butter
1 carrot, diced	4 tbsp. flour
½ tsp. powdered thyme	¼ c. cold water
2 tbsp. minced parsley	

Prepare duck as for roasting and sauté in bacon fat until brown. Add onion, carrot, thyme, parsley, salt, and pepper, and cover with water. Simmer until the duck is tender, then remove from stock. Blend flour and cold water together until smooth and add gradually to stock, stirring constantly. Pour gravy over the duck. Serves 4.

Braised duck with mushrooms: Omit bacon and carrot. Use ½ pound of sliced mushrooms and sauté in fat.

Roast Wild Duck

Clean the duck by wiping the inside and outside with a damp towel. Tuck back the wings and truss. Dust with salt, pepper, and flour. If there is not a lot of fat on the duck, cover breast with 2 thin slices of salt pork. Place duck in a pan and add 1 cup of water and 2 tablespoons of fat. Roast uncovered and breast down at 350° F, allowing 20 to 25 minutes per pound, according to rareness desired. Baste frequently. Turn the duck to breast side up when half done. Serve with slices of lemon or orange and a brown gravy. Wild ducks are served rare and are seldom stuffed when roasted.

Wild Fowl (Pheasants, Partridges, Quail, and Grouse) Cooking

A distinction must be made between white meat and dark meat in cooking game. Quail and partridges are white meat and, like chicken, must be thoroughly cooked. Ducks, pigeons or squabs, grouse (prairie chicken), and snipe and woodcock are dark meat and are cooked rare and served very hot.

All these birds are cooked by the same methods, varying only as to the degree of rareness desired. Pick out shot from birds with a sharp pointed knife. Wash quickly under running water. Small birds may be skinned when they are clean.

Broiled Birds

Season with salt and pepper and dust with flour. Brown the bird on both sides, allowing 8 to 12 minutes for quail and 25 to 40 minutes for partridges and pheasants. A strip of bacon, smoked ham butt, or salt pork may be placed over the top of each bird. When done, brush with melted butter. During broiling, if the breasts are quite thick, cover the broiling pan with another pan, lower the temperature, and lengthen the cooking time.

Roasted Birds

Clean and stuff the birds. Brush with unsalted melted fat. If the birds do not have a lot of fat, lay strips of salt pork across the breasts. Roast uncovered at 350° F until the meat is tender and the bird is well browned. Baste every 30 minutes with butter and water. Season the bird with salt when about half done. Place on a warmed platter and cover with gravy made from pan drippings. Garnish the platter with parsley. Allow ½ to 1 bird per person.

Sautéed Partridge Breast with Figs

4 boneless breast halves from
    partridge or ruffed grouse
6 dried figs, chopped
1 tbsp. butter or margarine
1 c. partridge stock or chicken
    broth

¼ tsp. dried thyme leaves
1 tbsp. balsamic vinegar
¼ c. butter, cut into 4 pieces
Salt and ground black pepper

In small saucepan, heat figs and stock to boiling. Reduce heat; simmer until stock thickens and darkens slightly, about 15 minutes. Remove from heat and set aside.

In medium skillet, melt 1 tablespoon butter over medium-low heat. Add breast halves. Cook until well browned on both sides but still moist in the center, 6 to 10 minutes. Remove from skillet. Set aside and keep warm.

Add balsamic vinegar after wiping skillet clean with paper towels; swirl vinegar around skillet. Add the reserved fig mixture. Cook over high heat until mixture is thick; stir in thyme. Remove skillet from heat. Add butter, 1 tablespoon at a time, stirring well between each addition. Add salt and pepper to taste. Slice the reserved breasts; pour sauce over breasts. Serves 2.

Doves or Quail in Cornbread Stuffing

8 dove breasts

Stuffing

½ c. chopped celery
¼ c. sliced green onion
2 tbsp. dry, snipped fresh parsley
    if available
¼ c. butter or margarine
3 c. cornbread stuffing mix

1 c. game bird stock or chicken
    broth
½ tsp. dried marjoram leaves
½ tsp. salt
⅛ tsp. pepper

Heat oven to 350° F. Lightly grease 2-quart casserole; set aside. In medium skillet, cook and stir celery, onion, and parsley in butter over medium heat until tender. Add remaining stuffing ingredients. Mix until moistened. Place half of stuffing mixture in prepared casserole. Arrange dove breasts over stuffing. Cover completely with remaining stuffing mixture. Bake, uncovered, until dove is cooked through and tender, about 1 hour. Serves 4.

To substitute quail for doves, use 6 quail and split in half. Proceed as above.

Stewed Partridge with Sage Dumplings

3 partridge, whole or cut up
1½ quarts water
2 bay leaves
1 tsp. dried thyme leaves
1 tsp. dried rosemary leaves
1 tsp. dried summer savory leaves,
    optional

2 tsp. salt
⅛ tsp. ground black pepper
4 carrots, cut into 1-inch pieces
3 stalks celery, cut into cubes
2 medium onions, cubed

In saucepan, combine partridge, water, bay leaves, thyme, rosemary, and savory leaves. Heat to boiling. Reduce heat; cover. Simmer for 1½ hours. Add 2 teaspoons salt, pepper, carrots, celery, and onions; cook until partridge and vegetables are tender, about 45 minutes. Remove from heat. Remove partridge and bay leaves from stock and vegetables; discard bay leaves. Cool partridge slightly.

Skim fat from broth. Remove partridge meat from bones and any skin. Tear meat into bite-size pieces and return to broth. Discard bones and skin.

Sage dumplings

1½ c. flour
2 tsp. baking powder
½ tsp. salt
½ to ¾ tsp. crushed sage

⅔ c. milk
3 tbsp. butter or margarine,
    melted

To make dumplings, combine flour, baking powder, ½ teaspoon salt, and sage in medium mixing bowl; stir with fork to combine. Add milk and melted butter; stir until flour is moistened. Set aside.

Heat meat, vegetables, and broth until the broth boils. Drop dumpling dough by heaping tablespoons onto broth mixture. Cook over medium-high heat for 5 minutes; cover and cook until dumplings are firm, about 10 minutes longer. Serves 4 to 6.

Roast Pheasant with Sauerkraut

1 whole pheasant, skin on
2 tbsp. butter, softened
2 slices bacon, cut up
1 16-oz. can sauerkraut, rinsed and
    drained

1 c. pheasant stock or chicken
    broth
¼ c. cognac or brandy
⅓ c. canned cranberries, rinsed
3 tbsp. butter or margarine

Heat oven to 375°F. Rub softened butter over pheasant. Place in small roasting pan; cover. Roast until pheasant is tender and juices run clear when thigh is pricked, about 35 to 45 minutes.

Prepare remaining ingredients while roasting pheasant. In medium skillet, cook bacon over low heat until lightly browned. Add sauerkraut and 1 cup pheasant stock. Cook over medium heat until most liquid evaporates, about 12 to 15 minutes. Remove from heat, set aside, and keep warm.

When the pheasant is done, transfer from roaster to heated platter; set aside and keep warm. Pour drippings from roaster into small bowl; set aside. In small saucepan, heat cognac gently over low heat until warm. Remove from heat and carefully ignite the cognac with a long match. When the flame dies, add 1 cup pheasant stock and cranberries. Cook over high heat until liquid is reduced by half, about 10 to 15 minutes. Skim fat from reserved drippings. Add drippings and 3 tablespoons butter to cranberry mixture; cook, stirring occasionally, until butter melts, about 2 minutes. Serve cranberry sauce with pheasant and sauerkraut and crusty French bread. Serves 2 to 3.

Pigeon and Squab Cooking

Domestic pigeons are the most desirable. Wild pigeons are likely to be tough. Squabs are the nestlings of pigeons, usually marketed at about 4 weeks of age. They are tender and delicately flavored. Both are prepared by the same methods as chicken, with pigeons taking a long, slow cooking time.

Broiled Squab

6 squabs
Salt and pepper

Butter
Toast

Wash birds quickly under running water, split the birds down back, flatten the breast, season, and broil. When browned, brush with melted butter and serve on toast. Serves 6.

Pigeon and Mushroom Stew

3 pigeons
1 tbsp. fat
2 c. stock or gravy
Salt, pepper, cayenne pepper

2 tbsp. mushroom ketchup
½ c. mushrooms
2 tbsp. cream

Clean and cut pigeons into serving portions. Sauté in fat, but do not brown. Add stock or gravy, salt, pepper, cayenne, and mushroom ketchup. Simmer 1 hour, or until tender. Add mushrooms, simmer 10 minutes more, and stir in cream. Serve on hot platter with mushrooms arranged around pigeons. Serves 3.

Bread Stuffing

Bread stuffing is popular for roast poultry. The following is one recipe for bread stuffing based on one quart of ½-inch crumbs cut or torn from the loaf or from sliced bread. A 4- to 5-pound bird will require about 4 cups of crumbs, while a 14- to 15-pound turkey will require 10 to 12 cups of crumbs. An ordinary 1-pound loaf of bread will make approximately 4 to 5 cups of crumbs. If boiled rice is used, it should be 1 cup less than the bread crumbs because the rice will swell.

⅓ c. butter/margarine/poultry fat
¾ c. chopped celery
3 tbsp. chopped parsley
2 tbsp. chopped onion

1 quart breadcrumbs
½ tsp. savory seasoning
½ to ¾ tsp. salt
Pepper to taste

Melt the fat in fry pan, add celery, parsley, and onion, and cook a few minutes. Mix lightly but well.

For variety: Oyster stuffing—omit celery and reduce parsley and onion to 1 tablespoon each. Add ½ pint oysters heated in their own liquid and drained.

Nut stuffing—omit parsley and savory seasoning and add ½ cup chopped nut meats, such as pecans, roasted almonds, filberts, or cooked chestnuts.

Large game animals, such as deer, elk, moose, antelope, and bighorn sheep, may be hunted in the wild or sourced from commercial production facilities that specialize in raising big game. Regulations apply to both commercially produced and hunted game, though. *Shutterstock/Richard Waters*

Chapter 7

VENISON, MOOSE, ELK, AND BIG GAME

Deer, moose, elk, antelope, and bighorn sheep are typically referred to as large game animals. Your ability to hunt and harvest these is dependent on the state or federal legislation that restricts the period when large game animals may be legally shot. Conservation efforts of past decades have provided for a more abundant population of each.

Large wild game animals have become an attractive addition to meal preparation for many families. Animals may be hunted in the wild or sourced from commercial production facilities that specialize in raising big game. Regulations apply to both

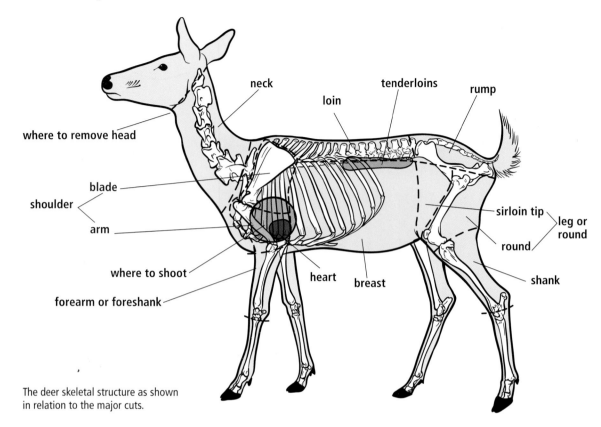

neck

loin

tenderloins

rump

where to remove head

blade

shoulder

arm

where to shoot

forearm or foreshank

heart

breast

sirloin tip

leg or round

round

shank

The deer skeletal structure as shown in relation to the major cuts.

commercially produced and hunted game, and if you choose to secure animals through either route, you are obligated to know and understand the rules and regulations governing them and to abide by them.

It is considered a privilege to hunt and receive licenses to secure game, so you are also obligated to minimize the suffering of the animal and to make a quick and efficient harvest to achieve optimal meat quality. You will also want to prevent or minimize waste of the carcass taken.

There are vast differences in size between big game animals, and these differences may influence your choice or your ability to handle a carcass in the field. It is much easier to harvest, clean, and cut up a 150-pound deer than a 500-pound elk, or an even larger moose.

You should plan ahead before embarking on a big game harvest to ensure that you can safely and efficiently dress and transport the carcass, sometimes over large distances. Planning for as many variables as possible in the wild will reduce the risk to yourself and possible contamination of the carcass if you have a successful hunt. These may include transport, weather conditions, distance from shelter, and equipment.

Safety

Without some precautions at the time of harvest, you may be at risk for injury or worse from the actions of a wild animal that suddenly comes back to life. You should approach all big game that has been shot with caution. Any wounded animal can turn aggressive,

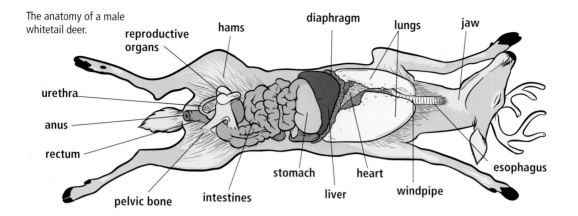

The anatomy of a male whitetail deer.

reproductive organs · hams · diaphragm · lungs · jaw · urethra · anus · rectum · pelvic bone · intestines · stomach · liver · heart · windpipe · esophagus

and those with antlers can be extremely dangerous for unsuspecting hunters.

Bleeding Deer

Having assured yourself that the animal is dead, you can consider bleeding it, although it is not necessary for deer unless it was shot in the head, and often not even then. Bleeding deer can be done by either cutting the jugular vein in the neck just behind the jaw or, in the case of a trophy-size buck, by cutting into the base of the neck several inches in front of the breast.

You can begin by inserting a hunting knife with a 5-inch blade into the breast with the point of the blade aimed at the tail. Insert the blade all the way and press it downward toward the backbone. With a slicing motion, withdraw the blade. Then elevate the hind legs to allow gravity to drain the blood.

Field Dressing

A clasp knife or a sheath knife work best for dressing deer in the field because they are easier to use than larger 10- and 12-inch knives. You can use small knives to make more precise and sensitive cuts if needed.

Temperature and insects are two variables that can affect the quality of any carcass

Field dress the animal immediately to drain the blood and dissipate the body heat. Wearing rubber gloves will protect you from any parasites or blood-borne diseases the animal may be carrying and make cleanup easier. Locate the base of the breastbone and then make a shallow cut that is long enough to insert the first two fingers of your hand, being careful not to puncture the intestines when cutting. *Creative Publishing international*

you dress in the field. You can minimize the effects of flies by wrapping the dressed carcass in cheesecloth. This will prevent flies or insects from entering the body cavity and laying eggs. Warm weather can cause spoilage in a short time, and getting the carcass to a refrigerated cooler within a day of killing it will prevent or minimize spoilage.

To dress a deer in the field, you can either tie the deer's legs to a tree with cords to give

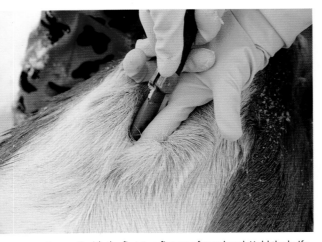

Form a V with the first two fingers of your hand. Hold the knife between your fingers with the cutting edge up. Cut through the abdominal wall to the pelvic area using your fingers to prevent puncturing the intestines. *Creative Publishing international*

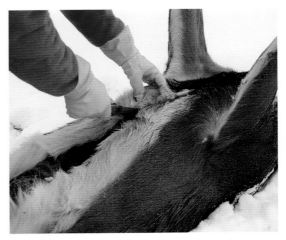

Straddle the animal, facing its head. If you do not plan to mount the head, cut the skin from the base of the breastbone to the jaw, with the cutting edge of the knife up. If you plan to mount the head, follow your taxidermist's instructions. *Creative Publishing international*

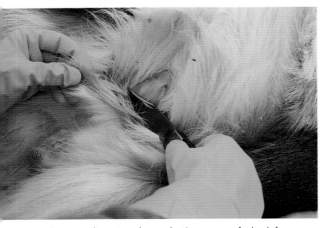

Separate the external reproductive organs of a buck from the abdominal wall, but do not cut them off completely. Remove the udder of a doe if it was still nursing. The milk sours rapidly and could give the meat an unpleasant flavor. *Creative Publishing international*

you room to work or while it's lying on its side if there is no place to elevate it.

First remove the genitals if you have shot a buck, but be careful when cutting the hide in the abdomen area. If you need to drag the carcass some distance later, you will want to make as small a cut as necessary to remove

the viscera. Dragging or carrying the deer will expose it to weeds, soil, and insects, which may contaminate it.

Once you have removed the genitals, cut a small opening in the hide in front of the aitchbone. If you have elevated the carcass, you can make a downward cut with the knife blade pointing outward and use the heel to slice down the inside. If your deer is lying on its side, elevate the pelvis to begin your cut down the abdomen. Then lay it back on the ground and use your free hand to push intestines away from your knife.

Cut until you reach the rib cage, and tilt the carcass sideways to drop the viscera and drain any blood from the body cavity. Cut around the anus and pull it back through the abdominal cavity after tying it closed to prevent fecal contamination.

These cuts should let you pull out the rest of the intestine and stomach from inside the body. You can then remove the heart, lungs, liver, esophagus, and windpipe by cutting as

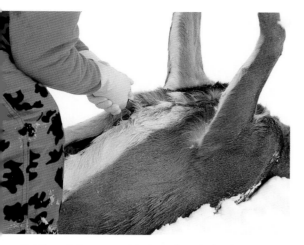

Cut through the center of the breastbone by bracing your elbows against your legs, with one hand supporting the other, and use your knees to provide leverage. An older animal may require using a game saw or small axe. *Creative Publishing international*

To free a buck's urethra, slice between the hams or split the pelvic bone on either a buck or doe. Make careful cuts around the urethra until it is freed to a point just above the anus. Be careful not to sever the urethra. Cut around the anus; on a doe, the cut should also include the vulva above the anus. Free the rectum and urethra by loosening the connective tissue with your knife. Tie off the rectum and urethra with sturdy string to prevent fecal contamination of the inside body cavity. *Creative Publishing international*

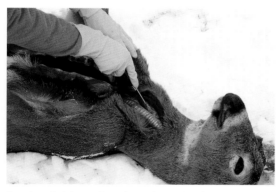

Free the windpipe and esophagus by cutting the connective tissue. Sever the windpipe and esophagus at the jaw. Grasp them firmly and pull down, continuing to cut where necessary, until freed to the point where the windpipe branches out into the lungs. *Creative Publishing international*

far forward in the chest cavity as possible. Cut the heart and liver free and save them for making sausage. Place the heart and liver in a portable cooler to keep them fresh.

Many hunters tag their deer after they have dressed it; some before. Either way, you will need to tag the deer before you load it into your vehicle. If the carcass is too large to drag or carry to your vehicle from where you dress it, such as with a large elk or antelope, you may have to split or quarter the carcass. Knowing and understanding the laws and regulations regarding the identification of and dressing of large game animals in your hunting area will eliminate potential problems if the carcass needs to be divided. Normally you will have a specified period of time in which to register your deer at a designated check station.

Carcass Disposition

If you intend to process the carcass yourself, be sure to keep it in temperatures that do not exceed 40 degrees Fahrenheit while it is aging. You can age a deer carcass for a week before cutting it up, as this should improve its tenderness and palatability. During aging, keep the hide on to reduce moisture loss or shrinkage and to avoid discoloration of the meat.

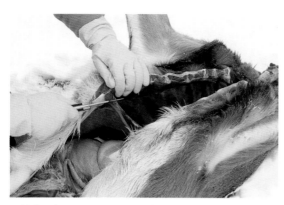

Hold the rib cage open on one side. Cut the diaphragm from the rib opening down to the backbone. Stay as close to the rib cage as possible; do not puncture the stomach. Repeat on the other side so that the cuts meet over the backbone. *Creative Publishing international*

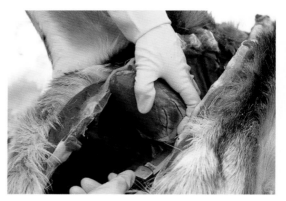

Remove the heart by severing the connecting blood vessels. Hold the heart upside down for a few moments to drain excess blood and then place it in a plastic bag. Some hunters find it easier to remove the viscera first, and then take the heart and liver from it. *Creative Publishing international*

Cut the tubes that attach the liver and remove it. Check for spots, cysts, or scarring, which may indicate parasites or disease. If any are present, discard the liver. If the liver is clean, place into a plastic bag with the heart. Place on ice as soon as possible. *Creative Publishing international*

Pull the tied-off rectum and urethra from the pelvic bone and into the body cavity, unless you split the pelvic bone, making this unnecessary. Roll the carcass on its side so that the viscera begin to spill out the side of the body cavity. *Creative Publishing international*

If you don't process the carcass yourself, you may be able to make arrangements with a local meat and locker service to do it. Federal and state regulations require that wild game not be processed in conjunction with domestic animals. If you are home processing, avoid handling wild and domestic carcasses at the same time. Be aware that a wild game carcass must be dressed before it enters the processing or refrigerated areas of a licensed facility. Also, it is essential that all equipment you use that comes in contact with wild game be thoroughly cleaned and sanitized before you again use it on domestic animal or poultry carcasses.

Skinning

Elevating the carcass allows you to skin a deer easily and effectively. Before raising it, cut slits in the skin between the rear leg bone and the tendon of the hock. Insert hooks and a strong piece of wood or metal bar into

Sponge the cavity clean, and prop open with a stick. If the urinary tract or intestines have been severed, wash the carcass with snow or clean water. If you need to leave the carcass, drape it over brush or logs with the cavity down, or hang it from a tree to speed cooling. *Creative Publishing international*

When moving the carcass, leave the hide on to protect it from dirt and flies. An intact hide prevents surface muscles from drying too much during aging. Drag a deer with each front leg tied to an antler to keep from snagging brush, or tie a rope around the neck if anterless. In dusty terrain, you should tie the carcass shut. A bear may be dragged on a heavy tarp to avoid damaging the hair. An elk or moose may have to be quartered to transport it from the field. Some hunters skin the carcass before quartering, so the hide can be tanned in one piece. To quarter an elk or moose, begin by bending a leg sharply and then cut the skin around the joint to remove the lower leg. *Creative Publishing international*

Firmly grasp the windpipe and esophagus, and pull down and away from the body. If the organs do not pull away freely, the diaphragm may still be partially attached. Scoop from both ends toward the middle to finish rolling out the viscera. *Creative Publishing international*

the slit. This will let you raise the carcass to a level that is comfortable to work with. If it is a buck and you wish to preserve the head, take extra care when you elevate it to a height where the horns no longer touch the floor or ground to avoid breaking them.

The hocks should be spread apart to give you easier access to the abdominal area. You can make the first cuts for skinning before you elevate the carcass. First, make a complete circular cut around each hock just

below the inserted hooks, and avoid cutting into the tendons. Place the blade tip on the top of the tendon and carefully slice toward the rectum. Do not cut into the hindquarter. Do the same for the other leg. From this point on, you will need very little knife work because the skin can be easily pulled and fisted from the carcass.

Remove the forelegs by making cuts just below the knee at the smooth joints. Then begin pulling the hide from the rounds or rump and inside the rear legs with even tension. You may have to work the inside skin free before pulling from the top part of the anus. Use your hand or fist to remove the skin from the sides as you pull it down the back.

If you plan to mount the head, you will need to retain enough of the hide for a cape.

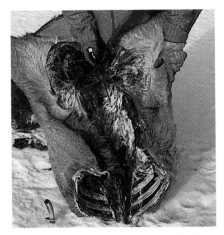

Hindquarters can be dragged out of the field by cutting a hole behind the first rib, and then threading a rope through and tying it. This lets you drag the quarter with the grain of the hair. To drag out a forequarter, tie a rope tightly around the neck. *Creative Publishing international*

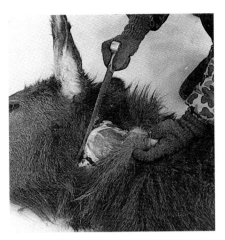

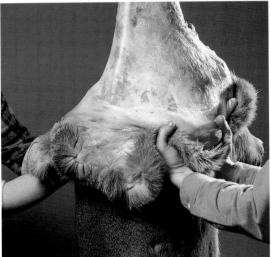

Open the skin on the top side of the neck and behind the shoulder to make enough for the cape. Leaving too much skin available for a taxidermist is better than too little.

To remove the head, you should cut at the atlas joint so that it and the cape of skin can be removed in one piece. After the head is removed, you can split the underside of the neck and remove the remaining esophagus, windpipe, and any other part, such as the lungs and heart, if they have not already been removed. Then brush and wash the inside body cavity with clean water to remove any hair or soil attached to it. After a thorough washing, you are ready to cut up the carcass.

Top: Skin the neck area before sawing off the head. Skinning the neck first will eliminate the chance of forcing hair into the meat with the saw. *Creative Publishing international*
Above: Skinning a deer, elk, moose, or bear is similar to that of a beef or pig. Start with cuts at the inner parts of the hind legs, peel the hide away, sever the tailbone, and continue peeling with your fist along the back, using your knife only when necessary, until reaching the head, which can be cut off at the atlas joint. *Creative Publishing international*

Head Mounting

If you desire to have the head mounted, you will need to care for it and the hide before taking it to a taxidermist. To help preserve it, you should liberally apply salt to the head and rub it into the skin side of the hide. Let the salt be absorbed for 24 to 48 hours before folding the skin together with the hair side out. Tie it and tag it according to the laws pertaining to your area before delivering it.

The evisceration process is similar to that used with deer. After the viscera are removed, cut between the third and fourth ribs, from the backbone to the tips of the ribs. Make your cuts from inside the body. *Creative Publishing international*

To separate the front half of the carcass from the rear half, use your saw to cut through the backbone after making your first knife cut. A quartered hide is still suitable for tanning. *Creative Publishing international*

Split the hide along the backbone on both halves, and then peel it back several inches on each side of the cut to expose the spine for cleaner sawing. *Creative Publishing international*

Begin sawing lengthwise through the backbone by propping one half against your legs. Be careful to saw down the middle of the spine and not through any of the loin. *Creative Publishing international*

Cutting the Carcass

You can divide the carcass by splitting the aitchbone and sawing down the center of the backbone. Remove the neck first before you split the carcass if you plan to use the neck for pot roast or neck cuts and don't need to keep the head.

Lay the carcass on its side on a clean table, abdomen-side down, and begin by removing the hind legs. You can now split one side into three pieces: hindquarter, ribs, and shoulder. Make your first cut just in from and close to the hipbone. Then separate the shoulder

continued on page 153

Keep the back off the ground as you continue cutting. Gravity will help pull the quarters apart so that your saw doesn't bind, as it would if the half were lying on the ground. *Creative Publishing international*

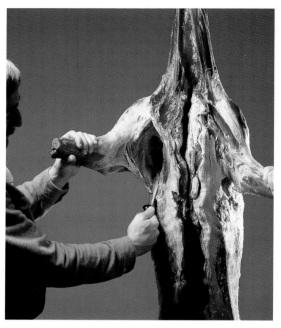

Begin fabrication by pushing the front leg away from the body and cut between the leg and the rib cage. Then continue until reaching the shoulder. *Creative Publishing international*

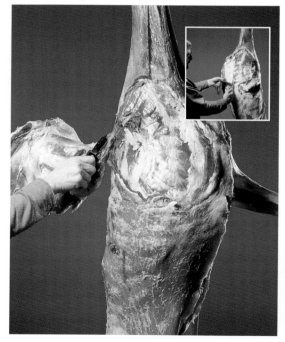

Remove the front leg by cutting between the shoulder blade and the back. Repeat with the other leg. Remove the layer of brisket meat over the ribs (inset). Moose or elk brisket is thick enough to be rolled for corning. Grind thin brisket for burger. *Creative Publishing international*

Cut the meat at the base of the neck to begin removing a backstrap. There are two backstraps, one on each side of the spine. They can be butterflied for steaks, cut into roasts, or sliced thinly for sautéing. The lower part, or loin, is the most tender. *Creative Publishing international*

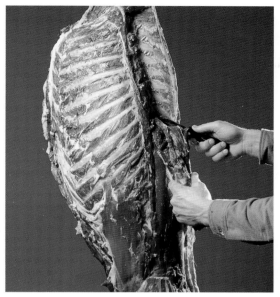

Make two cuts between the shoulder and rump bone along the spine and the other along the rib tops. Keep your knife close to the bones, removing as much meat as possible. Cut off this first backstrap at the rump, and then remove the backstrap on the other side of the spine. *Creative Publishing international*

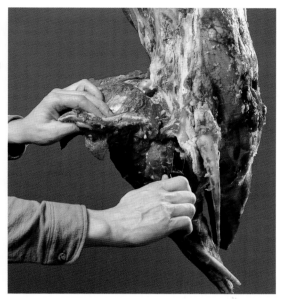

Begin cutting one hind leg away, exposing the ball-and-socket joint. Push the leg back to pop the joint apart, and then cut through the joint. Work your knife around the tailbone and pelvis until the leg is removed. Repeat with the other leg. *Creative Publishing international*

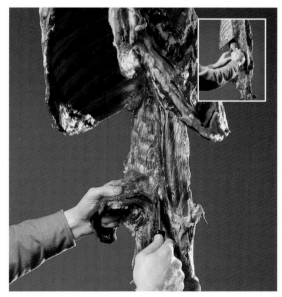

Cut the tenderloins from inside the body cavity after trimming the flank meat below the last rib (inset). The flank meat can be ground or cut into thin strips for jerky. Many hunters remove the tenderloins before aging the carcass, to keep them from darkening and dehydrating. *Creative Publishing international*

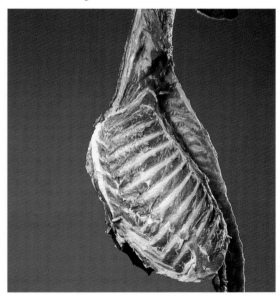

Remove the ribs if desired by sawing along the backbone. Cut around the base of the neck, and then twist the backbone off. Separate the neck and head. Bone the neck to grind for burgers or keep it whole for pot roasting. *Creative Publishing international*

Left: Trim the ribs by cutting away the ridge of meat and gristle along the bottom. If the ribs are long, saw them in half. Cut ribs into racks of three or four. If you don't want to save the ribs, you can bone the meat between them to grind for burgers or sausage. *Creative Publishing international* **Above:** Cut along the back of the leg to remove the top round completely. The top round is excellent when butterflied, rolled, and tied for roasting. Or cut it into two smaller flat roasts, cubes for kabobs, or slice for sautés. *Creative Publishing international*

Above left: Remove the rump portion. Cut the rump off at the top of the hipbone after removing the silverskin and pulling the muscle groups apart with your fingers. A large rump is excellent for roasting; a small one can be cut for steaks, kabobs, or sautés. *Creative Publishing international* **Above:** Cut the bottom round away from the sirloin tip after turning the leg over and separating these two muscle groups with your fingers. Next, carve the sirloin tip away from bone. Sirloin tip makes a choice roast or steaks; bottom round is good for roasting, steaks, or kabobs. *Creative Publishing international* **Left:** Large-diameter steaks can be made from a whole hind leg by cutting across all the muscle groups rather than boning as before. First, remove the rump portion, and then cut the leg into 1-inch-thick steaks. As each steak is cut, work around the bone with a fillet knife, and then slide the steak over the end of the bone. Continue steaking until you reach the shank. *Creative Publishing international*

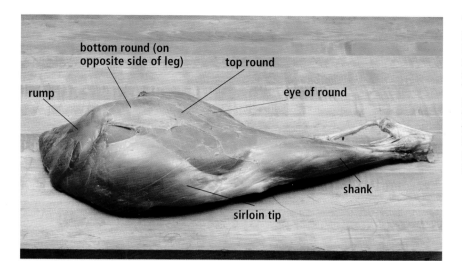

The hind leg consists of the sirloin tip, the top and bottom rounds, the eye of the round, a portion of the rump, and the shank. The sirloin, rounds, and rump are tender cuts for roasting or grilling; the shank is tough and best used for ground meat or soups. *Creative Publishing international*

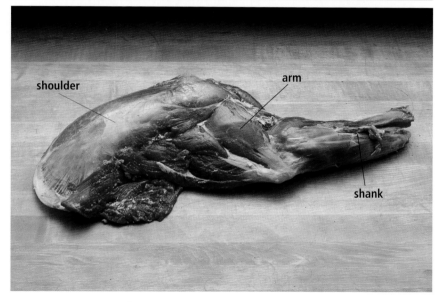

A front leg consists of the shoulder, arm, and shank. The meat from the front leg is less tender than that from the hind leg, and it is used for pot roasting, stews, jerky, or grinding. *Creative Publishing international*

Continued from page 149

from the ribs and loin by cutting between the fourth and fifth ribs. The breast or flank is removed by cutting across the ribs about 3 inches from the backbone, from front to back. Then you can separate the ribs from the loin by cutting directly behind the last rib.

To remove the rump from the leg, you can turn the aitchbone upward and make a saw cut parallel to it. You can then remove the flank with your boning knife.

The shanks, breast, and flank are generally boned and ground into burgers or mixed with pork fat for sausage. The neck slices can also be boned for ground meat and sausage. Venison rib chops, boneless tenderloins, round steaks, and rolled shoulder roasts are the most important cuts. Many of the

Quartered elk will look like this. Depending on the animal's size, elk quarters weigh 60 to 125 pounds each, moose up to 225 pounds. Where the law allows, some hunters bone the carcass in the field to reduce weight. *Creative Publishing international*

principles used for cutting a lamb carcass can be applied for deer processing.

Mutilated Areas

Portions of the carcass may have sustained damage from a gunshot or arrow wound, depending on the season. This damaged meat may have materials imbedded in it, such as hair, metal shards, and any mixture of blood, bone chips, and fecal matter. Carefully cut out damaged tissue and dispose of it.

Meat Volume

Some estimates can be made of the amount of edible meats that can be derived from deer carcasses. Many factors will influence the weight of the animal, including its age and diet, but the percentages will remain fairly typical. A 100-pound, field-dressed deer will typically be about 1.5 years of age and can dress out at up to 80 percent. This

yields a carcass weight to cut of 80 pounds. Roughly 50 percent of this, or 40 pounds, will be edible meat, while the other half will consist of bone, fat, and mutilated areas or areas affected by shot and the resulting blood damage.

Antelope, Elk, and Moose

Antelope, elk, and moose are all members of the deer family. Antelope are smaller than deer, which makes them easier to process. Elk are larger than deer and antelope, but much smaller than moose. This size difference, as well as the habitat in which they live, will largely determine the procedures you use in the field to handle them.

It is essential to cool the carcass of any large game animal as completely as possible to prevent spoilage. You may need to halve or quarter the carcasses of larger game, such as elk and moose, to get them out of the field and cool them within an acceptable period of time. The principles of cutting a large wild game carcass are similar to handling and processing large domestic animals.

Bighorn Sheep

Bighorn sheep are a very specialized big game animal hunted only by permits during a restricted season. Only a few states allow bighorn sheep to be hunted. In states that do, such as South Dakota, only a few licenses are issued, resulting in lotteries or auctions to fill them. In the United States, the permit prices can reach into tens of thousands of dollars. If you secure a license and bag a bighorn sheep, they can be processed in much the same way you would handle a deer. However, you need to be careful in handling the head, horns, and pelt because of their trophy value.

Roasting Big Game

The two basic ways to roast big game include dry and moist heat. Dry-heat roasting includes using high and low temperatures. The most common method of moist-heat roasting is braising, which includes pot roasting.

Use only prime roasts, such as top round, sirloin tip, backstrap, and rump roasts, for dry-heat, high-temperature cooking. Tenderloins from moose, elk, or deer may be cooked this way, but they typically do not need long, slow cooking because they are naturally tender.

High-temperature cooking requires a hot oven between 400° to 450° Fahrenheit, but roasts should only be cooked to rare or medium. Well-done cooking will dry out the meat and cause shrinkage. Low-temperature roasting can be used for prime cuts too. This involves using a slow oven at 300° to 325° Fahrenheit. Low heat allows for roasts to be cooked at rare, medium, or well-done degrees. Use a meat thermometer to check for doneness when roasting with dry heat.

Internal Temperature of Meat at Various Degrees of Doneness

Degree of Doneness	Internal Temperature (Fahrenheit)
Rare	130° to 135°
Medium rare	135° to 140°
Medium	140° to 145°
Medium well	150° to 155°
Well done	155° to 160°

Venison

Venison differs little from beef or veal, except that it has less fat. The flavor is gamey but not strong, and the texture of the meat is fine. The most desirable cut is the round, which may be used for steaks but is most satisfactory for roasting. Other roasting pieces are the saddle and the leg.

Roast Leg of Venison

Leg of venison
¼ c. fat salt pork

Salt and pepper
Flour

Wipe the leg carefully and remove any dry skin. Lard the lean side of the leg with strips of pork. Soften the fat, rub it over the meat, and coat with salt, pepper, and flour. Lay the leg on rack of roaster, sprinkling flour on the bottom of the pan. Roast uncovered at 300°F, allowing 20 to 22 minutes per pound. When flour in the bottom of pan is browned, add boiling water to cover the bottom of the pan. Baste venison frequently, renewing water in pan as often as necessary. Serve with gravy made from the juices in the bottom of the pan. Always serve with a tart jelly like currant, wild grape, or plum with venison. Allow ½ pound per person.

Venison Steak

3 lbs. venison steak
Sliced onions
1 c. tomato soup
1 tbsp. vinegar

½ c. water
1 tbsp. Worcestershire sauce
1 tbsp. brown sugar

Fry steak until well done. Cover steak with onions; simmer for 1 hour. Mix soup with vinegar, Worcestershire sauce, salt, brown sugar, and water. Pour over steak and onions. Bake at 350°F for 1 hour. Add more water if needed. Serves 8.

Venison Breakfast Sausage

1 lb. trimmed deer, antelope, elk,
   or moose meat
6 oz. lean bacon ends or slab
   bacon

¾ tsp. salt
1 tsp. dried crushed sage leaves
½ tsp. ground ginger
¼ tsp. pepper

Cut meat and bacon into ¾-inch cubes. Place in a medium mixing bowl. In a small bowl, mix salt, sage, ginger, and pepper. Sprinkle over meat; mix well. Chop or grind to desired texture. Shape into thin patties and fry over medium heat until browned and cooked through, turning once. Sausage can also be frozen uncooked.

Venison and Beans

1½ lbs. ground deer, antelope, elk,
   or moose
6 slices bacon, chopped
1 medium onion, chopped
16 ounces (1 can) pork and beans
16 ounces (1 can) kidney beans,
   drained

16 ounces (1 can) butter beans,
   drained
⅓ c. brown sugar
1 c. ketchup
2 tbsp. vinegar
1 tbsp. Worcestershire sauce
½ tsp. salt
½ tsp. prepared mustard

Heat oven to 350°F. Cook bacon until crisp. Remove with slotted spoon; set aside. Add meat and onion to pan with 1 tablespoon bacon fat. Cook over medium heat, stirring occasionally, until meat is no longer pink and onion is tender. Add reserved bacon and remaining ingredients to pan; mix well. Cook and bake until bubbly around edges, about 45 minutes. Serves 8 to 10.

Venison Meatloaf

2 lbs. ground deer, antelope, elk,
   or moose meat
2 c. soft breadcrumbs
½ c. beef broth or venison stock
½ c. chopped onion
2 eggs, slightly beaten
1 tsp. salt
½ tsp. Worcestershire sauce

¼ tsp. sugar
¼ tsp. celery salt
¼ tsp. dried crushed sage leaves
¼ tsp. dried oregano leaves
¼ tsp. pepper
2 small tomatoes, peeled, halved,
   and seeded

Heat oven to 325°F; grease 9x5-inch loaf pan and set aside. In a large mixing bowl, combine all ingredients except tomatoes; mix well. Pat half of the meat mixture into the prepared pan. Arrange tomatoes on the meat mixture, leaving ½ inch around the edges of the pan. Spread the remaining meat mixture over tomatoes, pressing around the edges to seal. Bake until well browned, about 1½ hours. Let stand 10 minutes. Remove to serving platter. Serves 6 to 8.

Moose, Elk, and Big Game

Peppered Antelope Roast

3 to 5 lbs. boneless rolled antelope
   or deer top round roast
2 medium garlic cloves

Vegetable oil
Cracked black pepper
8 to 10 slices bacon

Heat oven to 325°F. Cut each garlic clove into 4 or 5 slivers. Make 8 or 10 shallow slits in roast and insert a garlic sliver into each slit. Place roast on rack in roasting pan; brush with oil. Sprinkle pepper over roast. Cover roast with bacon slices. Roast to desired doneness, about 22 to 32 minutes per pound; remove roast when temperature is 5°F less than desired. Allow meat to rest for 10 to 15 minutes before carving. A pound equals 2 to 4 servings. You can substitute a deer or small elk sirloin tip or a deer, elk, or moose backstrap or rump roast for this recipe.

Fillet of Venison, Moose, Antelope, or Elk

1 whole tenderloin, 1 to 3 lbs.
1 to 2 tbsp. butter or margarine
1 tbsp. olive oil or vegetable oil

Salt and freshly ground black
pepper

Remove all surface fat and silverskin from tenderloin. Slice across grain into 1-inch thick fillets. In a medium skillet, melt butter in oil over medium-low heat. Add fillets; cook to desired doneness over medium-high heat, turning once. Salt and pepper to taste. Serves 2 to 3.

Big Game Baked Round Steak

2 to 3 lbs. boneless deer, antelope,
    elk, or moose round steak,
    1-inch thick
½ c. flour
2 tsp. salt
¼ tsp. pepper
1–2 tbsp. butter or margarine
2–3 tbsp. olive oil or vegetable oil

3 tbsp. finely chopped onion
Brown sugar
Ketchup
Dried basil leaves
1 tbsp. butter or margarine, cut up
¼ c. venison stock or beef broth

Heat oven to 350°F. Trim meat and cut into serving-sized pieces. Pound to ½-inch thickness with a meat mallet. Mix flour, salt, and pepper on a sheet of waxed paper. Coat steaks on both sides with the flour mixture. In a large skillet, melt 1 tablespoon butter in 2 tablespoons of oil over medium-high heat. Add coated steaks; brown on both sides. Arrange browned steaks in a baking pan. Sprinkle with onion. Top each steak with 1 teaspoon brown sugar and 1 teaspoon ketchup. Sprinkle lightly with basil. Dot with 1 tablespoon butter. Add stock to drippings in skillet. Cook over medium heat for about 1 minute, stirring to loosen any browned bits. Add to baking pan, and cover the pan with aluminum foil. Bake for 45 minutes. Remove foil and add water or stock to pan if dry. Bake until browned on top, about 15 minutes longer. Serves 6 to 8.

Moose Roast

3 lbs. moose meat
1 package onion soup mix
1 can golden mushroom soup

1 can water
1 c. sherry

Trim all fat and tallow from roast. Place in roaster; cover with all ingredients. Bake covered for 20 minutes per pound at 325°F. Baste occasionally. Gradually add 1 cup sherry during bastings.

Bear Stew

1½ to 2 lbs. bear stew meat
¼ c. flour
1 tsp. dried marjoram leaves
1 tsp. salt
⅛ tsp. pepper
2 tbsp. vegetable oil
1 16-ounce can whole tomatoes, undrained
1 c. water

¼ c. white wine or water
1 tbsp. vinegar
1 medium onion, cut in half lengthwise and thinly sliced
½ c. chopped celery
2 cloves garlic, minced
1 bay leaf
2 medium baking potatoes

Remove all fat and silverskin from meat. Cut into 1-inch pieces. Combine flour, marjoram, salt, and pepper; shake to mix. Dip pieces in mixture, coating all sides. In large saucepan, heat oil over medium-high heat until hot. Add meat and flour mixture. Brown the meat, stirring occasionally. Add remaining ingredients except potatoes; mix well. Heat to boiling. Reduce heat and cover. Simmer 1 hour, stirring occasionally.

Cut potatoes into 1-inch pieces. Add to saucepan. Heat to boiling. Reduce heat and cover. Simmer until meat and potatoes are tender, about 1 hour, stirring occasionally. Discard bay leaf before serving. Serves 4 to 6.

Elk Tenderloin Sauté

1½ lbs. elk tenderloin, thinly sliced
2 c. water
1 tsp. salt
½ pound fresh pearl onions (about 1½ c.)
¼ c. flour
½ tsp. salt
¼ tsp. pepper
2 tbsp. butter or margarine
2 tbsp. vegetable oil
1¾ c. beef broth

1 16-oz. can whole tomatoes, cut up and drained
½ c. burgundy wine
¼ c. tomato paste
1 tsp. Worcestershire sauce
¼ tsp. dried thyme leaves
1 or 2 cloves garlic, minced
2 bay leaves
½ lb. fresh mushrooms, cut into halves
Hot cooked rice or noodles

Heat water and 1 teaspoon salt in small saucepan to boiling. Add onions. Return to boiling. Reduce heat and cover. Simmer onions 15 minutes or until tender. Drain and rinse under cold water. Set aside.

Combine flour, ½ teaspoon salt, and pepper; mix. Add elk slices and coat all sides in the flour mix. In large skillet, melt butter in oil over medium heat. Add elk slices and cook over medium-high heat until browned but still rare, stirring occasionally. Remove with slotted spoon; set aside. Add remaining ingredients except mushrooms and rice to cooking liquid in skillet; mix well. Add mushrooms and reserved onions. Heat to boiling. Reduce heat and cover. Simmer 10 minutes. Stir in elk slices. Cook, uncovered, over medium-heat until slightly thickened, about 5 minutes. Discard bay leaves before serving over rice or noodles. Serves 4 to 6.

Field-dress rabbits, hares, and squirrels as soon as possible to prevent unpleasant tastes in their delicately flavored meat. *Shutterstock/Lincoln Rogers*

Chapter 8

RABBITS, OTHER SMALL GAME, AND FISH

A number of wild species can be harvested for home use, including rabbits, raccoons, fish, squirrels, bear, turtles, snakes, and feral pigs. Except for feral pigs and domestic rabbits, all the others are controlled through designated hunting seasons and licensing programs. You will need to learn and abide by all rules and regulations that apply to any particular area.

Rabbits

Wild and domestic rabbits can be dressed in a similar manner. Domestic rabbits are among the most efficient meat producers of all animals. They can reach market weights of 4 to 5 pounds by eight weeks of age while typically converting 2.5 pounds of feed into 1 pound of gain. They can be fed a high-forage (grass, legume), low-grain diet, which minimizes production costs without sacrificing growth rates. They are extremely prolific and can average 45 to 60 offspring per year.

Rabbit consumption has not significantly increased over time and remains fairly low when compared to all other meat animals. This may be a result of limited supply or the perception that they are a pet animal rather than one destined for a family meal.

Wild rabbits will have a darker-colored meat than domestic rabbits, largely due to diet and exercise. Unfortunately, wild rabbits are susceptible to a communicable disease known as tularemia, which causes rabbit fever, a very infective disease caused by bacteria that attack the internal organs. It can be transmitted from one rabbit to another by lice or ticks or to humans by handling the flesh of an infected animal, inhaling the bacteria during the skinning process, or through a tick bite. Because its entry is through cuts, abrasions, or inhalation, you will need to take precautions when skinning a wild rabbit carcass. However, this is not a condition that affects domestic rabbits. The bacteria are destroyed when the rabbit is thoroughly cooked.

You should wear rubber or latex gloves when dressing and skinning rabbits, as well as during the preparation for cooking. Always handle the rabbit carcass with care to prevent bruising. If hunted, rabbits are most likely dead by the time you dress them.

Tips for Rabbits

- Dipping rabbits in boiling water may help remove parasites in the fur or hide.
- Dipping rabbits in cold water will reduce risk of fur contacting the meat.
- It is illegal to hunt rabbits out of season; check local laws before hunting.
- Always cook rabbit meat thoroughly at minimum of 180 degrees Fahrenheit.
- Rabbits are active in early morning and at sunset, which are the best times for hunting them.
- Cold weather may reduce number of parasites but not eliminate them completely.
- Always wash your hands while preparing food, and keep raw meat away from other food.

Equipment for field-dressing small game includes a hunting knife, rubber gloves, plastic bags, paper towels, and a cord for hanging dressed animals. *Creative Publishing international*

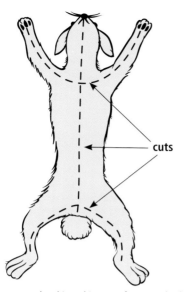

Small furred game can be skinned in one of two methods, open or cased skin. The cut marks on the rabbit show an open-pelt method.

Small furred game can be skinned in one of two methods, open or cased skin. Cased skin allows for the stripping of the pelt from the carcass. Begin with a shallow cut from the vent to the rib cage along the midline. Be sure not to puncture the intestines. Some hunters extend the cut through the rib cage to the neck. *Creative Publishing international*

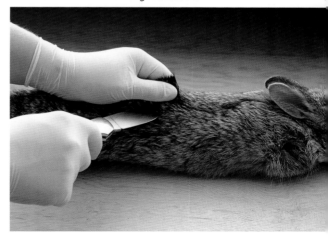

To skin a rabbit or hare, start by pinching the hide up and away from the middle of the rabbit's spine. Slit the hide from the spine down the sides, being careful not to cut the meat. When handling rabbits, wear rubber gloves not only for dressing and skinning, but also during all stages of kitchen preparation to avoid contracting any bacterial disease they may have. Thorough cooking destroys the tularemia bacteria. *Creative Publishing international*

For domestic rabbits, you can stun them with a hard blow to the head before severing their jugular veins to bleed them. After stunning the rabbit, make an incision at the rear hocks between the leg bone and the tendon to suspend the carcass by hooks through the hocks. One alternative is to suspend it only by one leg, leaving the other leg free to begin the skinning.

To sever the head, make a cut where the vertebrae joint meets the base of the skull. If you left one hind leg free, you can remove it at the hock join before removing the pelt. Remove the tail and the forelegs at the knee joints.

To skin the rabbit, make a cut on the rear side of the loose leg, slicing to the base of the tail and then back up the suspended leg. Pull the pelt away from the muscle and down the carcass. They should separate without needing to make any further cuts in the skin.

After the hide is removed, you can open the abdomen by cutting the midline of the

Grasp the hide with both hands and pull in opposite directions. Keep pulling until all the legs are skinned up to the feet. Then cut off the head, feet, and tail. If you did not field-dress the rabbit before skinning, slit the underside from the vent to the neck, and then remove all internal organs. *Creative Publishing international*

Clean the body cavity, removing any material left after dressing. Rinse briefly under running water and pat dry. Squirrels can also be skinned this way, but not as easily. *Creative Publishing international*

Pull out the viscera. Check a rabbit's liver for white spots indicating disease; if it's clean, save it in a plastic bag with the heart. Wipe the body cavity with paper towels. Small game can transmit diseases to humans. Such diseases are contracted by handling viscera or uncooked meat from infected animals because bacteria passes through cuts in a person's skin or through the mucous membranes. Never use an animal that appears sick or moved erratically. *Creative Publishing international*

belly from the anus to the rib cage, making sure not to puncture the intestines. Pull out the viscera before cutting off the other rear leg. Inspect the liver for white, yellow, or any other spotting, which could indicate tularemia. Wash and rinse the carcass thoroughly with cold water to remove any materials. If field dressing the carcass, you can use paper towels to clean the body cavity until you return home. Place the carcass in a cool water bath or ice chest during transport, particularly during warm weather.

You can cut the carcass into three sections: forequarters, loin, and rear quarters. Place the rabbit carcass on its back on a clean surface. Cut into the rear leg at a point near the backbone but stop before cutting through the bone. Bend the leg back to pop the ball joint of the hip. Cut through the joint to remove the leg.

The front legs can be split at the shoulders by cutting through the shoulder joints and severing them. The loin can be portioned by cutting off at the shoulder and at the hip joint.

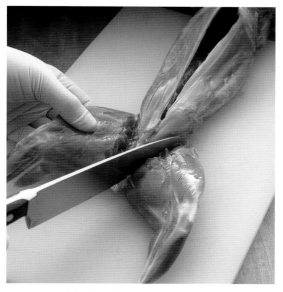

To portion a rabbit, begin by cutting into the rear leg at a point near the backbone. When you come to the leg bone, stop cutting. This portioning method works with squirrels, rabbits, hares, and raccoons. *Creative Publishing international*

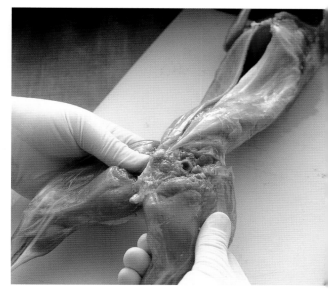

Next, bend the leg back to pop the ball-and-socket joint. Cut through the joint to remove the leg. Repeat with the other leg. On a large rabbit, hare, or raccoon, each rear leg can be split in two at the knee. The rear legs are the meatiest pieces, followed by the saddle or loin portion. *Creative Publishing international*

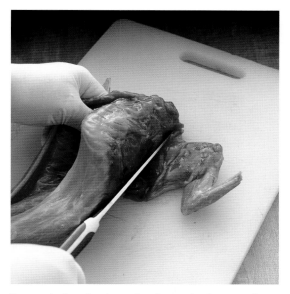

Remove the front legs by cutting close to the rib cage and behind the shoulder blades. The legs come off easier this way because you don't cut through joints. On a large animal, cut each leg in two at the elbow. The ribs contain very little meat, but they can be used for soup stock. *Creative Publishing international*

Cut the back into two or three pieces, depending on the animal's size. If you choose, remove the rib cage. When portioning a raccoon or large hare, split the back along the spine to make four to six pieces. *Creative Publishing international*

To portion a squirrel, begin by cutting it in half behind the ribs or along the backbone. If the squirrel is small, no further cutting will be necessary.*Creative Publishing international*

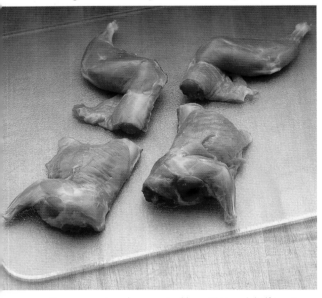

You can quarter a large squirrel by cutting each half apart. Quartered squirrels are easier to fry than halved ones, and they look more attractive when served. You can snip the meat around the bone if you are using a game shears. Game shears are an excellent tool for cutting up squirrels, rabbits, and hares. You may need a heavy knife to cut through the thick backbone of a raccoon. *Creative Publishing international*

The ribs can be trimmed because they contain very little meat, but they can be used for soup stock. The rear legs contain the most meat, followed by the loin and then the front legs.

Squirrels

Squirrels are considered rodents, and three major types can be used for meat: red or brown, gray, and fox squirrels. They can be trapped or hunted, but like many other game animals, you need to hunt in seasons and obtain a small game hunting license.

Skinning a squirrel is similar to rabbits because the pelt can be easily stripped off rather than trimmed. Begin by making a cut through the base of the tailbone on the underside of the tail. Stop when the bone is severed and make a circular cut around both rear legs. Do not cut the skin on the top side of the tail. Securely suspend the hind legs and peel the skin down the body, like peeling a banana, until reaching the front legs. Peel the skin on the rear legs back to the ankles.

To remove the hind feet, cut through the ankle joint with a knife or game shears. Pull each front leg out of the skin as far as the wrist joint. Then cut each foot off at that joint.

Finish pulling the skin down to the head, and in most cases this will also remove the head. If not, you will remove the pelt when you cut the head off. You can open the body cavity, clean it, and make the cuts as you would with a rabbit.

Raccoons

Raccoons can yield two useful products: meat and pelts. While the price of pelts can vary considerably depending on market conditions, their meat can be used at home. The most important cuts are found in the hind legs.

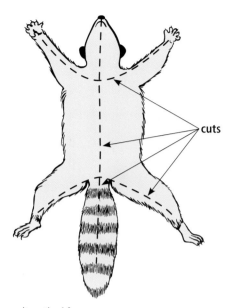

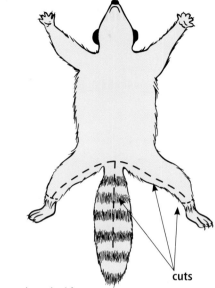

cuts

An open-pelt method for a raccoon.

cuts

A case-pelt method for a raccoon.

If the pelt is to be sold, you need to carefully skin the carcass. Begin by suspending the carcass by the hind legs and making circular cuts just above the hocks. Cut along the inside of each leg to a point below the tail. Make a circular cut around the anus to free all the skin on the rump. Peel the skin down the hind legs with even tension until you reach the tail. Cut through the tailbone close to the rump, leaving the tailbone inside the pelt.

Continue peeling off the pelt until you reach the shoulders. Next, make circular cuts above the knee joint on both front legs and then make an incision on the inside of each leg to a point at the brisket. Then make a singular cut from the brisket to the tip of the lower jaw.

Make circular cuts around the eyes and the rear base of the ears to free the skin from the sockets and ears. Peel the skin down the front until the head, where you will need to skin the face with a knife. The pelt should then be free.

Raccoons can be skinned to keep the pelt saleable. Begin by hanging it by the rear legs and cut the skin around the rear feet. Some raccoon populations carry a roundworm that may be found in the droppings and on the pelt. In very rare circumstances, this parasite can be transmitted to humans. Raccoon hunters should wear rubber gloves while dressing and skinning the carcass. *Creative Publishing international*

Cut along the inside of each rear leg to the base of the tail. Peel the pelt back to the base of the tail. Begin peeling the skin off the abdomen. *Creative Publishing international*

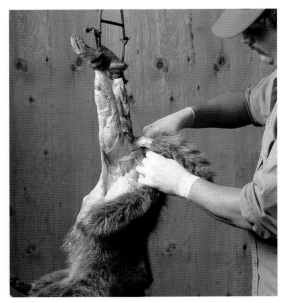

Use your knife to skin the pelt from the spine above the tail. Cut through the tailbone close to the rump. Leave the tailbone inside the pelt. *Creative Publishing international*

Continue peeling off the pelt until you reach the shoulders, using your knife only when necessary. Cut the skin around the front feet. *Creative Publishing international*

Pull the pelt off the front legs and then off the head, cutting carefully at the eyes and rear base of the ears. Cut the pelt off at the nose and turn it right-side-out to dry. Cut and peel the tail skin to remove the bone. *Creative Publishing international*

Remove the viscera by cutting down the center line of the abdomen, being careful not to puncture the intestine or internal organs. Once the intestines and internal organs are removed, you can wash the carcass with clean water.

Raccoons have several small scent glands located under the front legs and above the base of the tail that need to be removed. Use your knife point to trim them away from the flesh, being careful not to puncture or break them open with your knife or fingers.

After removing these glands, cut through the flank to the backbone. Then cut through the hip joints to remove each hind leg. The rest of the carcass will contain little meat and can be discarded or composted. Rinse the legs in clean water and place in salt brine for several days before use.

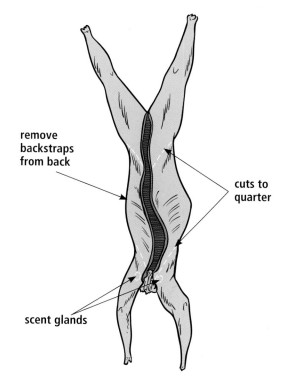

Small game can be quartered or cut into chunks.

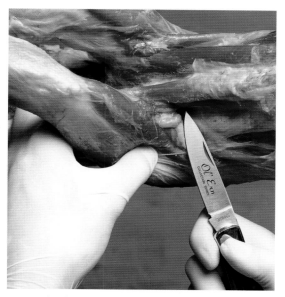

Remove the glands that lie under the front legs and above the base of the tail. Cut off the head and feet. Slit the abdomen from vent to neck. Remove the internal organs, rinse the raccoon, and pat it dry. This method of skinning can also be used for opossums and muskrats. *Creative Publishing international*

Opossum

The opossum is a large rodent-like animal found in North and South America. In recent decades, they have been expanding their territory, including into urban areas. Depending on their age and sex, opossums can range from 5 to 15 pounds. Their meat is light in color and fine-grained, but tends to carry a lot of fat within the muscles. This can make them difficult to cook. They can be skinned in similar ways to raccoon, rabbits, squirrels, and other small furred game.

After skinning and eviscerating the carcass, remove as much of the fat as possible. Be sure to remove the reddish gland located under the forelegs and at the small of the back before storing or cooking. The carcass can be placed in a salt brine of 1 tablespoon salt in 1 quart of water to remove some of the strong flavor of the meat.

Muskrat

The muskrat is a medium-sized, semi-aquatic rodent native to North America. It is found in wetlands but can range over different climates and habitats.

You can skin muskrats in a manner similar to other furred game. Be sure to check for any county or state regulations that may apply to hunting or trapping them.

The meat from muskrats can be fried or broiled, made into casseroles or sausage, or used in a variety of ways like other small game animals.

Snakes

Most common snakes are unprotected by hunting laws and can be used for meat. Many rattlesnakes are protected, and you should check your local or state regulations before capturing any wild snakes. Some snake species are venomous, and you need to use great care in capturing or handling them. If you are bitten by a snake, particularly a venomous one, immediately seek medical treatment. Reptiles also are known to spread salmonella, so be sure to wash hands and equipment thoroughly after handling.

Begin by removing the head, as it's easier to work with them because its reflexes will still allow it to "move." Snakes have been known to strike even when they are considered dead, and those with fangs can still be dangerous.

Wash the outside of the snake well and lay it on a clean, flat surface, belly-side up. Use the knife tip to cut an incision down the center from the head to the tail. Cut only

through the skin while avoiding cutting into the body.

Use your hands to pull the skin from the flesh with even tension, beginning with the head. The hide should be loose enough to detach it from the carcass. Trim areas if the flesh begins to tear as you peel off the skin.

Remove the tail and skin by severing them just in front of the cloaca. Remove the viscera by hand after making a centerline cut the length of the body and into the flesh. Try to avoid deep cuts at the lower end of the digestive tract.

After the viscera are removed, rinse the carcass in cool water and then cut it into segments. When cutting segments, make sure your cuts are between the ribs and not across them. This will avoid severing the ribs, which may be difficult to remove from the meat after it is cooked.

The flavor and texture of snake is somewhere between chicken and fish, and you may be able to make them taste like either, although this will detract from the uniqueness of having snake for its own flavor. The pieces may be placed in salt water for a day or two before cooking to remove any remaining blood or reduce the wild flavor.

Although cooking should remove all venom contained in any snake, you should check for any signs that the snake has been bitten by another. If you see bite marks on that snake, be careful with those areas of the meat and consider discarding the snake.

Turtle

Turtles are vertebrates that have two skeletons: an endoskeleton that consists of all the internal bones, and an exoskeleton, which is its outer shell. The endoskeleton is divided into two subsections called the axial and appendicular skeletons. The axial skeleton is

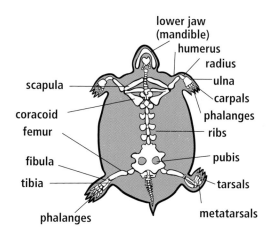

The turtle anatomy includes four different types and numbers of vertebrae: cervical (eight), dorsal (ten), sacral (two), and caudal (twenty to thirty).

made up of the skull and both the cervical and thoracic vertebrae, while the appendicular skeleton consists of the remaining bones, including the legs.

There are two parts to the shell: the carapace, which is the hard upper part, and the plastron, which sometimes is referred to as the belly. Both shells are made of many fused bones. Turtles have the ability of pulling the carapace and plastron together tightly while the animal retracts its body into the shell. This is the joint where you will cut to open up the shells.

Begin by decapitating the turtle, but realize that its reflexes will still be working. Avoid the head and feet so you don't get bitten or clawed. Place the body upside down in boiling water for 5 minutes to loosen the exterior layer of the skin.

Tail, neck, and all four legs are attached to the carapace. Separate them from the bottom shell, or plastron, by turning the turtle on its back and making a circular cut at the joint between them. As the plastron is loosened, trim until it is completely free from the body. This should expose the viscera, which can be removed by hand.

Most of the meat will be located in the carapace and include the legs, shoulders, loins, and neck. First, remove the legs by severing them at the shoulder and pelvic joints. Then remove the neck and tail. These can be boned later because the skin is not edible.

The loins or hams are located in the top part of the carapace and are protected by a rib-like structure made of hard cartilage. You will need a sturdy shears to cut through the cartilage before you can remove the loins.

After you have removed as much of the muscles as possible, separate them from fat particles and wash all the pieces in clean, cool water. You do not need to debone the legs, neck, or tail before you cook them as pieces, in stews, or soups.

Frogs

Frogs and other amphibians are cold-blooded animals that grow slowly whether in the wild or in intensive indoor frog farms. A number of frog species, including the green frog, leopard frog, and pickerel frog, are harvested from the wild and sold as luxury food, such as frog legs, in restaurants. The common bull frog is the largest native North American species, often reaching 8 inches in length, which makes it best for human consumption. However, wild populations of frogs are declining throughout the world as environmental pollution, development pressures, and other factors affect their habitats.

While some prefer to only use the hind legs for meat, the whole body can be utilized, especially if they are large frogs. To begin, you can kill the frog by inserting your knife into its lower jaw and thrusting up into its cranial cavity.

Begin by making a circular cut behind the ears, which appear as round spots behind each eye. Pull the skin out below the jaw and grasp it with your fingers or pliers. While holding the head, pull the skin down with your free hand. It should slip free of the front legs. Continue pulling until you reach the hips at the top of the hind legs. The skin is constricted at this point, so either cut a small incision in the skin or slowly work the skin over the hips with your fingers. Once the skin is past the hips, continue to pull it off the back feet. Now the skin should be completely removed.

Remove the four feet by cutting at the joint where each foot bends at the tip. Remove the head by cutting just behind the skull and around the bottom jaw. Either sever it or pull the head apart from the body.

To open the abdomen, insert the tip of your knife at a point slightly anterior to the pelvis and slice up to the ribs. A little pressure with a sharp knife should split the rib cage up through the breastbone.

Remove the viscera and esophagus if it does not come out with the head. Rinse the carcass with clean, cool water before you cook or refrigerate it.

Fish

Fish make up the largest and most diverse class of vertebrates. There are more than 20,000 species, but only a limited number are readily available for most anglers in the United States.

Although fish are caught in abundant numbers in lakes, streams, rivers, ponds, and other open water areas, fish farms are found in all 50 states. Raising fish in controlled conditions has provided an abundant harvest that may be more sustainable than if long-term fish supplies are only confined to the wild or the seas.

Fishing seasons help manage available stocks and are more plentiful and timely than

Fish are extremely perishable, and proper care insures firm flesh for cooking. Coolers filled with ice keep fish cold. Avoid placing fish in the sunshine or in a nonporous wrapping such as a plastic bag. Fish spoil quickly without air circulation. *Creative Publishing international*

Different techniques for dressing fish are used for different species, generally related to size and whether they will be cooked with their skin on or not. A basic approach starts with removing the gills by cutting the throat connection and then cutting along both sides of the arch so that the gills pull out easily. *Creative Publishing international*

Insert the knife in the vent and run the blade tip to the gills. Pull the viscera and gills out of the cavity. Most fish that are filleted do not need their scales removed. Those that are cooked whole or with their skin on should have their scales removed. *Creative Publishing international*

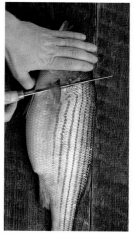

Cut the membrane along the backbone. Scrape out the kidney or bloodline underneath the membrane. Use a mesh glove on your free hand to prevent accidental cuts from your knife and to protect it from the external spines. *Creative Publishing international*

Anglers use a variety of filleting techniques. One way is to begin by lifting the pectoral fin with your knife and angle it toward the back of the head to start your cut to the backbone. *Creative Publishing international*

Turn the blade parallel to the backbone and cut toward the tail with a sawing motion until the fillet is cut off. Having a sharp knife is essential to making easy cuts. *Creative Publishing international*

Remove the rib bones by sliding the blade along the ribs. Turn the fish over and remove the second fillet. Cutting through rib bones will dull knives quickly. Keep a steel handy to touch up your knife when needed. *Creative Publishing international*

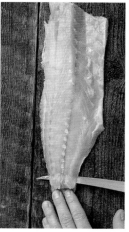

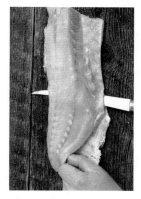

Above left: Remove the thin strip of fatty belly flesh on oily fish such as salmon and large trout. Any contaminants ingested by the fish will settle into this fatty tissue. Discard the viscera and belly. *Creative Publishing international*

Above right: Skin the fillet, if desired, by cutting into the tail flesh to the skin. Turn the blade parallel to the skin. Keep the skin on fillets that will be charcoal grilled. This helps prevent the flesh from falling apart, sticking to the grill, and overcooking. *Creative Publishing international*

Above left: Finish by pulling the skin firmly while moving the knife in a sawing motion between the skin and the flesh. Clean the fillets by wiping with paper towels or rinse quickly under cold water and then dry thoroughly. *Creative Publishing international*

Above right: Northern pike, muskellunge, and pickerel have a row of Y-shaped bones that float just above the ribs and run lengthwise along the fillet, ending above the vent. They can be cut out by guiding the knife blade along the bones and scraping lightly. Some flesh is lost when Y-bones are cut out but may make for more pleasurable dining. They can be left intact and removed after cooking. *Creative Publishing international*

hunting seasons. This allows you to secure your favorite fish for long periods during the year, in contrast to other species with limited harvest seasons.

The quality of a fish begins to decline as soon as it is caught. Like other species, fish should be handled with care to avoid bruising and kept out of sunlight to prevent further deterioration. They should be cleaned, dressed, and washed before being refrigerated or frozen.

Sharp fillet knives work best for cutting fish. You should use a chain mail glove to protect your free hand from knife slips while filleting them.

If you are going to skin the fish, you will not need to remove the scales. However, to remove the scales, use a fish scaler or a dull knife to scrape from tail to head, or in the opposite direction that the scales lay.

There are several ways to cut up fish. Four methods are described here, but you may use others. Fish can be left whole, dressed, steaked, or filleted, depending on your use and preference.

To keep the fish whole, you will only need to remove the viscera and wash the inner body cavity and outside with clean water. Your decision to remove the scales may depend on whether you will use your fish at the earliest opportunity or freeze it.

Dressing a fish involves the removal of the viscera, head, tail, and dorsal, pectoral, pelvic, and anal fins. You can make fish steaks by using the dressing procedures. Then cut the body crosswise into portions about 1-inch thick. Generally, steaking is only done with large fish, such as northern pike and salmon.

It is easier to fillet fish by first removing the viscera and retaining the head (especially on most large fish, such as walleye, northern pike, or bass, so you have something to hold on to the fish while cutting it). Fish are also easier to cut if the viscous covering is thoroughly washed off the scales.

Make your first cut just behind the gill behind the head. Turn your knife at an angle and slice down the backbone using the heel to guide your cut. As the knife slides along the backbone, it will cut through the ribs until you reach the tail. If you skin the fillet, you can stop your cut at the tail, leaving a portion of skin attached to the fish. Then turn the fillet over skin-side down and flatten the knife on the skin and run the knife forward to separate the flesh and skin. Then do the same for the other side. If done properly, the end result will be an entire carcass left without the meat fillets. Finally, pack the fillets in ice or refrigerate them until cooked or preserved.

Final Considerations

While small furred animals can provide meat for exotic or adventurous tastes, you should give thought to the effect that harvesting these animals has on local wildlife populations. The diversity of species in the wild is often dependent upon their ability to sustain their populations. Overhunting or trapping can decimate populations to the point they become unsustainable. If you decide to pursue these game animals, use as much of the carcass as possible so their contribution to your table is not wasted.

In many states, it is lawful to capture and possess no more than a few wild native animals or amphibians for private use. It is not lawful to sell, barter, or trade any that you hunt or trap. Permits or licenses for hunting or trapping wild game are required in most, if not all, states, and you are responsible for knowing, understanding, and abiding by any regulations or statutes.

Small Game Cooking Considerations

Simplicity is the greatest asset in obtaining good taste from cooking small game. Following several basic principles will help determine how your game tastes and how it should be prepared to maximize flavor.

The chronological age of the game animal will have a great influence on the flavor and cooking method used. Young animals born of that year, or yearlings, can be cooked by roasting, broiling, or frying. Older animals, large adults, or animals that have been subjected to a chase will require slow cooking either by stewing, pot roasts, or fricassees.

Secondly, fat typically needs to be added during cooking to compensate for the leanness of most game meat and to bring out the flavor. Very active small game animals, such as squirrels and rabbits, typically have fat reserves that only accumulate during certain seasons. The result is a lean-muscled animal that will make tough chewing at certain times of the year unless some fat is added. Some animals such as opossum possess a natural oiliness that helps the cooking process.

Adding fat to small game cooking is referred to as oiling and is most generally done by rubbing the individual cuts with pork fat. Bacon can be used when it is cut into slabs or small pieces and laid over the small game cuts.

The taste of game meat is also influenced by the food habits of the animal. Most are favorable and become characteristic of regions and times of year. This may influence the method of cooking used for a specific species at a particular time of year. Roasting may be more favorable at one time and stewing at another time.

Roast Rabbit

1 rabbit   Poultry fat or oil
Salt and pepper   Currant jelly
Sausage stuffing

Wash the dressed rabbit under running water and dry. Season with salt and pepper, stuff, and sew shut. Roast uncovered at 325°F for 1½ to 1¾ hours or until tender. Baste with fat. Serve on hot platter with brown gravy and currant jelly. Garnish with parsley or watercress. Serves 4 to 6.

Hasenpfeffer

1 rabbit
1 quart vinegar
2 tbsp. salt
1 tbsp. pickling spices
1 tbsp. peppercorns
2 large onions, sliced

2 tbsp. fat (bacon grease)
1 c. cold water
2 tbsp. flour
1 tsp. cinnamon
½ tsp. allspice

Cut rabbit into serving portions. Place in crock and cover with vinegar, combined with salt, spices, peppercorns, and 1 onion. Let stand in a cool place 24 hours. Drain, cover with boiling water, and simmer until tender, about 1½ hours. Remove meat and strain broth. Melt fat or bacon grease in frying pan. Blend in flour and add water, stirring constantly. Cook until thickened. Add rabbit, strained broth, cinnamon, allspice, and remaining onion; simmer for about 1 hour.

Squirrel

3 small squirrels
¾ c. salad oil
¼ c. lemon juice
2 c. bread crumbs
½ c. milk or cream
½ c. mushrooms, diced and
   sautéed

½ tsp. salt
⅛ tsp. pepper
½ tsp. onion juice
4 tbsp. olive oil or bacon fat
1 tsp. Worcestershire sauce
Paprika

Wash and clean squirrels in several cups of water and dry. Cover with salad oil mixed with lemon juice and let stand for 1 hour. Combine bread crumbs with just enough milk or cream to moisten, mushrooms, salt, pepper, and onion juice. Stuff the squirrel with this mixture, skewer, and truss. Brush with olive oil or bacon fat and roast uncovered at 325°F for 1½ to 1¾ hours or until tender. Baste every 15 minutes with fat from bottom of pan. When tender, make gravy with remaining broth, adding Worcestershire sauce and paprika to taste. Serve gravy in separate dish. Serves 6.

Brunswick Stew

2 squirrels
1 tbsp. salt
1 minced onion
2 c. fresh lima beans
6 ears corn
½ pound salt pork

6 potatoes
1 tsp. pepper
2 tsp. sugar
4 c. sliced tomatoes
½ pound butter

Cut squirrel into serving pieces. Add salt to 4 quarts of water, and when boiling, add onion, lima beans, corn cut from the cob, pork, potato, pepper, and squirrels. Cover and simmer 2 hours, add sugar and tomato, and simmer 1 hour more. Ten minutes before removing from heat, add butter cut into pieces the size of a walnut and rolled in flour. Bring to a boil. Serve in soup plates for 6. The characteristic Brunswick stew is made with squirrels. Chickens and rabbits can be used in place of squirrels.

Opossum

1 opossum

The opossum is a very fat animal with a peculiarly flavored meat. Wash thoroughly inside and out with hot water after dressing and skinning. Cover with cold water to which 1 cup of salt has been added and let stand overnight. Drain off the salted water and rinse with clean, boiling water.

Dressing

1 large onion, minced
1 tbsp. fat
Opossum liver, chopped
1 c. bread crumbs

1 sweet red pepper, chopped
Dash Worcestershire sauce
1 hard cooked egg, chopped
Salt

Brown the onion in fat. Add liver and cook until liver is tender. Add bread crumbs, pepper, Worcestershire sauce, egg, salt, and water to moisten.

Stuff opossum and place in roaster; add 2 tablespoons water and roast at 350°F. Baste every 15 minutes with drippings. Skim fat from pan gravy; serve gravy separately with baked yams or sweet potatoes. Serves 10.

Raccoon

1 raccoon

Dressing

8 to 10 slices dry bread	½ tsp. ground cloves
Stock from raccoon	1 tbsp. salt
2 eggs	2 tbsp. sage

Cut raccoon into small pieces and salt to taste. Cook in inset pan of pressure cooker for 1 hour at 15-pounds pressure. Cook longer if the meat is tough. When tender, arrange pieces in baking dish and cover with dressing. Mix ingredients and put on top of cooked raccoon meat. Bake at 350°F until dressing is browned. This can also be used for opossum.

Cranberry Braised Raccoon

2½ to 3 lbs. raccoon pieces, fat and glands removed	1 tsp. grated orange peel
1 c. cranberries, finely chopped	¾ tsp. salt
1 c. apple cider	⅛ tsp. ground cloves
¼ c. honey	⅛ tsp. ground nutmeg

Place raccoon pieces in large saucepan. In small mixing bowl, combine remaining ingredients; mix well. Pour over raccoon pieces. Heat to boiling. Reduce heat; cover. Simmer until raccoon is tender, about 2 to 3 hours; stirring occasionally. Serves 3 to 4.

Fried Frog Legs

6 frog legs
Salt and pepper
Lemon juice

1 egg
Fine bread crumbs

Skin the legs and wash them in cold water; dry well on a towel or napkin. Season with salt, pepper, and lemon juice. Beat the egg and season it with salt and pepper; dip the legs into egg, then into dried bread crumbs or fine cracker crumbs. Fry in hot, deep fat at 390°F for 2 to 3 minutes. Serve with tartar sauce. Serves 2.

Turtle Ragout

2 lbs. turtle meat, diced
1 onion, chopped
2 tbsp. butter
1 tbsp. flour

1 bay leaf
1 clove garlic
1 c. water
¼ c. sherry

Cook onion in butter; blend in flour. Add remaining ingredients and simmer 30 minutes. Serves 6.

Turtle Soup

2 c. turtle meat or tail
1 medium chopped onion
1 crushed garlic clove
1 bay leaf
Salt and pepper
1 c. carrots, cubed

1 c. celery, chopped
1 medium rutabaga, cubed
1 c. potatoes, diced
1 c. green beans
½ c. whole corn
½ c. parsnips, cubed

Boil turtle meat, onion, garlic clove, bay leaf, salt, and pepper until meat separates from bone; remove from kettle. Remove meat from bone. Put meat back in kettle. Return to heat and add remaining ingredients. Simmer about 1½ hours. Add salt and pepper to taste.

Salmon Quiche

Crust

3 c. flour
1 tsp. salt

⅔ c. vegetable oil
¼ c. plus 2 tbsp. milk

Filling

1 to 1½ c. salmon, cooked and
   flaked
5 eggs
1 c. Monterey Jack cheese,
   shredded

2 c. half-and-half
¾ tsp. salt
⅛ tsp. pepper
Dash ground nutmeg
2 tbsp. parsley flakes

Heat oven to 350ºF. In medium mixing bowl, mix flour, salt, oil, and milk lightly with fork until blended. Pat into 13x9-inch baking pan, patting dough 1 inch up side of pan; bake for 8 minutes.

Sprinkle cheese over hot crust, then sprinkle with fish. In small mixing bowl, blend eggs, half-and-half, salt, pepper, and nutmeg. Pour over fish. Sprinkle with parsley. Bake until knife inserted in center comes out clean, 30 to 35 minutes. Cool for 10 minutes. Cut into 2 to 1½-inch pieces. Serves 36 appetizers.

Salmon Salad

2 c. salmon, cooked and flaked
1 c. small shell macaroni,
   uncooked
⅓ c. black olives, sliced
¼ c. green pepper, finely chopped
1 tbsp. grated onion

¼ c. vegetable oil
2 tbsp. red wine vinegar
¼ tsp. dried oregano leaves
¼ tsp. salt
⅛ tsp. pepper

Prepare macaroni as directed on package. Rinse under cold water; drain. In medium bowl, combine macaroni, salmon, olives, green pepper, and onion. In small bowl, blend oil, vinegar, oregano, salt, and pepper. Pour dressing over salad, tossing to coat. Refrigerate at least 1 hour before serving. Serves 4 to 6.

Baked Walleye and Ratatouille

2 to 3 lbs. walleye
1 medium onion
2 cloves garlic, minced
¼ c. olive or vegetable oil
1 eggplant (about 1lb.)
3 medium zucchini (about 1 lb.)
1 medium green pepper
2 c. sliced mushrooms

1 16-oz. can whole tomatoes,
   drained, cut up
1 tsp. salt
¾ tsp. dried basil leaves
½ tsp. dried oregano leaves
¼ tsp. pepper

Heat oven to 350°F. Cut onion into thin slices and separate into rings. In saucepan, cook and stir onion and garlic in olive oil over medium heat until onion is tender, about 5 minutes. Peel eggplant and cut into ¾-inch cubes. Cut zucchini into ¼-inch slices. Core and seed green pepper; cut into ½-inch strips. Stir eggplant, zucchini, green pepper, mushrooms, tomatoes, salt, basil, oregano, and pepper into onions. Cook over medium heat, stirring occasionally, for 10 minutes. Set aside.

Place fish on large sheet of heavy-duty aluminum foil. Spoon vegetables over and around fish. Wrap tightly. Place on baking sheet. Bake until fish flakes easily at the backbone, about 35 minutes. Serves 2 to 4.

Tomato-Baked Walleye Fillets

1½ lbs. walleye or other lean fish
   fillets
1 medium onion
2 tbsp. olive or vegetable oil
1½ c. fresh mushrooms, sliced
7½ oz. whole tomatoes, drained,
   cut up
⅓ c. white wine

½ tsp. salt
⅛ tsp. pepper
⅛ tsp. garlic powder
1 medium tomato, thinly sliced
½ tsp. dried oregano leaves
2 tbsp. parsley

Cut onion into thin slices and into rings. In 9-inch skillet, cook and stir onion in olive oil over medium heat until tender-crisp, about 5 minutes. Set aside.

Heat oven to 350°F. Place fish in 13x9-inch baking pan. Top with onion rings. Sprinkle mushrooms over onions. Set aside.

In small bowl, combine canned tomatoes, wine, salt, pepper, and garlic powder. Spoon evenly over fish and vegetables. Top with tomato slices. Sprinkle oregano and parsley over tomato. Bake until fish flakes easily at thickest part, 25 to 30 minutes. Serves 4 to 6.

Creamy Northern Pike Casserole

2 c. northern pike or other lean
  fish, cooked and flaked
1 10¾-oz. can condensed cream of
  shrimp soup
1 c. celery, thinly sliced
1 tbsp. butter or margarine
1 c. frozen green beans, fresh if
  available

1 5.3-ounce can evaporated milk
1 4-oz. can sliced mushrooms,
  drained, or fresh if available
1 3-oz. can French-fried onion
  rings, crushed
⅛ tsp. pepper

Heat oven to 350°F. In small skillet, cook and stir celery in butter over medium heat until tender, about 6 minutes. Set aside.

In 2-quart casserole, mix fish, cream of shrimp soup, green beans, milk, mushrooms, ½ cup of crushed onion rings, and pepper. Stir in celery.

Bake for 30 minutes. Top with remaining onion rings. Bake until hot and bubbly, 15 to 20 minutes. Serves 4 to 6.

The liver is a brown-colored organ that metabolizes sugars into glucose, providing energy to the body systems. The gallbladder is greenish-colored and is attached near the liver. It must be removed and discarded. The liver should have a bright, healthy look, free of abscesses. It can be sliced and fried or used in sausage making.

Chapter 9

MEAT BYPRODUCTS AND FOOD PRESERVATION

———— •❖• ————

Early peoples used as much of the animal's carcass as possible for food, clothing, tools, weapons or bindings, and ornaments, among other things. Stomachs, bladders, and skins were fashioned into containers. Nothing was wasted following a successful hunt for meat. Today's commercial meat processors make a similar use of the entire carcass. Modern society still utilizes the nonmuscle portions and transforms them into many products, including pharmaceutical uses.

All parts of the animal that are not included in the carcass are called byproducts. These include such parts as skin, bones, hair, teeth, feathers, claws, fat, brains, and nonconnective tissues and tendons. Your use of byproducts may depend on whether you have a need for them. Skins may be sold or tanned for leather, feathers can be used for ornaments, and fats can be used in sausage making or rendered into lard.

Edible byproducts, such as livers, hearts, tongues, testicles, kidneys, oxtails, stomachs (tripe), and intestines, may find uses in your meals in one form or another. These are sometimes referred to as variety meats. You may develop a taste for a particular byproduct part, as most can be included in specialized dishes or can be ground into meat for making sausage.

Several, such as liver, kidney, and heart, are high in protein content and highly nutritious. These variety meats are generally more perishable than other meats and should be frozen or cooked soon after harvest or purchase.

The paragraphs below detail these byproducts, how they can be cooked, and for what purpose.

Liver: After removing all connective tissue surrounding the liver, it can be thinly sliced and cooked in a variety of methods. These include frying, broiling, sautéing, and braising. You can grind or chop liver and use it as an additive to sausages, loaves, spreads, and other dishes.

Heart: The heart from different animals can be used. For fowl and small animals, such as squirrels or rabbits, they can be cooked with moist heat or ground and used in sausages. The heart is generally less tender than liver, although it has an excellent flavor. Large animal hearts can be sliced open for inspection and then may be filled with a dressing, stitched shut with cooking thread, and then roasted with moist heat, like a turkey.

The heart is less tender than the liver, but it has excellent flavor. Small animal hearts can be ground as an additive for sausages. After the heart is removed from the body, you should slice it open and wash out any remaining blood.

Tongues can be thinly sliced after braising for cold sandwich meats. You can remove the tough outer membrane by blanching (short exposure to boiling water) prior to long-term, moist-heat cooking. Sweetbreads include the beef and veal thymus and pork pancreas glands and are similar to tongues in that they need to be precooked to remove the outer membranes and sliced thinly before dipping in batter or flour and deep fried.

The kidneys can be used in casseroles and stews, or they may be broiled and skewered. While in the carcass, they are often surrounded by fat, which should be peeled away before use. Lamb and veal kidneys are more tender than beef kidneys.

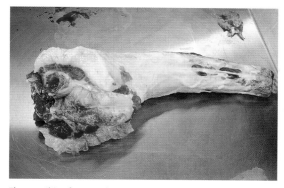

The oxtail is often used in soup stock. It is the top portion of the tail that attaches to the posterior end of the spine. It can contribute a rich, meaty flavor.

The honeycomb edible portion of a beef animal's stomach is called tripe. Before use, it must be opened, the contents thoroughly cleaned out, and then cooled. After the inner surface membrane is removed, it can be sliced and cooked with moist heat, or used in soups.

Tongue: Tongues from large animals, such as cattle or pigs, can make cold sandwich meats after being braised and thinly sliced. You can remove the tough outer membrane of the tongue by blanching, followed by moist heat cooking for an extended period. Once this membrane is trimmed, the rest can be cooled and sliced.

Kidneys: Lamb and veal kidneys may be broiled and skewered and are more tender than beef kidneys. They can be included in meat casseroles, stews, and other dishes.

Oxtail: The oxtail is the upper portion of the tail that attaches near the lateral end of the spine. It is often used as soup stock. The tail sections can be browned first, if desired, then simmer until the meat is tender and separates from the bone. Remove the bone parts and use the meat as soup ingredients. Oxtail has a rich, meaty flavor and texture, and it can also be used in stews.

Tripe: The edible portion of stomach tissues is called tripe. Tripe comes from the first and second stomachs of cattle and the stomach of pigs. To use tripe, you must cut open the stomach to remove all contents. Then it must be thoroughly washed before quickly chilling it. Remove the inner surface membrane. It will have a firmer texture than other variety meats and is less tender. You can use it in various meat dishes, such as kidneys, or added to soups. It is best cooked with moist heat and may be served with sauces and dressings.

Intestines: If the intestines are not used as casings for sausage making, they can be utilized for specialty dishes. The intestines, especially those from pigs, can be cleaned

The intestines can be used for casing in sausage making. Pig intestines are the most commonly used after being thoroughly washed and brined. They can also be cooked and cut into small pieces, breaded with raw egg and crumbs, and then deep fried.

Blood contains about 17 percent protein and can be used for making blood sausage. Pork or beef blood is most often used. It is added with fillers such as meat, fat, barley, oatmeal, and bread until it is thick enough to congeal when cooked. Any blood that comes in contact with the surface of the carcass or is otherwise contaminated should not be used.

and thoroughly washed and cooked with sauces. These are sometimes referred to as chitterlings. They can also be cut into small pieces, breaded with raw eggs and bread crumbs, and deep fried.

Blood: Blood contains approximately 17 percent protein and can be used in sausage making; blood sausage makes the best use. The U.S. Department of Agriculture regulations do not allow any blood that comes in contact with the surface of the body of an animal or is contaminated in any other manner to be used for food purposes. Only blood from inspected animals can legally be used for meat food products that are sold to the public. Some societies, such as the Masai tribes, will mix blood with milk as part of their diet, but blood is generally discarded in home butchering. Cattle have the largest amount of blood, and a 1,200-pound animal

will typically yield about 46 pounds of blood; a pig will yield about 7 percent of its live body weight, and sheep will yield about 3 percent of its live body weight.

Fats: Animal fats have had many uses over the course of human history. They have served as a food energy source, been rubbed into animal hides to make tepee leather supple and waterproof, and, in the case of bear grease during the nineteenth century, provided a sheen and unique aroma to human hair. Fats also have been used for making soaps and providing fuel for oil lamps in the days prior to kerosene or gasoline.

Animal and plant fats differ mainly in melting point and saturation. Fats and oils contain both saturated and unsaturated components. Saturated fats are firmer and have a higher melting point than the softer, unsaturated fats.

Cooking and table fats available for use range from liquid oils, derived mainly from plants, to solid fats, which come from animals and other sources.

Lard is the fat most often used in home cooking and is rendered from the clear and edible tissues of pigs. Recent decades have witnessed a decreased in use of lard production due to health concerns and competition from vegetable fats. However, lard provides a source of energy, and linoleic fatty acid is an essential component of the human diet.

Lard has a melting point that is near body temperature, making it easily digested. This low point allows a cook or baker to use it in a variety of ways, such as cooking fat, shortening, a flavor ingredient, and a source of nutrition.

Rendering is the process of extracting fat from the tissues using heat. The raw fat and meat is either cooked or heated to turn the fat into a liquid. The melted fat is then drawn off.

This process increases the shelf life of the fat by killing the microorganisms that were present and removing most of the moisture.

You can render pork fat at home whether it comes from butchering a pig or is purchased at a local market. If you are using one of your pigs, remove the raw fat from the skin to obtain better quality.

Begin by chopping the fat into fine pieces. For each pound of fat, allow ½ cup of water. Place the fat and water in a cooking vessel and heat to boiling, but do not exceed 240 degrees Fahrenheit. Stir as it warms to avoid scorching. As it boils, the steam will remove extraneous odors. Boiling will not occur until the fat liquefies. Allow the fat to cook until the solid material reaches a golden or amber color, then drain into storage containers.

Use several thicknesses of cheesecloth or similar material that can be placed over clean, dry, nonmetallic storage containers suitable for use with hot liquids. Slowly pour the hot fat into the cloths until the containers are fitted to a desired level. Cool the lard rapidly to produce a firm, smooth-textured product. As the lard cools, stir it occasionally when it reaches the creamy stage to reduce the oils separating out and avoid developing a grainy texture. Store at temperatures of 40 degrees Fahrenheit or lower. Lard may be frozen but should be packaged in airtight containers and used within six months. This will reduce changes in flavor or aroma due to oxidation.

If you choose to render fat in your home, you need to use caution during the entire process. You also need to avoid spills because hot grease can cause severe burns to exposed skin. If the fat is spilled on clothing, it will cling to it and can also cause deep, severe burns. Never allow children anywhere near your processing area or as the containers are cooling.

Food Preservation Options

Whether butchering domestic animals or hunting wild game for meat, it is likely you will have more meat available than you can eat at one meal. The rest will have to be preserved to keep it usable for later. Different preservation methods serve different purposes. You should decide on a plan of distribution of the meat into one or several of these methods before you proceed with processing. Do you want to freeze all or part of the carcass that is not used immediately? Do you want to make some into sausages? Develop a plan before you begin and you will eliminate waste.

Food preservation, in relation to meat products, is the process of handling it in a way that stops or retards the growth of microorganisms, making it safe for long-term consumption. There are many forms of food preservation, including freezing, canning, drying, salting, and pickling to name the major processes used in homes. Large commercial applications employ methods such as vacuum packaging, irradiation, sugaring, and using lye, modified atmosphere, and high pressure, but those will not be discussed here.

Freezing is one of the most commonly used preservative methods and has several advantages. It is a fast and simple way to stop microbial growth. The nutritional value of the meat does not deteriorate through freezing, although some texture and quality can be affected by long-term storage, resulting in freezer burn.

Canning involves cooking food to a boiling point for a specified time as a form of sterilization. This is done while sealed cans or jars are submerged in boiling water or placed in a pressure cooker. The advantages of canning include a ready-to-heat meal after the can or jar is opened, it can serve as a backup

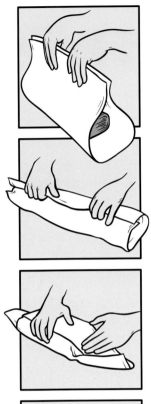

Begin by placing the meat near the center of the wrap and then bring the edges together at the top.

Make a short fold at the top and repeat folds until last fold is tight against the meat.

Even out the fold wraps and smooth the ends as you make triangle folds.

Fold the ends under the package and seal with freezer tape. Label with date, type of meat and cut, and weight.

A moisture- or vapor-proof freezer wrap that seals out air and locks in moisture will make material to use for meat to be stored in a freezer. Choose heavy-duty, pliable wraps, such as freezer paper, aluminium foil, and freezer bags that can be used with bulky or irregular-shaped cuts of meat.

in case of freezer malfunction, and it allows useful preservation when insufficient freezer space is available.

Drying is perhaps the oldest method of food preservation and involves dehydration of the meat. The removal of water from the meat significantly reduces the water activity to prevent, inhibit, or delay bacterial growth. Reducing the amount of water in meat also reduces the total weight, making it easier to transport.

Salting is used to cure meats by drawing moisture out of the tissue through a process of osmosis. Salt or sugar can be used separately or in a combination. Salted fish or meat was a staple in the diets of many early settlers who were on the move or lacked other methods to preserve food.

Pickling is the use of a brine, vinegar, or any spicy edible solution that is used to inhibit microbial action. Pickling can involve two different forms: chemical pickling, which uses a brine solution, or fermentation pickling, such as making sauerkraut. The edible liquid used in chemical pickling typically includes agents such as a high salt brine, vinegar, alcohol, and vegetable oils, particularly olive oil. The purpose is to saturate the food being preserved with the agent. This may be enhanced in some cases with heating or boiling. Common foods that are chemically pickled include corned beef, peppers, herring, eggs, and cucumbers. Fermentation pickling is generally not used with meat but can be used with foods that offer a good compliment to meat during a meal, such as sauerkraut. Fermentation pickling is assisted by the food being preserved as it produces lactic acid.

Until the middle of the last century, jugging was a popular method of preserving meat. This method involves the process of stewing meat in an earthenware jug or casserole. The meat is cut into pieces, placed in a tightly sealed jug with brine or gravy, and stewed. Sometimes red wine is added to the cooking liquid.

Pickling involves the use of brines or vinegars to preserve meat products through fermentation. It is mostly used for fruits and vegetables, but it can be used for animal and fish products, such as pig's feet, pork hocks, corned beef, herring, northern pike, or other large game fish.

Freezer Effects on Meat

Freezing has a physical effect on meat, but it remains one of the best preservation methods available for long-term storage while not destroying vitamins or the meat's nutritional value. Freezing meat almost completely inactivates the enzymes and inhibits the growth of spoilage organisms.

When processing a carcass, it is important to remember that meat temperatures must be brought down to 40 degrees Fahrenheit within 16 hours to prevent growth of spoilage microorganisms that lie deep within the carcass tissues or in the centers of containers of warm meat. If the meat has not been cooled but is going directly to a freezer, it must reach a temperature of 0 degrees Fahrenheit within 72 hours to prevent the growth of putrifying bacteria.

You should make cuts to be frozen into smaller, individual sizes that are ready for cooking rather than to freeze them as large portions that need to be further deconstructed once they are thawed. Smaller cuts freeze more quickly and evenly than very large pieces or chunks. It is better to minimize the number of times the meat needs to be handled and exposed to surfaces after it is thawed and used.

Canning

Canning is the second most commonly used preservation method for long-term storage of meat. Canned meats are generally of two types: sterilized and pasteurized. Sterilized meat products do not need refrigeration and can sit on shelves for extended periods as long as the container remains intact. Pasteurized products require refrigeration to inhibit spoilage.

When canning meat for home use, you should use the appropriate procedures to ensure quality and safe storage. Canned meats are preserved by hermetically sealing the container, which prevents air from escaping or entering it. By applying heat to the sealed meats, you destroy the microorganisms that are capable of producing spoilage. Using proper sanitation during the breakdown of the carcass will help minimize the number of organisms originally present at canning time.

Canning involves a time-temperature relationship in destroying most microorganisms. A specific internal temperature must be reached and held for a minimum amount of time to destroy the microorganisms present. This method is most often applied to destroy

Glass jars are used for canning meats and vegetables. Inspect all jars for rim cracks or chips, and discard any jar when they are found because they will not create a good, safe seal. Also, inspect each rubber ring or metal lid with gaskets to be used and discard any that are defective.

the spores that can lead to botulism. These times and temperatures are at the high end of any other methods. A safe cook, which is considered to be one that destroys the botulism organisms, requires a minimum of three minutes at 250 degrees Fahrenheit. Achieving this sterilizing temperature will require the use of a pressure cooker. These typically operate under pressure of 12 to 15 pounds per square inch. Pressure changes the boiling point of water and allows it to rise above the normal boiling point of 212 degrees Fahrenheit.

There are many advantages to using the sterilization method of canning meat products. The best is a long storage life over a wide temperature range. Canned meats that are properly done can last several years and still be edible, although some flavor deterioration may occur. Providing the container has remained intact and the seal or exterior

has not been damaged, canning can provide an effective preservation method when refrigeration storage or electrical power disruption occurs. Some popular products that can be canned include roast beef, beef stews, canned beef, potted-meat products, and pickled pig's feet.

The two most important aspects of canning are providing sufficient heat and creating a perfect seal of the container. Only the best and freshest meats should be used because canning only preserves the meat; it does not improve the quality of the meat used.

Glass jars are typically used in a method called the hot pack. This involves packing the meat into the jars and processing the jars in boiling water or steam. The advantages of this method are that the jars are completely sealed and the meat has no further exposure to outside influences or organisms.

Glass canning jars come in several sizes but are most generally found in pints or quarts. Covers or lids that can be firmly tightened before being placed in water are needed. Rubber rings and metal lids with a sealing gasket attached to it are two popular options. New rings and seal lids must be used each year; discard used lids or rings.

Many models of pressure cookers are commercially available, such as stovetop and electric models, and they are usually made of aluminum or enameled steel. Whichever model you choose, the same principles apply. It should be substantially constructed and should have a pressure indicator, a safety valve, and a petcock or vent.

Begin by thoroughly washing each jar in hot soapy water and rinse it in clear, hot water. The jars can air dry by placing them on clean towels. Inspect the jars and test the cooker before you begin. Examine the jars

Pressure cookers are used to create a higher cooking temperature than is possible under normal cooking conditions. Water heated under pressure increases the temperature quickly. Be sure the gauge is accurate, the handles are securely fastened before heating the water, and the petcock functions appropriately to ensure safe use of a pressure cooker.

stay open until steam has poured out steadily for 10 minutes or more. Then close it to allow the pressure to rise to the level directed in the owner's manual, usually 10 pounds.

To begin the processing, place a small amount of water in the bottom of the cooker. Add the meat-filled jars to the cooker and clamp on the air-tight lid. The cooker is then set over heat or heat is applied electrically.

The pressure raises the temperature higher than that used in ordinary cooking, and the food cooks more quickly. A gauge on the lid shows the number of pounds of pressure, indicating the temperature. A safety valve releases pressure after cooking is completed. It will also release excess pressure. The petcock provides an outlet for steam and air.

When the appropriate pressure is reached, you should adjust the heat to keep the same pressure without variation. For meats, process for three minutes at 250 degrees Fahrenheit.

When the processing time is completed, the cooker should be taken off the heat and left alone until the pressure goes down to zero. Then open the petcock to release the remaining steam. Liquid may be lost from the jars if the pressure varies during processing or if the steam is released too quickly. Jars should not be reopened and refilled under any circumstances unless being immediately used. Do not let the cooker sit unopened for any length of time after the steam is down. This may create a vacuum, which will make it difficult to open the lid. If this happens, reheat the cooker for a few minutes until it is loose.

Take the jars out of the cooker and hand-tighten their lids if necessary. Place the jars on a rack or towel to cool, but keep them away from drafts. Some canners turn the jars upside down as they cool to check for any leaks or bubbles, which indicate a poor seal.

and lids for nicks or cracks. If they appear intact, fit a new ring to each jar, partly fill with hot water, and adjust the lid and seal. Invert each jar and watch for leakage or small bubbles rising through the water as it cools. An imperfect seal means you should discard the jar or the lid, depending from where the bubbles originate. You can also test the rubber rings by doubling them over. If any crack, discard them.

Fill the jar half to three-quarter full with small raw cubed-sized pieces of meat. Do not tightly pack down the meat into the jar. Fill each jar with clean water to within 1 inch of the rim. Place the jars on the rack inside the cooker. The water level should reach the bottom of the rack, which keeps the glass off the chamber base and allows the water and steam to completely surround the jars. Place the jars so they do not touch one another. The lid or cover should be adjusted carefully and fastened tightly so that no stem can escape through the petcock. The petcock should

After drying, label the jars with the canning date. After ten days, recheck the jars. Immediately discard any that exhibit cloudiness or signs of spoilage. Do not eat their contents under any circumstances.

Meat Cooking Methods

The cooking method you use depends on the kind and quality of the meat to be cooked. Only tender cuts of meat can be cooked by dry heat. Less tender cuts require moist heat and long, slow cooking. The kind of cooking methods include the following:

Baking: To cook in an oven or oven-type appliance. Covered or uncovered containers may be used.

Barbequing: To roast slowly on a spit or rack over coals or under a gas broiler flame or electric broiler unit, usually basting with a highly seasoned sauce. The term also is commonly applied to foods cooked in or served with barbeque sauce.

Boiling: To cook in water or mostly water, at boiling temperature (212 degrees Fahrenheit at sea level). Bubbles rise continually and break on the surface.

Braising: Braising is cooking by moist heat. It is used for the less tender cuts, which require long, slow cooking in the presence of moisture to bring out the full flavor and make them tender. Many pork cuts are cooked by braising rather than broiling or pan-broiling because pork requires thorough cooking. Brown the meat in a small amount of fat, then cover tightly and cook slowly in juices from the meat or in added liquid, such as water, milk, or cream. Add only a small amount of liquid occasionally and do not let boil but keep at a simmering temperature. Pork chops and pot roasts can be cooked by braising.

Broiling: Broiling is cooking by direct heat and may be done over hot coals or under a flame or an electric unit. This method may be used for tender cuts that have adequate amounts of fat. Veal and pork should not be broiled since they are too low in fat.

Caramelizing: To heat sugar or food containing sugar until a brown color and characteristic flavor develop.

Creaming: To work a food or a combination of foods until soft and creamy, using a spoon, wooden paddle, or other utensil.

Fricasseeing: To braise individual serving pieces of meat, poultry, or game in a little liquid such as water, broth, or sauce.

Frying and sautéing: Some meats such as chops and cutlets may be crumbed and fried in deep fat or oil. Ham, liver, and some other meats can be sautéed in a small amount of oil or fat at low temperatures after the first searing.

Marinating: To let foods stand in a liquid (usually a mixture of oil with vinegar or lemon juice) to add flavor or to make them more tender.

Pan-broiling: To pan-broil, place the meat in a sizzling skillet or pan, and brown on both sides. Reduce heat, pour off fat as it accumulates, and cook until done, while occasionally turning it. Pork is generally not pan-broiled.

Parboil: To boil until partly cooked.

Pot roasting: To cook large pieces of meat by braising.

Roasting: To roast meat, place it on the rack in a roasting pan, fat side up, and cook in a slow oven, uncovered and without water, until cooked as desired. The large tender cuts of meat are cooked by this method.

Scalding: To heat liquid to just below the boiling point.

Simmering: To cook in liquid just below the boiling point, at temperatures of 185 to 210 degrees Fahrenheit. Bubbles form slowly and break below the surface.

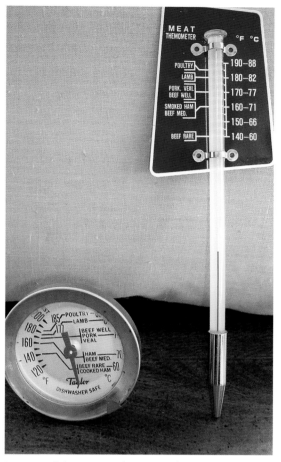

Instant-read thermometers have stems that are inserted into large pieces of meat, such as hams or roasts, to monitor internal temperatures. They are essential for accurate cooking and smoking processes.

Stewing: To boil or simmer in a small amount of liquid. Cut the meat into cubes and brown on all sides in hot fat, if desired. Cover with boiling water and cook at simmering temperatures in a covered kettle until meat is tender. Less tender cuts containing much connective tissue are best cooked by stewing, which softens both tissue and fiber. The best cuts for stews are those containing both fats and lean and some bone. The shank is the most economical of all cuts for this

purpose. Other cuts used are the neck, plate, flank, heel of the round, and short ribs. The brisket and rump are sometimes used.

Wrapping

Rancidity is the bad taste or smell derived from fats or oils that have spoiled. It develops differently in animal carcasses, depending on their fats' ability to absorb oxygen from the air. Rancidity can affect the taste, odor, and palatability of the fat and adjoining tissue. Different animal species produce different fats. Pork fat is high in unsaturated fatty acids, which have the ability to absorb oxygen resulting in a shorter storage life. Beef and lamb have a higher proportion of saturated fatty acids and are less susceptible to oxygen absorption and generally have a longer storage life.

You can reduce oxidation effects by eliminating air exposure to the meat. One good way for home use is to properly apply a wrapping material that is airtight and moisture proof.

Loss of meat moisture is referred to as shrinkage or dehydration. The loss of moisture from the frozen surface of the meat is called freezer burn. Freezer burn results from surface moisture loss due to using an unsuitable grade of wrapping paper, holes in the paper, or improper wrapping. Severe dehydration results in lower quality cuts, and the increase in oxygen exposure to fats can make them rancid.

To avoid freezer burn and reduce oxygen effects, you should use a good grade of meat wrapping paper that is moisture proof and use proper wrapping and handling procedures that eliminate tears or cuts in the paper. There are many American companies that supply meat wrapping paper, often referred to as butcher paper.

Bacon comes from the pig belly and is cured and smoked before it is sliced into strips for use. Squaring up the piece before smoking will allow you to cut more uniform slices.

Chapter 10

MEAT CURING AND SMOKING

The curing or salting of meat is the oldest preservation method used by humans. Salt was used for preserving meat and fish as early as 3000 B.C. Through the centuries that followed, civilizations used salt as a way to extend the use of meat products when traveling great distances and creating a longer "shelf-life." Salt became such a valuable commodity that it was zealously protected and bartered for, serving as a currency in some instances. The purpose of curing then, as now, was to create a product that could be safely eaten at a later date.

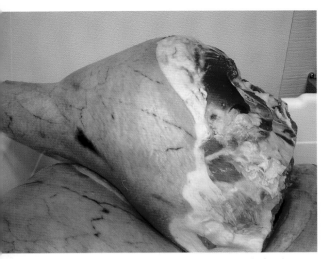

Hams should be rinsed or soaked in cold water before being cured and smoked. This removes excess salt on the outside and eliminates the formation of salt streaks on the meat when exposed to the heat of the smokehouse.

Native Americans hung strips of meat in the tops of the tepees to keep them out of reach of small animals and dogs. As these strips dried and took on the smoky flavor from the campfire inside their tepee, they became very hard. The dried meat strips were beaten into powder with stones and mixed with dried fruits, vegetables, and berries to make pemmican. This dried meat could be easily transported when their community moved to another area.

Modern-day meat curing and smoking practices are used primarily to create more and varied products, develop unique flavors and colors, extend shelf life, and inhibit the growth of spores that cause botulism, a lethal form of food poisoning. Home curing can be a part of your food preservation plan and can be done safely and effectively.

The use of salt and nitrite in curing meats are important ingredients in preventing botulism food poisoning. By inhibiting the growth of bacteria, meat products have

a longer shelf life before spoilage occurs. Cured meats also offer a versatile product that has a salty flavor enjoyed by many. One good example of a smoked meat product is sausage. It is smoked and heated to pasteurize it, extend its shelf life, to give it a smoky flavor, and to improve its appearance. Smoking and heating also fixes the color and causes protein to move to the surface of the sausage so it will hold its shape when casing is removed.

Curing

The term *curing* is sometimes interpreted to mean both curing and the subsequent smoking of meat. However, curing is not smoking, although these two processes work together. Strictly speaking, curing applies only to dry salt, brine submersion, or pickling with a vinegar base. However, in a wider sense, curing applies to any saline or alkaline preservation solution with some modifications.

Salt is the essential ingredient in a successful curing process. It draws moisture from the muscle cells while entering the cells by osmosis. This process distributes the salt through the tissue. It also inhibits the action of certain harmful bacteria and inhibits the function of several types of enzymes. If too little salt is applied to the meat, bacteria that can grow in the presence of some salt will not be fully stopped and spoilage can follow. If too much salt is used, the meat can become hard, dry, and taste overly salty.

Generally speaking, several weeks are required for the salts or brine to reach sufficient concentration in the tissues to protect the center of hams, shoulders, and other large chunks of meat. This means you will need a storage space where your meat can be kept away from insects, animals, and children while the curing processes work.

Drying

Prior to smoking meats, it is critical that the meat's surface is slightly moist to ensure that the smoke volatiles will adhere properly. Smoke will not adhere to dry surfaces, so you will need to dry the surface enough to remove the excess moisture while still leaving enough moisture to absorb the smoke.

Smoking

The purpose of smoking meats is to give them a unique smoke flavor, an even external color, and lower the moisture content in the meat, which reduces the opportunity for bacterial growth. Country-cured hams and similar cured and smoked meats that do not require refrigerated storage owe their stability to a combination of low moisture, high concentrations of curing agents, and heavily smoked surfaces. Three factors affect the amount of time a meat product needs to be smoked: the type of meat product, the density of smoke generated within the smoking unit, and the ability of the meat surface to absorb the smoke properties.

Options you can use for smoking include natural wood, charcoal, or electric units specially designed for smoking meats. The products you use for creating the smoke will have a significant effect on the meat.

Natural wood smoke is generally produced from hardwood sawdust, wood chips, or logs. Hickory wood is the most popular for use in smoking, although other hardwoods, such as oak, maple, ash, mesquite, apple, cherry, and other fruit woods, are also used. You should avoid using pine and other coniferous trees because of their high tar content and bitter flavor.

Natural wood smoke contains three major components: solids, such as ash and tar; air and combustion gases and acids;

Dried beef is generally derived from extremely lean round or sirloin cuts found in the rear quarters of beef. These are less tender cuts because of the high amount of connective tissue found in them. When fully cooked, smoked, and thinly sliced, dried beef is an excellent meat for sandwiches. Although relatively dry, dried beef products should still be refrigerated.

and carbonyls, phenolics, and polycyclic hydrocarbons. The ash, tar, and gases do not contribute very much to the flavor, aroma, or preservative properties of smoked products. The phenolics have been identified as the primary source for aroma and flavor and preservative properties, while the carbonyls are the source of the amber-brown color generated from the smoking process.

The length of time that the smoke fills the chamber will largely determine the amount of smoke deposited on the surface of the meat. Variations in smoke density will also affect how much the smoke components adhere to the meat.

Heat will dry the surface of meat, which will then inhibit the amount of smoke it will absorb. An even temperature should thus be maintained during the smoke cycle.

After the smoke cycle is completed, you can gradually increase the temperature inside the chamber to cook the meat. Avoid a rapid increase in temperature, as this will dry and overcook the surface before the desired internal temperature is reached. Increasing the temperature in increments will conduct the heat through the meat to minimize the difference between the surface and internal temperatures. A long, slow cook of the meat will tenderize it to maximum effect.

If possible, try to cook pieces that have a similar or uniform size, as this will allow you to cook them at a specific temperature for an equal time and have a uniform result. Unevenly matched pieces may be overdone and too dry or undercooked, depending on temperature and time. You may be able to circumvent these problems by using individual temperature probes to determine when target internal temperatures have been reached and the cooking cycle should be stopped. This may not be practical, so several cooking sessions may be needed. As a rule, high smoke house temperatures (110 degrees Fahrenheit and above) with a light smoke will speed up the drying while lower temperatures (80 to 110 degrees Fahrenheit) with a dense smoke will intensify the smoky flavor in meat.

The type of cured and smoked meat product you want to produce will determine the level of smokehouse temperature. If you are storing meat at air temperature, it should be smoked at a temperature of 135 degrees Fahrenheit until the inside of the meat reaches 110 degrees. You can then lower the smokehouse temperature to 110 degrees and maintain that until the desired color is reached.

Remove the meat after it has been cured and wash it to remove salt and fat streaks from the surface. Cooked meat products should be cooled quickly to 40 degrees Fahrenheit or less. At this point, it is important to maintain sanitary conditions and avoid contact with uncooked meat or surfaces that have come in contact with uncooked meat. This will minimize recontamination of the cooked products with organisms that may create spoilage.

Cured and Smoked Products

Many different meat cuts can be smoked and cured to produce a variety of flavors and textures. Bacon, ham, beef cuts, pork shoulders, ribs, hocks, jowls, poultry, and wild game can be smoked and cured into specific products. These include the following listed below.

Bacon: Pork bellies are usually trimmed into a rectangular shape and smoked and cured before being sliced into strips. Although it has been smoked and heated, bacon must be cooked before it is consumed. Cooking methods may include frying, grilling, broiling, or cooked in the microwave.

Dried beef: The beef round, the sirloin tip, and the larger muscles of the chuck may be used to make dried beef. Dried beef has a lower moisture content than many other beef products. It is smoked to varying degrees but is fully cooked and ready to eat after curing.

Beef jerky: These are dried meat strips that may be produced using a combination of curing, smoking, and drying. Take lean beef and cut into strips of about 1-inch in width and ⅛-inch or less thick, with varying lengths. Marinating the strips overnight in a refrigerator will allow the marinade's flavor to penetrate the meat. A salt-nitrite cure mix can be added to other flavorings and spice when making jerky. Cured strips should be rinsed of excess ingredients and placed on a screen in a smokehouse to be smoked, cooked, and dried. The drying and cooking should be done slowly. Dried jerky does not

Beef jerky is made from lean meat cut into thin strips of varying lengths, about 1-inch wide and ⅛-inch thickness. With a combination of curing, smoking, cooking, and drying, jerky strips normally do not need refrigeration. Jerky processing techniques may be used for strips of game, lamb, beef, pork, and mutton meats.

need refrigeration if it is packaged to prevent it from absorbing moisture and contamination from its surroundings during storage. Jerky processing techniques may also be used for wild game and lamb.

Hams: Hams are a popular smoked meat product that may be boneless or boned. Because of their larger size than other meat cuts, hams will take longer to cook, cure, and smoke.

Poultry: You can cure and smoke whole birds by controlling the smoke intensity and duration, both of which will affect the final smoke flavor. Hollow birds will cook more rapidly than solid hams or other cuts. Ducks and geese have larger amounts of carcass fat than other birds. You should trim as much fat as possible to reduce the amount of grease that will drip away. Fat from these birds has a low melting point, and it may streak the smoked surface during the cooking phase.

Wild game: Most game animal and fowl meats may be cured and smoked to add variety. Salt, spices, seasonings, and other ingredients may be applied to suit your tastes.

Smokehouses and Equipment

A smokehouse is a simple version of a heat processing unit used by today's meat industry. The size may be vastly different, but the principles are the same: it is an enclosed area where the temperature and smoke level may be controlled with acceptable accuracy. If you decide to build a smokehouse, it does not need to be an elaborate structure to do an effective job. However, it must be adequately built and have the ability to be monitored so that the meat is properly cooked to minimize health risks.

The purpose of a smokehouse is to enclose heat and smoke, and reduce, but not entirely eliminate, airflow. Depending on how much smoking you want to accomplish, you may construct your own smokehouse or purchase a commercial unit. Because smokehouses are generally located outdoors, you should check if any local ordinances or fire codes apply before you begin construction of any new structure.

Many types of smokehouses can be used successfully to smoke meats, fowl, and fish. Smokehouses can include such simple equipment as a charcoal grill for very small amounts of meat, metal barrels, water and electric smokers, and, in more extensive units, those of frame or concrete construction. The more elaborate structures will cost more to build. By understanding your end goals, you can make a reasonable assessment of which type will work best for you. Depending on where you live, you may be able to get your smoke work done with a local meat shop that smokes its products. The paragraphs below detail the different types of smokehouses to consider.

Charcoal grill: One of the least expensive methods to smoke small amounts of meats and sausages is on your covered charcoal

A charcoal grill is one of the cheapest methods of smoking small amounts of meats and sausages. You will need an oven thermometer to monitor the temperature.

by premoistened woodchips rather than charcoal. This will provide a more constant temperature and may require less attention during smoking. The sizes of electric smokers vary with some accommodating up to 40 pounds of sausage at one time.

Barrel smoker: A clean, noncontaminated 50-gallon metal barrel, with both ends removed, can be used as a smoker for small quantities of meat, fowl, and fish. Set the open-ended barrel on the upper end of a shallow, sloping, covered trench or 10- to 12-foot stovepipe. Dig a pit at the lower end for the fire. Smoke rises naturally, so having the fire lower than the barrel will aid its movement toward the meats. Mound the dirt around the edges of the barrel and the fire pit to eliminate leaks. You can control the heat by covering it with a piece of sheet metal.

Use metal or wood tubes as racks from which to suspend your sausages in the

grill. This will require an oven thermometer to monitor the temperature. You can fill the bottom of your grill with briquettes and burn them until gray ash appears. Separate the coals onto two sides of the grill and place a pan of water between them. Place the grate over the top and place your sausages above the water. As the sausages heat and cook, the fat will drip into the heated water and create steam that will help destroy harmful bacteria. Keep the vents open on the cover. For hot smoking, you will need to maintain an air temperature between 225 to 300 degrees Fahrenheit throughout the process.

Vertical water and electric smokers: A vertical water smoker is built with a bottom fire pan that holds charcoal briquettes and generally has two cooking racks near the top. The water pan positioned above the coals supplies moisture and helps regulate the internal temperature. An electric smoker is similarly constructed, except the smoke is controlled

Vertical water and electric smokers can be used when small amounts of meat and sausages are to be smoked. Some electric smokers can hold large amounts of sausage at one time.

excessive shrinkage of the meat. Use moist wood chips, sawdust, or charcoal for starting your fire. You want a lot of smoke but very little flame. Once your fire is going, you can add green sawdust or green hardwood to cool the fire and make more smoke. **Never** *use gasoline or other accelerants to start your fire.* Besides their explosive potential, which can cause serious injury, the fumes and residues will contaminate your sausage.

Metal strips can be attached to the cover, to help hold it in place, trapping the smoke near the meat. You can monitor the inside temperature by suspending a thermometer from one of the meat racks.

Frame or concrete smokehouse: You can build a smokehouse out of wood or concrete blocks. While these are more elaborate structures, they will accommodate larger quantities of meats at one time and will last for many years. They have the advantage of making temperature control easier and reducing fire hazards. Their tight construction and well-fitted ventilators can control air flow past the meat. A larger-size building will provide space for several tiers of racks. This will let you adjust the hangers to the size of the pieces of meat being smoked. Meats can be crowded into a smokehouse, but the only rule is that no piece of meat be able to touch another or the wall.

A barrel or wood smoker is easy to construct and can be used for small amounts of meat, fowl, and fish. Use metal racks to place or suspend your sausages. Wood is held in one part, and the smoke transfers to the large chamber. Set a container of water inside the large chamber to slow the drying process.

barrel. At the beginning of the smoking, you want a rapid flow of air past the meat to drive off excess moisture. Less rapid air movement near the end of the smoking period prevents

holes

metal cover

wood dowel

55-gallon drum

10 to 12 feet

cover

fire pit

6-inch plumbing pipe

A basic plan for a barrel for metal drum smoker.

A basic plan for a wood
structure for smoking meat

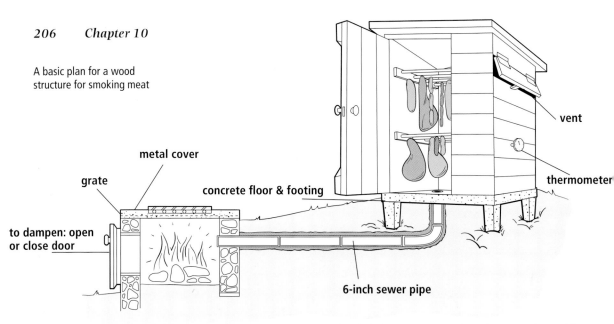

vent

metal cover

grate

concrete floor & footing

thermometer

to dampen: open
or close door

6-inch sewer pipe

Any building you construct should have four features: a source of smoke, a place to hold the smoke, a method to hold the meat in the smoke, and a draft regulator near the top or bottom. A smokehouse is a very slow oven in which the temperature does not exceed 200 degrees Fahrenheit. Even though you will use and maintain low temperatures, build your smoke house in a safe location from other buildings, particularly your home, and away from all combustible materials. Check with local ordinances and fire codes before you begin any construction.

The size of your smokehouse can be calculated based on the amounts and weights of meat used. These requirements vary with the weight of the cuts. To estimate the capacity of your smokehouse, use an accepted measure of 12 inches in width, front and back, and 2 feet in height for each row. Construction plans for smokehouse are generally available from university extension offices or commercial supply companies.

While smokehouses are excellent for processing meats, they do not make a good storage area for smoke-finished meats. After your smoking processing is complete, flies will eventually get in either on a piece of meat or when the door is open. Smokehouses can be used for storage, however, if each piece of meat is properly wrapped, bagged, and hung separately, provided everything is fly and insect proof.

Smoking Pork

Smoking pork raises certain considerations. If you are smoking pork and want to eat it without further cooking, you smoke it to an internal temperature of 137 degrees Fahrenheit to make sure you kill any trichinae, which are the cause of trichinosis. You can use a meat thermometer to check the temperature. The meat in the smokehouse is approximately 10 to 15 degrees less than the smokehouse air temperature. Raise the smokehouse temperature to 155 degrees, just to be safe.

Dutch Ovens

A Dutch oven is a traditional piece of cooking equipment used outdoors. It has a long history of use, and its easy application make it a favorite of many outdoor hunters.

Historically, small permanent frame or concrete structures were used for smoking a variety of meat products. Today, they are often more detailed in construction and can hold a larger quantity of meats and sausages to be smoked. Materials used for constructing a smokehouse need to be able to withstand temperatures up to a minimum of 160 degrees Fahrenheit.

One advantage is that it can deliver a low, moist heat over long periods of time to allow the meat to mellow and develop its own unique taste. Low heat and slow cooking tenderize the meat because juices within the cell walls are slowly released during the heating process. Fast cooking purges these juices too quickly.

A second advantage of using a Dutch oven is its versatility. Bread, roasts, and stews can all be cooked in it, making it an excellent camp utensil. Dutch ovens are easy to use and remove much of the uncertainty of cooking small game. Cooking in them does not require you to pay as close attention as in a regular home oven. Many models are available, and you should investigate which one may best suit your purposes.

Final Considerations

You may become enthused or enchanted by your smoking ability and like the flavors you create. However, do not replace your normal cooking procedures and dietary needs with this practice. Eating too much smoked meat can be a cause of some health concerns. The problems generally are found in the smoke, which contains coal tars that are considered carcinogenic. You may want to use your smoked meats as special treats rather than for daily meals.

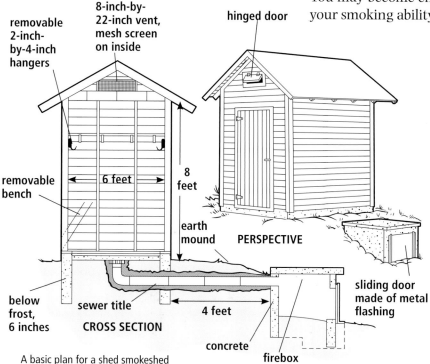

A basic plan for a shed smokeshed

Cooked summer sausage should first be put through a fermentation cycle at 95 to 100 degrees Fahrenheit if a lactic acid starter culture is used. Then the temperature should be slowly raised until an internal temperature of 158 degrees Fahrenheit is reached during the next three to four hours to finish cooking. Smoking takes place during cooking, and the amount can vary depending on your preference. Once cooking is finished, the sausage should be cooled to complete the process.

Chapter 11

SAUSAGES

———✦———

Sausage has been a highly prized meat product throughout much of mankind's history and is one of the oldest known forms of processed food. The history of sausage production extends back to the ancient Babylonians, who produced and consumed sausages 3,500 years ago. Even Homer's *Odyssey*, written in the eighth century, B.C., referred to sausage.

Europe saw the production of a variety of sausages by the Middle Ages. The cooler climates of Germany, Austria, and Denmark produced more fresh and cooked sausages because preservation was less of a problem. More temperate and warmer climates, such as in Italy, Spain, and southern France, developed dry or semidry sausages, which remain today.

The discovery of and subsequent demand for spices in Europe made them very important and valuable commodities and eventually allowed European sausage makers to become skilled at creating new and distinctive products bearing their influences. Some of these included types that are still well

Many sausages consist of less valuable parts of animal carcasses, such as meat trimmings and fats that are less edible or might otherwise be discarded, which have accumulated from carcass fabrication. Fats add juiciness and flavor to sausages but add little nutritional value to the final product.

known today, such as bologna from Bologna, Italy, and braunschweiger from Brunswick (Braunschweig), Germany.

Sausage making did not develop in the United States on an industrial scale until after the Civil War, although early Native Americans produced a type of sausage called pemmican. This was made by combining meat with dried berries and pressing it into a cake or a skin that was smoked or sundried.

The influx of European immigrants after the end of the Civil War brought many German, Polish, Italian, Dutch, Danish, and other nationalities with sausage-making skills to the United States. As these groups settled throughout the country, they brought their recipes with them, extending their influence and tastes wherever they went.

Today's sausage industry is diverse in size and type of production. Most major sausage processing plants in the United States are highly mechanized and automated to handle large volumes of products with speed and efficiency.

A niche production venue has been slowly developing with home sausage making. This chapter will provide information about basic types of sausages that can be produced at home and their characteristics; the safety and sanitation issues involved; spices, additives, and casings used; and the stuffings used in the process.

Homemade sausages are popular among hunters, who prefer to use all parts of the wild game they bring home. While home sausage making typically has been associated with rural areas, urban residents can shop in a market and make delicious and distinctive sausages with enough expertise.

Sausage Varieties

Of all the varieties of sausage produced in this country, the U.S. Department of Agriculture (USDA) only classifies them as two types: uncooked, which includes fresh bulk sausage, patties, links, and some smoked sausages; and ready-to-eat, such as dry, semidry, and cooked sausages.

Like other fresh meat, fresh sausages are highly perishable and must be refrigerated or frozen until ready to be cooked. Fresh sausages must be cooked prior to consumption to avoid health risks. Ready-to-eat sausages have been processed and preserved with salt and spices and may be dried or smoked. These types of sausages, such as jerky or sticks, can be eaten out of hand or cooked and heated, like hot dogs.

Fresh Sausages

Fresh sausages are made from uncooked and uncured cuts of meat. These sausages include those seasoned and stuffed into casings, or those in bulk form that will be

Thin, light-colored casings manufactured from beef collagen are often used for fresh sausages. Certain types cannot be used for smoking because they can dissolve during the cooking phase and the sausage will fall out.

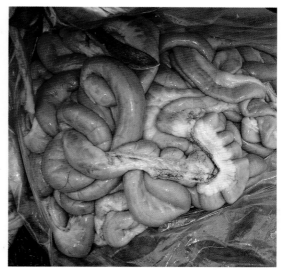

Natural casings are made from animal intestines, particularly sheep, pork, and beef. When using intestines for casings, they must be thoroughly cleaned and washed. The intestinal membranes are strong, flexible, and resilient, but they tend to lack the uniformity of manufactured casings.

pressed into patties. However, they are not cured or smoked. Fresh sausages should be eaten within three days of processing or purchase (or frozen), and they should be thoroughly cooked before being served. Examples include the following:

Bockwurst: A German-style sausage made from ground veal or veal and pork combined. It is typically flavored with onions, parsley, white pepper, paprika, or cloves and often sold fresh. Cooked bockwurst has an increased shelf life and is usually cooked by simmering, although it can be grilled.

Bratwurst: A German-style sausage made from pork, beef, and veal. It looks like a big hot dog and is flavored with allspice, caraway, and marjoram, although recipes can vary between regions and countries. It can be produced as fresh or cooked.

Chorizo: Originating in Spain, the term encompasses several types of pork sausage. It

Cut the intestines into 2- or 3-foot sections and strip the fecal content from them. Flush with clean water and then soak in a salt brine to neutralize the remaining contaminants. Keep immersed until used because if they dry out, they will crack and break when stuffed with sausage. Natural sausage casings should be packed in salt for storage.

can be fresh or cured. Fresh chorizo is similar to Sicilian sausage but is much spicier. Cured or dried chorizo can resemble pepperoni in size and shape but has a sharper taste and smell. Different countries have different recipes for making chorizo, and some have a sweet or spicy flavor.

Country-style or breakfast sausage: One of the most common kinds of sausage found in the United States. It is known by several names, can be made into patties or small links, and is flavored with sage, savory, and thyme.

Pork sausage: A fresh, uncooked sausage made entirely from pork and seasoned with salt, pepper, and sage. It is often sold in bulk, in a chub or link form, or as patties.

Kielbasa: Similar to Italian sausage in that its name is more of a generic term than a reference to a specific sausage. In the United States, it refers to a Polish or Polish-style sausage. It is typically made from coarsely ground lean pork and is sometimes combined with beef or veal, or both. Commercial kielbasa is usually an uncooked, smoked sausage with a medium red color.

Italian-style sausage: A fresh sausage that must be fully cooked before eating and can have either a hot or sweet taste. It is traditionally a pure pork sausage with pepper, fennel, and other spices as the added ingredients for flavoring.

Liverwurst: A popular German-style sausage. It is made from finely ground pork and pork liver. It can be stuffed into a non-edible casing but must be thoroughly cooked before being served. Spices such as ground black pepper, marjoram, allspice, thyme, ground mustard seed, and nutmeg are used to provide distinctive flavors. The term is sometimes interchanged with braunschweiger because of the similarities between the two in production, taste, and texture.

Thuringer sausage: A lightly smoked, German-style sausage similar to summer sausage. It is often semidry and is more perishable than other cured sausages, even though, technically, it is cured. Some are not fermented and are sold fresh. It is mostly made from pork, but beef and sometimes veal can be used. Flavorings that are used to make Thuringer sausage are used in fresh pork breakfast sausages but without the sage.

Haggis: A Scottish traditional food made from the heart, lungs, and livers of sheep or calves. It is highly seasoned, mixed with oatmeal, onions, suet, spices and salt, and then stuffed into a sheep's or pig's stomach. It is then boiled for about three hours. Haggis is perhaps the only sausage that is involved with the sport of hurling it for distance, called haggis hurling.

Cooked and Smoked Sausages

Cooked sausages are usually made from fresh meats that are cured during processing, fully cooked, and/or smoked. Cooked sausages should be refrigerated until eaten. They will generally keep seven days after being opened. Because they are fully cooked, they are ready to eat once opened, although you may prefer to serve them warm or hot. Examples include the following:

Frankfurters: Also known as the common hot dog, these are touted as the most consumed sausage in the world. Processed hot dogs contain mostly water and fat and have a soft, even texture and flavor. Homemade frankfurters can be made with a blend of beef, pork, and/or poultry meat. In the United States, if fillers are used, such as cereal or soy, the name must be changed to "links" or their addition must be identified on any sales label.

Bologna: A generic term for a fully cooked, mildly seasoned sausage made from low-value pieces of beef, pork, or both. It can be eaten cold or reheated. Bologna is usually produced in large-diameter rings or chubs, which give it several distinctive styles and shapes although they are constitutionally much the same as hot dogs. Beef bologna is an all-beef version and will appear a more red color because it does not have a mixed meat composition. It can also be made from pork, turkey, or chicken.

Vienna sausage: Sometimes called garlic sausage, it is made in the general shape of a hot dog, although it can be longer and somewhat thinner. It is a sausage with a creamy meat texture and is made primarily from pork and beef, although chicken and turkey can be used. Veal is sometimes added to create a milder flavor. The predominant flavors include onions, mace, and coriander. Sometimes pistachio nuts are added for seasoning.

Beerwurst or bierwurst: A large sausage, usually 2 to 3 inches in diameter or larger, of a dark red color. It is stuffed into veined natural casings or vein-decorated artificial casings. It is made from coarse-ground beef and pork and spiced with garlic, black peppercorns, paprika, and mustard seeds. Contrary to its name, it does not contain any beer. It is usually sold as sandwich meat.

New England sausage: Also known as Berliner, this sausage is made from coarse-ground pork with pieces of ham or chopped beef interspersed within it. Generally, it is stuffed into large casings, similar to beerwurst.

Braunschweiger: A creamy-textured, German-style liver sausage of pure pork origins. It has a mild flavor that includes onions, mustard seed, and marjoram. It is nearly always smoked and generally served cold as a spread for toast or used as a filling for sandwiches.

Mettwurst: A strongly flavored German-style sausage made from raw minced pork and preserved by smoking and curing. It contains ginger, celery seed, and allspice. Although it is smoked, it needs to be cooked thoroughly before being served. Mettwurst

Artificial or manufactured casings come in several sizes, thicknesses, and color for different types of sausages. Most manufactured casings must be soaked in clean water before use to make them pliable.

can have either a soft or hard texture, depending on the length of smoking time used.

Dry and Semidry Sausages

Dry and semidry sausages are made from fresh meats that are ground, seasoned, and cured during processing. They are stuffed into either natural or synthetic casings, fermented, often smoked, and carefully air-dried. True dry sausages are generally not cooked and may require long drying periods of between 21 to 90 days, depending on their diameter.

The distinctive flavor of these sausages is due to the lactic acid produced by fermentation. This fermentation occurs after the meat is stuffed into casing and the bacteria metabolize the sugars, producing acids and other compounds as byproducts and the resulting tangy flavor.

Semidry sausages, such as summer sausage, are often fermented and cooked in a smokehouse. Both dry and semidry sausages are ready to eat and do not require heating before serving, although a cool temperature or refrigeration is recommended for storage. Dry and semidry sausages include summer sausage, pepperoni, salami, and Landjäger, among others. These are detailed in the paragraphs below.

Summer sausage: A general term for any sausage that can be kept without the need of refrigeration. It is typically a fermented sausage with a low pH to slow bacterial growth and provide a longer shelf life. It is usually made from a mixture of beef or beef and pork. Venison can also be used to make summer sausage. It resembles some of the drier salamis but is milder and sweeter in flavor. Summer sausage can be either dried or smoked, and although curing agents can vary considerably, some sort of curing salt is almost always used.

Pepperoni: A hotly spiced Italian-style sausage made from coarse-ground, fermented pork with ground red pepper as the main flavor ingredient. It is a dry sausage and increases in flavor as it progresses through the drying process.

Salami: Not necessarily a specific sausage but most often refers to those products that have similar characteristics and is made from beef, pork, or both. Salamis can be found in many sizes and shapes, and they may be dry and quite hard. Most are made with garlic, salt, various herbs and spices, and some minced fat. Salamis are made by allowing the raw meat mixture to ferment for 24 hours before it is stuffed into either a natural or synthetic casing and then hung to dry. Most are treated with an edible mold culture that is spread over the outside, which prevents spoilage during curing. Pepperoni is one type of salami, and others include Genoa, kosher, Milano, Sicilian, Novaro, and Sorrento.

Landjäger: A traditional Swiss-German dried sausage that is a popular snack food. Its taste is similar to dried salami, and it can be boiled and served with vegetables. It is made from equal portions of beef and pork, with fat or lard and sugar and spices added. The meat is pressed into small casings for making links, usually 6 to 8 inches lengths. They are then pressed into a mold before drying. This gives the strips their characteristic rectangular shape. After drying, they can keep without refrigeration if needed.

Specialty Sausages

This group of sausages may include cured, uncured, smoked, and nonsmoked meats that do not readily fit into other groups. These include luncheon meats that may be cooked in loaf pans or casings, or water cooked in stainless-steel molds. Some specialty sausages include headcheese, olive loaf, scrapple, and souse.

Headcheese: Actually not made from cheese but, rather, from meat pieces from the head of a calf, pig, sheep, or cow set in a gelatin base. It may also include meat from the feet, tongue, and heart. It originated in Europe and is usually eaten cold or at room temperature as a luncheon meat. In the United States, headcheese is available in two styles: French and German. French headcheese is made from cured pork pieces suspended in a vinegar-flavored gelatin with small bits of pickles and pimentos added for flavor. There is no casing. The German style, also composed of cured pork and beef pieces, differs in that the gelatin is produced by heating to resemble an emulsion and, because of this, requires a casing.

Olive loaf: In reference to meat, olive loaf refers to a type of bologna that is composed of cured pork and beef, seasonings, sweet pickles, diced pimentos, and green olives. It is served as a luncheon meat and can also contain garlic, basil, and sweet peppers.

Scrapple: Not a sausage per se, but rather a cornmeal-based mixture or mush of head meat, pork sausage, or both. It can also contain pork scraps and trimmings that can't be used elsewhere. Meat scraps that come from the head, heart, liver, or attached to bones are boiled to make a broth. When they are finished cooking, the bones and fat are discarded, and the meat is then mixed with dry cornmeal and added to the broth, which is then boiled. Seasonings such as sage, thyme, savory, and black pepper are added. This mush is formed into a semisolid congealed loaf and allowed to cool until thoroughly set. Then slices are pan fried before serving. It has a Pennsylvania Dutch origin with strong regional recognition, although it can be found throughout the country.

Souse: A loaf product similar to head-cheese. It typically contains cured or cooked meat from the head, tongues, lips, and snout of pigs, which are added to gelatin. Pickles and pimentos are added for color and flavor.

Venison Sausage

Venison sausage can come from deer, elk, bison, moose, or other large game animals. Because of these animals' feeding habitat, their meat tends to be very dry. Pork and pork fat are typically added to enhance venison's flavor and palatability. It may be prepared as fresh, dried, or smoked sausage in ways similar to domestic animal-based sausages.

Other Sausages

It is estimated that there are more than two hundred types of sausage and related products produced today, with many variations of each. While you may start with producing only one or two types of sausage, in time you may venture to others. The list may include the following:

Alesandri: An Italian-style member of the salami family made with highly seasoned cured pork.

Arles: A French-style salami that contains coarsely chopped pork and beef seasoned with garlic.

Berliner: A pork and beef sausage mildly flavored with salt and sugar.

Blood and tongue sausage: Contains cooked lamb and pork tongues and hog blood.

Bloodwurst or blood sausage: Sausage made of pig blood, pork meat, ham fat, gelatin-based meats, salt, pepper, clover, allspice, and onions.

Boterhamwurst: A Dutch-style veal and pork sausage.

Corned beef: Made from cured and spiced beef brisket.

Cotto salami: Cooked salami enhanced by whole peppercorns.

Easter nola: An Italian-style mildly seasoned, salami-type dry sausage.

Garlic sausage: Similar to the frankfurter in taste and texture but with a more pronounced garlic flavor.

Farmer sausage: Originated with farmers of northern Europe and is a mildly seasoned dry or semidry sausage made of 65 percent beef and 35 percent pork. Chopped medium fine, seasoned, stuffed into beef middles casings, and heavily smoked.

German salami: Similar to the Italian-type salamis but more heavily smoked.

Goteborg: A Swedish-style cervelat that is heavily smoked and made from coarsely chopped pork and beef which is flavored with cardamom.

Ham and cheese loaf: A specialty product containing pieces of cheese imbedded within finely ground ham.

Holsteiner: Similar to farmer sausage, except that the ends are tied together like a horseshoe. Dried and smoked.

Honey loaf: A mixture of pork, beef, honey, and spices but can also contain pickles or pimentos, or both.

Hungarian salami: A mild, dry salami made of lean pork and backfat.

Knackwurst: Similar to the frankfurter in texture and mixture and is fully cooked but with more garlic added.

Linguisa: A Portuguese pork sausage cured in brine, seasoned with garlic, and spiced with cinnamon and cumin.

Liver loaf: A sandwich-shaped liver sausage that is similar in flavor to liverwurst.

Longaniza: A dry Portuguese sausage flavored similarly like chorizo.

Macaroni and cheese loaf: Contains chunks of cheddar cheese and pieces of macaroni mixed with ground beef and pork.

Mortadella: A dry sausage containing pork, beef, and cubes of pork fat, seasoned with anise.

Pastrami: The cured, smoked plate of beef that is usually thinly sliced for sandwiches.

Pinkel: A sausage made of beef, oats, and pork fat.

Salsiccia: A fresh Italian sausage made of finely ground pork.

Smoky links: Smoked, cooked links made from pork and beef spiced with pepper.

Straussburg: A liver and veal sausage that contains pistachio nuts.

Vienna sausages: The small hors d'oeuvre or cocktail-style frankfurters or hot dogs.

Weiswurst: A fresh German-style sausage that is mildly spicy and made of pork and veal.

Selecting Ingredients, Additives, and Spices

The ingredients, additives, and spices you add, and their quality, will greatly affect the taste and texture of your final sausage products. For sausage making, ingredients you add may be raw meat and nonmeat materials. The interaction between the ingredients and meat materials used will determine the different flavors and textures between sausages.

You control the ingredients and spices you add to your sausage. By understanding the properties of each, you will be able to create products that meet your requirements and tastes, whether it is to limit the preservatives you eat or to avoid high fat products routinely available at retail markets.

You should keep one simple rule in mind when creating your sausages, regardless of which kind they are: your finished product is only as good as the ingredients it contains. The meat you start with should be fresh, have a proper lean-to-fat ratio, and exhibit good binding qualities. Clean meat that has been cut in sanitary conditions is a prime requirement. The meat used should not have been contaminated with bacteria or other microorganisms at any stage of processing or cutting.

Ingredients

Most of the ingredients you will use are readily available for purchase at local supermarkets or meat markets, or from other specialized commercial businesses. Licensed retail outlets that specialize in such products are another source. Internet businesses that sell ingredients for meat processing can provide them for sausage making. If buying ingredients from businesses outside your area, be sure to check their licenses and ask about the sources they access for their products. Always check their labels to be sure you know what you are adding to your meat.

The main ingredients for your sausage making are likely to be based on meat derived from pork, beef, and perhaps veal, either separately or in a combination. Other ingredients may include hearts, tongues, livers, kidneys, and stomachs. If you don't raise your own livestock for home use, be sure the meat you buy comes from a reputable source or that it has been USDA inspected. If using your own animals for processing, be certain they are healthy and disease free. Cuts with the lowest economic value are generally used for sausage making.

Several nonmeat ingredients are used to provide flavor, inhibit bacterial growth, and increase the amount of sausage produced. These may include water, salt, sugar, nonfat dry milk, soy products, extenders and binders, and spices.

Binders and Extenders

Several ingredients are often added during commercial sausage production that are referred to as binders and extenders. Some of these products are used for both purposes. Binders are used to help the meat particles adhere to each other or to prevent them from separating during the production process. Extenders are used to increase the moisture content and texture of the product, as well as stretch the amount of product derived from a certain volume of meat.

Extenders often include non-fat dry milk and similar dried products of milk origin including dried whey. Binders can include many derivatives of milk plus cereal flours, wheat gluten, and soy flours.

Other components of sausage production that are often added are:

Water and ice: Added sometimes to add moisture and keep the sausage cold during processing. Cold temperatures delay bacteria growth and add to the final product quality. Water also helps dissolve salts for better distribution within the meat.

Salt: Serves three functions in the meat: preservation, flavor enhancement, and draws out protein to help bind the mixture. Sodium nitrate and nitrite are used for curing meat as they inhibit growth of a number of pathogens and bacteria that cause spoilage, including those that cause botulism. Nitrate and nitrite are the most regulated and controversial of all the sausage ingredients. It is strongly recommended that a commercial premixed cure be used when nitrate and/or nitrite is called for in the mixture.

Sugar: Used for flavor and to counter the bitter taste of salt. It helps reduce the pH in meat because of the fermentation of the lactic acid.

Ascorbates and erythorbates: Vitamin C derivatives that speed the curing reaction. They can be used interchangeably in cured sausages to which nitrite has been added.

Spices, Seasonings, and Flavorings

Many different spices, seasonings, and flavorings are used in sausage production to increase taste. For home sausage making, they are generally added by personal preference and taste or to follow general guidelines for a particular product recipe. By combining different levels of various spices, you can create unique and distinctive sausages.

Spices, seasonings, and flavorings are not usually included to add to the nutritional value of the sausage, although some minute traces of nutrition are provided by them. Spices vary greatly in composition and may be added as whole seeds, coarsely ground, or in powdered form. Some of the major spices used include:

Allspice: A reddish brown pimento berry sold whole or ground. Pungent, clove-like odor and taste. Used in bologna, pork sausage, frankfurters, hamburgers, potato sausage, headcheese, and other products.

Basil: Marketed as small bits of green leaves, whole or ground. Aromatic, mildly pungent odor and used in dry sausage such as pepperoni.

Bay leaves: Elliptical leaves marketed whole or ground. Fragrant, sweetly aromatic with slightly bitter taste. Used in pickling spice for corned beef, beef, lamb, pork tongues, and pigs' feet.

Caraway seed: Curved, tapered, brown seeds sold whole. Slightly sharp taste and used in Polish sausage.

Cardamom seed: Small, reddish brown seeds sold whole or ground. Pleasant, fragrant odor; used in bologna, frankfurters, and similar meats.

Cloves: Reddish brown, sold whole or ground. Strong, pungent, sweet odor and taste. Used in bologna, frankfurters, headcheese, liver sausage, corned beef, and pastrami. Whole cloves can be inserted into hams and other meats during cooking.

Coriander seed: Yellowish brown, nearly globular seeds sold whole or ground. Lemon-like taste. Used in frankfurters, bologna, knackwurst, Polish sausage, and other cooked sausages.

Cumin seed: Yellowish brown oval seeds sold whole or ground. Strong, bitter taste; used in chorizo and other Mexican and Italian sausages; used in making curry powder.

Dill seed: Light brown oval seeds sold whole or ground. Warm, clean, aromatic odor used in headcheese, souse, jellied tongue loaf, and similar products.

Garlic, dried: White color ranging in forms of powdered, granulated, ground, minced, chopped, and sliced. Strong, characteristic odor with pungent taste. Used in most beef sausages and salamis.

Ginger: Irregularly shaped pieces brownish to buff-colored; sold whole, ground, or cracked. Pungent, spicy-sweet odor; clean, hot taste. Used in pork sausage, frankfurters, knackwurst, and other cooked sausages.

Mace: Flat, brittle pieces of lacy, yellow to brownish orange material sold whole or ground. Somewhat stronger than nutmeg in odor and flavor. Used in bologna, mortadella, bratwurst, bockwurst, and other fresh and cooked sausages.

Marjoram: Marketed as small pieces of grayish green leaves either whole or ground. Warm, aromatic, slightly bitter and used in braunschweiger, liverwurst, headcheese, and Polish sausage.

Mustard: Tiny, smooth, yellowish or reddish brown seeds sold whole or ground. Used in bologna, frankfurters, salamis, summer sausage, and similar meat products.

Nutmeg: Large, brown, ovular seeds sold whole or ground. Sweet taste and odor. Used in frankfurters, knackwurst, minced ham sausages, liver sausage, and headcheese.

Onion, dried: Similar to garlic. Used in luncheon loaves, braunschweiger, liver sausage, headcheese, and other meat products.

Oregano: Marketed as small pieces of green leaves, whole or ground. Strong, pleasant odor and taste. Used in most Mexican and Spanish sausages, fresh Italian sausage, and sometimes in frankfurters and bologna.

Paprika: Powder form ranging in color from bright red to brick red. Slightly sweet odor and taste. Used in frankfurters, fresh Italian sausage, bologna, and many other cooked and smoked sausage products.

Pepper: Black, red, white in color and sold whole or ground. Penetrating odor and taste, ranging from mild to intensely pungent. Black pepper is the most used of all spices, but white is substituted when black specks are not wanted, such as in pork sausage and deviled ham. Red pepper is used in chorizo, smoked country sausage, Italian sausage, pepperoni, fresh pork sausage, and many other meat products.

Rosemary: Needle-like green leaves available whole or ground. Fresh, aromatic odor, somewhat like sage in taste. Used in chicken stews and other poultry products.

Saffron: Orange and yellowish in color, sold whole or ground. Strong odor and bitter taste. Most expensive of all spices and used primarily for color in a few sausages.

Sage: Grayish-green leaves sold whole, ground, or cut. Highly aromatic with strong, slightly bitter taste. Used in pork, pizza, and breakfast sausages.

Savory: Sold as dried bits of greenish brown leaves. Fragrant, aromatic odor and used primarily in pork sausage but also in other sausages.

Thyme: Marketed as gray to greenish brown leaves, whole or ground. Fragrant, odor with pungent taste. Used in pork sausage, liver sausage, headcheese, and bockwurst.

Whether they are added by volume or weight, herbs and spices are a very small percentage of any sausage but have an enormous influence on character and flavor of the end product. In either case, the best herbs and spices are those that are purchased fresh or homegrown and those used soon after harvesting. If you purchase either or both, try to buy new products rather than older ones because new vintages will have retained their potency more than older ones. Store herbs and spices in a cool, dry area away from heat and light. Freshly dried herbs and spices rarely retain their optimum flavors longer than six months.

Salt and Pepper

Salt and pepper add flavor and aroma to sausages. Many different types of salt are available, but those without additives, such as iodine, provide maximum flavor. Pepper can be purchased as whole peppercorn and ground when needed. Recipes may make distinctions between three forms of pepper: finely ground, medium grind, and coarse grind. Finely ground is a fine powder with no large pieces in it. Medium grind refers to flakes that will pass through a typically shaker. Coarse grind has small bits that may be ground in either a pepper grinder with a coarse setting or with a mortar and pestle.

Sodium Nitrite and Potassium Nitrate Concerns

Many recipes that have been handed down through the years called for saltpeter, or potassium nitrate. Most sausage supply companies no longer sell saltpeter, but you may find other commercial products that will accomplish similar results, such as Morton Salt's "Tender Quick" mix. It is a fast-cure containing 0.5 percent sodium nitrate and 0.5 percent sodium nitrite and is used in some recipes at the ratio of 1 teaspoon per pound of meat.

The University of Minnesota published findings in 1992 that a fatal dose of potassium nitrate for adults is in the range of 30 to 35 grams (slightly more than one ounce) consumed in a single serving. The fatal dose of sodium nitrite is in the range of 22 to 23 milligrams per kilogram of body weight. Nitrates are found in vegetables such as spinach, beets, radishes, celery, onions, and cabbages, and so they are not uncommon substances.

The concerns of consuming too many nitrates or nitrites in meat center on the quantity eaten rather than its inclusion as a preservative. The Minnesota report concluded that nitrite as it is used in meat such as sausages is considered safe because the known benefits outweigh the potential risks. You can consume uncured sausages if you are concerned about limiting nitrites and nitrates in your diet.

Casings

It is not necessary to stuff fresh sausage meat into a casing. It can be left in bulk form or made into patties. But if ground into bulk form, it will have to be used within one or two days to retain its freshness and quality. Most sausages are made by inserting the ground ingredients into some forming material that gives them shape and size and holds the meat together for cooking and smoking, or both. This material is called a casing.

There are two types of casings used in sausage making: natural and manufactured. Although their purposes are the same, their origin is very different.

Natural sausage casings are made from parts of the alimentary canal of various animals that can include the intestinal tracts from pigs, cows, or sheep. One advantage for using them is that they are made up largely of collagen, a fibrous protein, whose unique characteristic is variable permeability. This allows smoke and heat to penetrate during the curing process but without contributing undesirable flavors to the meat. Natural casings can be purchased from companies that offer sausage-making products or they can come from an animal that you are butchering. Packing houses that save casings will flush them with water and pack them in salt before selling them to casing processors. The casing processor does the final cleaning, scraping, sorting, grading, and salting before you purchase them. If using your own animal casings, it is important they are thoroughly flushed and cleaned and are placed in a salt brine prior to use.

Cleaning Casings for Home Use

You can clean your own hog and sheep casings for sausage production after they are removed from the body cavity. Because they are unlikely to be the first parts you work with from the carcass, they need to be set in cold water to reduce their temperature to prevent spoilage. If working alone, you should set up the cold water tub prior to beginning the butchering process. If working with others, you can designate another to handle this part.

There are several things to consider if using the intestines for meat casings. The first is sanitation. The intestines will likely be filled with excrement that contains *E. coli* bacteria and needs to be kept away from any organs that you plan to use later. If you plan to use several or all of the organs attached within the viscera, you will need to cut them away from the mass of intestines and stomach prior to placing them into the cold water to reduce the chances of contamination. Cut the heart, liver, spleen, kidneys, or any other organs away from the intestines and stomach and place them aside in a clean container. The stomach and intestines should then be separated by making a cut at the point where the stomach and large intestines meet. If you have used a cord or string to tie off the end of the intestine at the anus when you made your cuts to remove it, then one end should still be tied. After making your cut at the stomach and intestine junction, place that end in an empty pail or other container and allow the intestinal materials to drop into it. Depending on the species and size of the animal you butchered, there may be much intestine to work with or relatively little. You may have to use your hand to strip as much of the excreta out of the intestine as possible. When finished, you can place the intestine in a cold water bath primed with salt and work with it later after you deal with the more valuable meat cuts of the carcass.

Intestines make very good natural casings for your sausages because they are largely collagen and will easily break down during the curing process, yet they still are strong enough to hold the meat during the stuffing process. Their flexibility makes them an attractive alternative to synthetic casings. But good casings are also clean casings and you will need to prep them for use by removing all of the excrement and intestinal linings before using them.

To begin properly cleaning your casings, you will need to invert the intestine by turning it inside out. After removing any cord or string that has closed one end, start by turning one end of the intestine inside out to create a lip much as you would roll down your socks, except that you are not making a rolled up mass. You want to pass the rest of the intestine through this roll as if you were peeling a banana without breaking it. When the inside of the intestine has completely become the outside, you can thoroughly wash it in a cold 0.5 percent chlorine solution. Use a soft-bristle brush to very gently scrub the excess fat, connective tissue, and any residual foreign or fecal materials off the intestine. Although the intestine can withstand some good scrubbing, you need to be careful not to overdo it or you may leave little tears in the membrane that can rupture and break during the stuffing process.

After thoroughly cleaning the intestine, rinse it with clean, cold water and invert it back to its original form. Use a saturated salt solution (1 gram salt/2.8 ml water) for storage overnight. If you are not using the casings for several days, they can be kept in this solution with cold temperatures. If not using them for two weeks or longer, you can freeze them in this salt-saturated solution. This solution will also inhibit the growth of bacteria that thrive on salt, as well as other bacteria that may have survived the chlorine solution bath. Before using your stored casings, gently flush them in lukewarm water to remove any clinging salt. They are then ready for use.

Generally, the larger the animal butchered, the larger the size of the intestinal tract you will have. The kind of sausage you want to make may have some bearing on the size of casings you use. Typically lambs and sheep are the smallest, followed by pigs, and then cows. Sheep casings are more delicate and can be used for hot dogs, frankfurters, and pork breakfast sausages.

Hog casings have a wide variety of use and are considered to be an all-purpose casing. They have five classes: bungs, middles, smalls, stomachs, and bladders. Bungs and middles are best used for dry sausage; smalls for fresh sausage, such as chorizos, bratwurst, bockwurst, and Polish; stomachs for headcheese; and bladders for minced luncheon meats. Small hog casings, from the small intestine, are probably the most widely used and easiest to find at a local meat shop.

Beef casings are larger and are classed as bungs, rounds, and middles. Rounds are the most common of all beef casings and come from the small intestine. They are used for ring bologna, Holsteiner, and mettwurst. Beef bungs are large casings that come from the cecum or appendix and may have diameters of 3 to 5 inches, making them good for use stuffing bologna. They can contain from 12 to 20 pounds of sausage.

Manufactured and Artificial Casings

The alternative to natural casings is a group of manufactured or artificial casings that are made from edible or inedible materials. Fibrous casings are popular because they are uniform in size and easy to use. They are made from a special paper pulp mixed with cellulose, are inedible, and must be peeled away before eating. However, they provide the most strength of any casing available. Three of the most common types of manufactured casings include collagen, cellulose, and artificial.

Collagen casings are made from the gelatinous substances found in animal connective tissue, bones, and cartilage and mechanically formed into casings. Because of their lower structural strength, these casings generally are made into small diameter products and are ideal for breakfast links or fresh, smoked, and dried sausages. Unlike large cellulose and fibrous casings, collagen casings should not be soaked in water before use. They are easier to work with when dry.

Cellulose casings are made from cotton linters, the fuzz from cotton seeds, which are dissolved and reformed into casings. Cellulose casings are crimped into short strands, and an 8-inch length may stuff as much as 100 feet of sausage. Small cellulose casings work well for skinless wieners and other small diameter skinless products.

Artificial casings are frequently made from plastic and are inedible. They can be used for sausages cooked in water or steam, such as bologna and braunschweiger.

If you are not using your own casings, you can purchase any of the manufactured or artificial casings from meat-packing companies, sausage supply businesses, local butcher shops, or through ethnic markets.

Essential Equipment

You only need a few pieces of equipment to make sausage in your home whether or not you butcher your own animal. The three most important pieces of equipment you will need include a meat grinder (but not if you only purchase bulk sausage meat), a sausage stuffer, and a thermometer. Other pieces that you may find useful include a mixing tub, a scale, and a smoker if you want to do your own meat smoking and preservation. Sausage-making equipment is usually available from meat equipment supply companies.

Meat grinders reduce large pieces into a soft, pliable mass into which spices, fats, or other additives can more easily be mixed. Grinders can be hand- or electric-driven and come in many different designs and shapes.

An old-style sausage stuffer was made of cast iron and operated by using a hand crank that pressed the plate, forcing the meat through the funnel opening at the bottom and into the casing.

A modern sausage stuffer relies on the same principle as the old style, but it is made of aluminum or stainless steel. It is lighter in weight than its predecessor and has multiple funnels for different-sized casings. Be sure to thoroughly wash, sanitize, and rinse the stuffer and funnels or horns prior to and following each use and between different sausage-making sessions.

Meat grinders

A meat grinder is used to reduce the size of the meat pieces into a pliable mixture. They can be operated by hand or by electricity. Some food processors can do a good job of chopping meat, and some heavy-duty mixers may have a grinding attachment that will work.

Hand grinders have been used for generations and usually have several different-sized grinding plates or chopping disks, ranging from fine, with holes ⅛-inch in diameter, to coarse, with holes ⅜-inch in diameter. All hand grinders will have a screw augur that is attached to the outside handle. A disk cap screws over the top of the grinding plate

to hold it in place while the meat is forced through the holes by the auger. It is a simple process once you have it set up. Hand grinders typically have a tightening screw at their base so that they can be mounted to a table or sturdy support frame.

If you are making small amounts of sausage, a hand grinder should be sufficient. Some large grinders make use of a small motor with belt attached. This is a fast, efficient way to grind a very large amount of meat in a very short amount of time. Food processors can be useful in producing finely ground or emulsified sausages, such as frankfurters, bologna, and some loaf products.

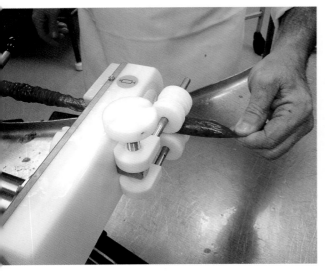

Begin by placing the casing over the stuffer funnel or horn and tying the end. Use whatever function your stuffer has, hand crank or electric, and push the sausage into the casing.

For larger casings such as summer sausage, use the same procedure by twisting each section after the desired amount has been added.

Push until the desired amount is added; stop and give the casing a twist to separate it into links or small sections. Continue until the end of the casing and tie the end.

Sausage Stuffers

You should consider buying a sausage stuffer if you plan on making your own sausages. There are several types available, including hand, push, crank, and hydraulic-operated by air or water. They can be made of plastic, stainless steel, or cast iron. Many small meat grinders are capable of supporting a small stuffing horn.

The piston-type stuffer is one of the most common for home use. It is operated by air or water pressure and will press the sausage quickly into the casing, producing fewer air pockets than hand-operated, screw-style stuffers.

A push stuffer is quick to reload but has a small capacity. With this type of stuffer, you manually push down on a handle to force the meat into the casing. A crank stuffer has more capacity than a push stuffer and takes less effort to press the sausage into the casing because of the pressure created by your combined arm and screw action.

Digital thermometers are very popular for home cooking. However, because they are less resistant to high external temperatures, they should not be used inside ovens.

Sausage Funnels or Horns

The sausage funnel or horn constricts the movement of the sausage from the meat tub into the casing. As the casing fills, it pushes itself away from the funnel as it elongates. The size of the funnel is directly related to the size of the casing. Funnels are straight tubes, not tapered, and may range from 4 to 6 inches in length. To decrease the possibility of tearing the casing, coat the funnel with water or grease to help slip the casing over it.

Other Equipment

There may be other items you'd like to keep on hand during your sausage processing, including measuring instruments such as a scale, measuring cups, and thermometers.

Scales

For weighing meats and other ingredients, a reliable scale is essential. A scale that measures both in pounds and ounces should be sufficient for most of your needs. For recipes or curing chemicals where weights are measured in grams or ounces, a smaller scale may be necessary. If curing ingredients are being used, particularly sodium nitrite, it is very important to use a scale that can measure to the nearest tenth of a gram.

Measuring Cups and Spoons

Measuring cups and spoons, ranging from ¼ teaspoon up to 1 tablespoon and ¼ cup to 1

Instant-Read Thermometers

An instant-read thermometer is a probe containing two different metal coils bonded together. The coil is connected to the temperature indicator that expands when heated, moving the dial. Insert the probe about 2 inches into the center of the meat to insure a safe, accurate reading. Instant-read thermometers are used to assess when a specific temperature has been reached to assure safe eating and in making smoked sausage. They are good for use in sausage making because they can measure the temperature of a food within 15 to 20 seconds. Although they are not used during the cooking process, they can be used at or near the end of it to check the final temperature. This will allow you to monitor the cooking progress without overcooking the product.

An oven thermometer can be set on one of the racks to monitor the temperature within the oven during the cooking time. One disadvantage may be if you do not have a window to check the thermometer, you may have to open the door to check the temperature, allowing heat to escape and prolonging the estimated cooking time.

Always sanitize thermometers before each use and when moving from one meat to another to avoid cross contamination. The thermometers can be washed in hot, soapy water, then rinsed and dried.

cup for liquids or dry measure, will be useful for adhering to specific recipes.

Thermometers

Thermometers are essential to help monitor and maintain appropriate temperatures during the processing and cooking of sausages. Several types are available including instant-read and oven thermometers.

Calibration

Regardless of the type of thermometer used, make certain the calibration is correct to achieve accurate cooking temperatures. You should calibrate thermometers before first use or whenever they are dropped. They are sensitive and can lose calibration from extensive use or when going from one temperature extreme to another. Inaccurate thermometers will give incorrect cooking temperatures and can be responsible for under or overcooked foods. Undercooked foods can pose health risks.

Two different methods can be used to calibrate thermometers: using ice water and using boiling water. In the ice water method, use the following steps:

- Fill a 2-quart measure with crushed ice and water and stir well.
- Let sit four to five minutes to provide an environment of 32 degrees Fahrenheit.
- Completely submerge the sensing area of stem or probe, but keep it from touching the sides or bottom of container.
- Hold for 30 seconds or until dial stops moving.
- If thermometer is not within plus or minus 2 degrees Fahrenheit of 32 degrees, adjust accordingly. The ice water method permits calibration within 0.1 degrees Fahrenheit. Some digital stemmed thermometers have a reset button, which can be pushed.
- Repeat process with each thermometer.

For the boiling point method, follow these steps:

- Fill a container with distilled water and bring to rolling boil.
- Insert thermometer to completely submerge stem or probe sensing area without touching sides or bottom.
- Hold for 30 seconds or until dial stops moving.
- If thermometer is not within plus or minus 2 degrees of 212 degrees Fahrenheit, adjust until it does. The boiling point method permits calibration to within 1.0 degrees Fahrenheit. Some digital stemmed thermometers have a reset button that can be pushed.
- Repeat process with each thermometer to be used.

The boiling point of water is about 1 degree Fahrenheit lower for every 550 feet above sea level. If you are in high altitude areas, adjust the temperature by calibration. One example is if you are at 550 feet above sea level, the boiling point of water would be 211 degrees Fahrenheit.

Any food thermometer that cannot be calibrated can still be used by checking it for accuracy using either method. You can take into consideration any inaccuracies and make adjustments by adding or subtracting the differences, or the thermometer can be replaced, which will provide greater assurance of accurate cooking temperatures.

Sanitation and the Three Cs

Strict sanitation is critically important in sausage making and must be maintained to prevent bacterial contamination and food-borne illnesses. It is essential to handle raw meat in a safe manner that reduces the risk of bacterial growth. No meat product is completely sterile, but using proper procedures will minimize your risks. The most basic sanitation procedure involves using and maintaining clean surfaces before and after processing sausages. It is easy to remember the three C's of sanitation: keep it clean, cold, and covered.

Once all the sausages are finished, they can be placed on racks for smoking. Regardless of the number of sausages, their size, or the type of smoker used, keep the individual pieces spaced so that they do not touch one another or any part of the smoking unit.

Keep It Clean

Wash all surfaces that you use with a diluted chlorine bleach solution of 10 parts water and one part bleach, as well as antibacterial soap. Nothing will replace vigorous scrubbing of the surface area with these products. This removes any grease or unwanted contaminants from the preparation area. Keep the area free of materials that do not relate to meat preparation or that will be used later but may accidentally come in contact with the meat. Utensils to be used and your hands should be thoroughly washed before beginning. Be sure to remove any rings, jewelry, or other metal objects from your hands, ears, or other exposed body parts.

Keep It Cold

Bacteria grow best in temperatures between 40 degrees and 140 degrees Fahrenheit. If you are cooking or cooling meat for cooked sausages, be sure your product passes through this range quickly because meat can be kept safe when it is cold or hot, but not in between. The meat you process should pass through this temperature range, whether being cooked or cooled, within four hours, but preferably less. This includes any butchering time involved. Cooling the fresh carcass is essential to a good meat product and is discussed elsewhere in this book.

During processing, cooked sausages should have an internal temperature of 160 degrees Fahrenheit, as this effectively kills pathogenic bacteria. Poultry meat should be cooked to 180 degrees Fahrenheit because of a more alkaline final pH. Ground meats are more likely to become contaminated than whole pieces because they have increased surface area exposure and go through more processing steps.

After cooking, you will need to cool the sausages quickly. This will prevent bacteria from attaching themselves and having an opportunity to grow while handling them.

The shelf life of any sausage has a limit. To minimize bacterial growth, you should store your sausage in a refrigerated or frozen

Food Safety Tips

- Always wash your hands with soap and water before handling meat or beginning work. Rewash between tasks and after sneezing, using toilet facilities, or handling materials not part of your processing work.
- Before and after use, thoroughly clean all equipment, knives, utensils, thermometers, bowls, and anything else used to cut or store meat. Clean and sanitize all surfaces that will be used.
- Keep raw meat separate from other foods. Avoid cross contamination between pieces of raw and processed meats. Avoid mixing of fluids and juices from other cuts or vegetables to be used.
- Keep meat below 40 degrees Fahrenheit during processing.
- Monitor temperatures at all stages of your processing.

state. Fresh or uncooked sausage can be kept safely refrigerated for several days while cooked sausages should be used within one week, unless frozen. Always remember that sausages are highly perishable products that don't get better with age. Never eat or serve sausage that has developed a slimy texture or an off smell. There is a good biological reason that your nose is placed near your mouth. If it doesn't smell right, it is better to discard it than risk eating it.

Keep It Covered

Meats, carcasses, and wholesale or retail cuts should be covered during any time you are not working on them. Your processing equipment should be properly stored in between use, as well as in any area used

where butchering is done. Maintain screens, barriers, or traps to keep out vermin and reduce access for flies and insects.

Game Meat Sausage

While the majority of sausages made use pork or beef separately or in combination, game meat can be used and substituted instead to create unique and original flavors. Most any meat from wild animals can be used, but, like meat from domesticated animals, it is important that it is handled properly after the animal is killed. The same awareness of temperatures is required, and dressing the animal as soon as possible while keeping the meat under 40 degrees Fahrenheit will help limit bacteria growth, reducing the chance of a food-borne illness.

Game meat is typically aged after it is dressed to increase tenderness. This is not a necessary step if the meat is to be used for sausage because it will be tenderized and broken down through the grinding process. Using the less tender cuts and trim pieces from wild game in sausage increases the volume available.

Game meat contains a distinct flavor that comes from the fat and not necessarily the meat itself. Removing all external fat prior to grinding will allow you to process game meat in the same way as beef or pork. However, game meat is leaner and contains less fat in the muscle. This will make a dry and unpalatable sausage unless you add unsalted pork fat when grinding. The pork shoulder butt is often used as a fat for game sausages. Generally, you will need to mix in a fat content of 15 to 20 percent to have a desirable flavor and texture. Blending different meat and fat percentages will affect your final product. Experimentation will be the best way to discover what you like best.

Making Jerky Safely

Temperature is very important when making jerky. The USDA Meat and Poultry's current recommendation for making jerky safely is to heat the meat to 160 degrees Fahrenheit before the dehydrating process to assure that any bacteria present will be destroyed by wet heat. Recent research at the University of Wisconsin demonstrated that the time-temperature combinations below are effective at killing *E. coli* 0157:H7 in jerky products. Although the lower temperatures are considered effective at killing bacteria, it is recommended that dehydrator temperatures of 145 degrees Fahrenheit or higher be used. Monitor the temperature of the dehydrator by placing the metal stem of a dial thermometer between the dehydrator trays or create an opening for the stem by drilling a hole through the side of the tray.

Drying Temperature (Fahrenheit)	Minimum Drying Time
125°	10 hours
135°	8 hours
145°	7 hours
155°	4 hours

Source: Wisconsin Cooperative Extension Service Meat and Animal Science Department, University of Wisconsin–Madison

Beef Jerky

5 lbs. lean beef
1½ tbsp. salt
1 tbsp. black pepper
1½ tsp. cardamom
2 tsp. marjoram

1½ tsp. cure (pink color)
2 tsp. cayenne pepper
1 tbsp. garlic powder
½ c. liquid smoke
½ c. water

Mix all spices together with meat until meat is tacky. Grind and press into a loaf pan lined with foil. Put in cooler or freezer to firm product for slicing. Slice as thin as desirable and lay on oven racks. Spray oven racks with oil and place the slices on a rack. Spray with liquid smoke and garlic mixture. Bake in an oven at 170°F for 2 to 3 hours.

Sweet Italian Sausage

90 lbs. pork trim (70 percent lean)
3 quarts water
3 c. salt
1 c. sugar
6 tbsp. cure
7 tbsp. plus 3 tsp. cracked fennel seed
3 oz. paprika

⅓ c. black pepper
⅓ c. cayenne pepper
⅓ c. garlic powder
2 tbsp. oregano
1 tbsp. sweet basil

Coarse-grind the meat trimmings. Add salt, water, sugar, cure, and spices. Regrind through ¼-inch diameter plate and stuff into pork casings. No smoking is necessary, as this is a fresh sausage. Cook before serving.

Dried Beef

50 lbs. lean beef
4½ c. salt

6⅓ c. sugar
1¾ tbsp. cure

Using ⅓ to ¾ ounces per pound of meat, rub the salt, sugar, and nitrate mixture onto the beef, making sure all areas are well covered. Rub the beef twice at 3- to 5-day intervals. Allow 2 days per pound of meat for the cure to complete. After the beef is cured, rinse it with cold water several times and allow to dry for 24 hours. Apply a light or heavy smoke as desired. Hang in a dry, well-ventilated room for further drying. Lamb or venison can be substituted for beef. Use large lean pieces, such as the round or legs, and separate into top, bottom, and tip. If you prefer to have a cooked product, smoke and cook to an internal temperature of at least 160°F.

Source: North Dakota University Meats Laboratory

Braunschweiger

10 lbs. 50/50 pork trim	3 oz. soy protein (optional)
10 lbs. pork liver	1 medium size onion
1 lb. fat bacon	1 tsp. nutmeg
7 oz. (⅔ c.) salt	1½ tsp. ginger
4 tbsp. white pepper	1 tbsp. cure (6 percent)

Grind pork trimmings, liver, and other ingredients to a very fine consistency. Mix in spices, salt, and cure. Stuff in moisture-proof fibrous casing and cook in 165°F water bath for 1½ hours or until internal temperature of sausage reaches 155° F. Chill rapidly in water.

Source: North Dakota University Meats Laboratory

Haggis

5 lbs. pork hearts	2 to 3 medium onions
3 lbs. pork liver	⅓ c. salt
2 lbs. beef suet	2½ tbsp. white pepper
21 c. oatmeal (3½ lbs.)	1 tbsp. nutmeg

Cook hearts and liver in 180°–190°F water until tender; do not boil. Remove cooked pieces. Reserve broth. Grind hearts and liver with beef suet through an ¼-inch plate. Chop onions finely. Bring the broth to a boil and sprinkle in oatmeal. Stir vigorously. To the hot mass, add the cooked meats, onions, salt, and spices. Stuff in moisture-proof casing and cook for about 3 hours in 170°F. water, or until internal temperature reaches 160°F. Chill in ice water and keep at 30°–34°F. Haggis is quite perishable. You may reduce amount of oatmeal if desired.

Blood Sausage

1 pint blood
1 pint milk or water
½ tsp. pepper
¼ tsp. nutmeg
1½ tsp. ground cloves

1½ tsp. ground allspice
1 tbsp. salt
1 c. quick cooking rolled oats
5 to 6 c. flour

Mix above ingredients together. Drop large spoonfuls into a large kettle of salted boiling water. Cook until brown throughout. Remove from water. It may be eaten hot with butter and syrup.

Italian Hot Sausage

5 lbs. pork trim
5 lbs. lean beef trim
20 cloves garlic, crushed
4 tsp. red pepper
4 tsp. fennel seeds, crushed

2 tsp. thyme
8 bay leaves
3 tbsp. salt
1 tbsp. black pepper
½ tsp. nutmeg

Grind meat through a coarse plate, then add spices and mix thoroughly. Grind again through a medium plate. Stuff into hog casing. Smoke at 140°F for proper color development and raise temperature to 170°F until internal temperature reaches 155°F. Excellent on pizza.

Potato Sausage

10 lbs. potatoes, peeled and
 grated
3 lbs. meat (pork head)

2 onions, ground
Pepper, salt, sweet marjoram to
 taste

Cook meat until done. Cool and grind. Mix together with other ingredients. Add some of the broth used to cook meat until mixture looks like cooked oatmeal. Stuff in casings. Heat in hot water.

Fresh Pork Sausage

45 lbs. fresh pork trimmings (70
 percent lean)
2½ quarts water
1⅓ c. salt

15½ tbsp. white pepper
¼ c. rubbed sage
½ c. sugar

Coarse-grind pork; mix in seasonings and grind product to desired size. Stuff into sheep casing. Smoke for 2 hours at 120°F. for smoky flavor. This must be cooked before serving.

Polish Sausage

40 lbs. lean pork trimmings
    (80 percent lean)
3 lbs. lean beef trimmings
    (80 percent lean)
1 quart water
3 tbsp. cure

1⅓ c. salt
½ c. black pepper
4 tbsp. mustard seed
4 tsp. marjoram
3 cloves garlic or ¾ tsp. garlic
    powder

Coarse-grind meat trimmings. Add salt, water, cure, and spices; mix thoroughly. Regrind through ¼-inch plate and stuff into pork casings. Smoke to desired color and heat to an internal temperature of 141°F. This must be cooked before serving.

Beef Summer Sausage

15 lbs. beef
10 lbs. pork trimmings
⅔ c. salt
1½ tbsp. cure
2½ tbsp. mustard seed

½ c. black pepper
½ c. sugar
1 tbsp. marjoram
3 tbsp. garlic powder

Mix salt and cure with coarse-ground meat. Pack in shallow pan and place in cooler for 3 to 5 days. Mix in remainder of spices, regrind, and stuff in 3-inch fibrous casings. Smoke to 140°F. for 2 hours; raise temperature to 160°F for 2 hours, and finish at 170°F until internal temperature reaches 155°F. Lamb or venison can be substituted for the beef.

Smoked Bratwurst

30 lbs. pork trim (70 percent lean)	1⅓ tbsp. cayenne
1 quart water	⅔ tbsp. nutmeg
1 c. salt	⅔ tbsp. thyme
½ c. sugar	⅔ tbsp. ginger
2 tbsp. cure	⅓ tbsp. rosemary
¼ c. white pepper	⅓ tbsp. mace

Coarse-grind meat trimmings. Add water, salt, sugar, cure, and spices. Mix thoroughly. Regrind through ¼-inch plate. Stuff into pork casings. Smoke product to desired color and heat to an internal temperature of 141°F. This must be cooked before serving.

Emulsified Products

Different products can be made using the same formulation of meat to spices. Generally, emulsified meat products contain the less valuable cuts and scraps not usable elsewhere. One example includes:

15 lbs. bull meat
12½ lbs. 50/50 beef trim
10 lbs. 60/40 pork trim
5 quarts water
2½ lbs. flavorings, consisting of:
  • 20 oz. salt
  • 8 oz. corn syrup solids
  • 5.5 oz. mustard
  • 1.6 oz. cure
  • 1.6 oz. ground black pepper
  • 1.1 oz. coriander
  • 1.1 oz. nutmeg
  • 0.7 oz. dehydrated onion and garlic
  • 0.3 oz. sodium erythorbate

A stainless-steel drop pan on wheels can be used for catching viscera and other internal organs in a home-butchering business. They are easy to clean, move around, and provide an easy viewing area to check the health of any organ.

Chapter 12

BUILDING A BUTCHERY BUSINESS

The past decade has witnessed a resurgence in consumer interest for locally grown foods. This interest also includes knowing where food originates, the conditions under which the animals are grown, how meat products are processed, and what, if any, additives are used. Part of this concern relates directly to health issues, personal preference, and a growing awareness and desire to support local producers rather than large industrial-size commercial businesses.

These concerns open opportunities for those who want to develop a butchering and slaughtering business. There are challenges to developing one that can be successful, but for those with enough determination, there can be personal and financial rewards.

A professional slaughtering and butchering business may be a welcome addition to a local community that doesn't have one or is located a significant distance from one. A slaughtering and butchering service has certain requirements in order to be established, including having equipment, licenses, and expertise in handling and deconstructing carcasses of many different sizes and weights. There are other basic issues involved in getting a meat service business started, and being aware of them will help you gauge your interest in pursuing this path.

Like any business venture, you will need to establish the entire concept and develop the initial plans for your business before anything else can happen. You will be responsible for developing your own clients, setting your prices, and having facilities that ensure a quality finished product for your customers.

You will need to acquire expertise in many areas, such as killing large and small animals; handling carcasses efficiently while reducing any potential bruising; fabricating the carcass; breaking it down into market-ready cuts; having environmentally acceptable access for the disposal of unwanted or unused viscera, hides, fat, and bones; relating with customers; and setting prices. Other considerations may include billing for work completed, which will require some accounting; hiring additional help, which may involve understanding and following safety protocols involving employees; and perhaps buying a mobile slaughter unit.

Two Types of Businesses

A farm slaughtering business can take two forms: home and mobile. Home slaughtering is where you process your own animals or have local producers bring their animals to your facility. A mobile business is where you go to farms at their request to process their animal. Neither of these necessarily requires that you do anything more than kill, skin, eviscerate, and cool the carcass, unless contracted to fabricate them further. Once the carcasses have been sufficiently cooled, they may be picked up by the owners, who may take it to their home and cut it up themselves.

You will need a cooler to hang carcasses for proper cooling and aging. It requires sufficient space and height to keep them from coming in contact with each other as well as touching the floor. A solid roof and beam construction is required to hold the anticipated number of carcasses stored at one time. You should plan a ceiling rail system that is sturdy, safe, and easy to move carcasses from the cooler to the workspace. If animals are quartered, the ceiling will not need to be as high.

Creating a Business Plan

Before purchasing any equipment to start your business, take time to develop a business plan to provide you with a reasonable indication of whether it is economically feasible to pursue it or not. Developing this plan helps you define your business, provides you with direction to make sound decisions, helps you set target goals, and provides a means to measure progress. It also increases your chance for success.

Business plans do not need to be extensive, but they must answer several questions that enable you to focus your efforts. Developing and writing your plan forces you to examine the resources you have available and the ones you need to acquire. You can also evaluate the capital investment and additional materials required.

Having a sound business plan with cost and income projections supports a knowledgeable case for a loan, should you need to raise startup funds.

Your business plan should have a realistic view of your expectations and long-term objectives. Developing a plan forces you to clearly understand what you want to achieve and how you can do it.

A local financial advisor, bank service department, or county or state agricultural extension personnel can be sources for helping you develop a business plan that fits your needs. While Internet resources can be helpful in developing a basic plan, it is always good business to discuss it with another person who has expertise in this area.

Experience

Experience is second only to a business plan in developing a successful slaughtering business. Being knowledgeable about different animal species and their physical conformation and parts, including the circulatory, skeletal, muscular, and digestive systems, is essential to success. Not knowing how to accurately process a killed animal or breakdown a carcass into different cuts, is a recipe for disaster and short-lived business prospects.

Where can you gain experience? There are several approaches you can take. The first is to work for or with an established slaughtering business. This may be located in a town or village near where you live. Be aware that in this type of situation they may perceive your interest as competition to theirs. But often there is enough business to go around so that may not become an issue.

Experience often equates with reputation. The better you are at your job, the more likely others will want to use your service. This builds your reputation, which, once established, you should endeavor to protect by maintaining customer satisfaction.

A second option is to enroll in courses that may be offered at universities, technical schools, culinary schools, or other educational programs that provide instruction on meat processing. Charts and photos are often available for many species to provide rudimentary lessons of where cuts are derived.

A third way of gaining experience is to slaughter and butcher your own animals. Although the number of animals you need to acquire a comfortable level of expertise may exceed your family's requirements for food, you may consider marketing your meat products as a supplement to developing your business. Or you could work cooperatively with several neighbors to develop a better understanding of what is involved. Starting with small animals, such as poultry, will give you an initial orientation on which you can build your experience.

Reading and studying as much as possible about the slaughtering and butchering industry will help familiarize you with all aspects of your potential business. You may even consider consulting older residents with expertise in home butchering who may be willing to pass on their knowledge.

A lack of experience does not preclude you from developing a slaughter and butchering business, but it is essential to find a way to gain some before you venture into one. How long it takes to become competent will often depend on your commitment and dedication to succeed.

Licences

In most states, some form of licensing is required if you are developing a business for the sale of meat products off your premises. Slaughtering and butchering animals for home use does not require licensing. Before you begin, check with your county agriculture extension office or state department of agriculture for licensing regulations that may apply to your planned business.

Equipment

To establish a successful business, you will need equipment that is durable and appropriate for your job. Nothing can be more frustrating or detrimental to your business reputation than to have carcasses fall to the ground.

For a mobile business, you will need such items as an open-end truck to which you can attach a boom arm, winch cable, gambrel, and slaughtering tools. Chains or cables wrap around hind legs to lift the carcass once it's killed to begin the bleeding and evisceration processes. Proper heavy-duty equipment provides for a safe, neat, fast, and efficient operation.

A metal catch chute is one useful restraining method for holding large animals just before harvest. The animal enters from the rear, and the lock gate in front restrains it for stunning. Many of these units are portable and can be moved from one location to another. A sturdy pen should be built to hold animals brought to your facility before directing them into the catch chute.

The greatest challenge you may face with home or mobile slaughtering is your willingness to kill animals. Unless you are able to put aside your emotions and feelings for the animal standing before you as you are about to kill it, then perhaps this type of business is not for you. That does not exclude you from the rest of the process, however. You still may be able to offer the rest of the service for your customers.

One important aspect to consider for the slaughter and butchering of large animals, such as a beef or pig, if you are on a farm or ranch is to have an area where it can be securely restrained so that it cannot injure itself, you, or anyone helping you. Missing the opportunity for a clean kill, which is discussed elsewhere, will likely provoke the animal into trying to escape from the threat. Yet this confinement area needs to be quickly accessible once the animal is dead so that little time is lost in proceeding with the butchering process. If working on someone else's property, examine the logistics beforehand and decide on a course of action that is safe and will meet your needs.

If you have created facilities at your home for slaughtering and animals are brought to you, you can design holding pens and restraining areas to fit your needs. Plans for these can usually be obtained with the help of county agriculture extension offices or university agriculture departments.

Fees

The success of your slaughtering business will depend largely on two factors: the number of animals processed and the charges you make for your work. At the beginning, it may be difficult to calculate or anticipate the number of animals you will process for customers. However, the price you charge will need to be realistic for the amount of work you do and competitive with any local meat market offering a slaughtering service.

Customer Relations

Understanding your customer's wants and needs is one important aspect of good customer relations. Discussing the customer's expectations and requirements beforehand will eliminate misunderstandings as you develop your business.

Identifying the animal to be slaughtered seems simple enough, but at times you may

An electric stunner is useful for hogs and can be wall-mounted, which limits its range and mobility but will provide reliable service. Have the electrical circuit installed by a qualified and licensed electrician, and read and fully understand the operator's manual instructions for safe use.

A handheld stun gun is a humane way to kill animals for butchering. This model uses a .22-caliber rim firepower blank load. The operator's trigger fires the shell that drives the steel rod into the skull.

be responsible for sorting out the animal to be killed. An owner may leave at the time of the kill, so the correct animal should be separated from the rest of the group before proceeding or before the owners dismiss themselves from the scene. Many do not like to stay to watch what happens next but will return when the killing is over.

The more animals you slaughter, the better you will become at it. One reason you may do more animals is that small-scale farmers tend to have limited experience with the whole process. Also, as more urban residents move into the countryside and raise animals, their level of expertise at slaughtering and butchering animals is likely to be limited. Providing a good service will increase your business.

Home Meat Business

If you enjoy cutting up your own animals, you likely have the talent and knowledge to start a business at your home. Your biggest costs likely will be for equipment that will make your work easier and more uniform, a cooling appliance, and a work area where you can process the carcass safely, quickly, and under sanitary conditions.

You should have a work area that is separate from your home or kitchen. Professional quarters will assure potential customers that you are committed to providing a quality service. A spacious environment that has been designed to include room for handling large carcasses, as well as refrigeration appliances, will make cutting and cooling meat easy, where it would likely be more difficult if it was attempted in your kitchen.

Your business plan may include constructing a structure that includes cold storage, a freezer, a meat cutting room, a smoking room, and washing and toilet facilities. Plans for such structures may be available through county agriculture extension offices or university animal science departments. You will also need lighting, heat, water, counter space, cabinets, cutting tables, chairs, stools, a wrapping table, and a ceiling rail for hanging and moving carcasses. Before beginning any construction, check local or county ordinances and regulations

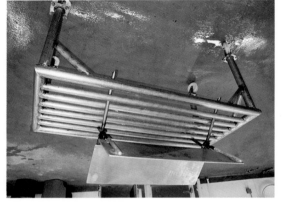

Your worktable should be sturdy, of an appropriate height for ease of cutting, and made from material that is easy to clean. It should be large enough to hold a half carcass of beef at one time. A cutting-board top prevents your knives from becoming dull.

A sturdy bar trolley with a V-rack attachment can be adapted for use with different-sized animals. The V-rack can be removed and placed on the floor for use with pigs, goats, sheep, veal, and deer. With rollers attached to the trolley, it can be easily moved.

larger structure at the beginning rather than remodeling and expanding later. A basic rectangular structure measuring 24x26 feet will provide sufficient area for creating separate rooms for specific purposes.

The roof rafters and ceiling should be built strong enough to carry the weight of several carcasses, particularly in the cooler. You should construct a rail system that allows you to easily move hanging carcasses from the cooler to the cutting table. You will need to install hanging scales for weighing carcasses. The floor should be cement, and the walls and ceilings should be built from materials that are easily cleaned. There must be a potable water supply of hot and cold running water.

It is a good idea to have a floor that slopes slightly to a drain to allow for easy floor washing. You will have to address the final disposition of where the water drains after leaving the building. You may create a separate septic pit that can be pumped out, but the water from this building should not be connected to the septic system of your residence.

Space Requirements

The largest carcasses you will likely work with are beef or, perhaps in some cases, bison. Using a beef carcass to determine the square footage of a structure will generally provide adequate space to move most large animal carcasses. It will also allow you to determine the number of smaller carcasses you can handle in the same space, such as deer, pigs, or lambs.

As a rule, you will need approximately 12 square feet of ceiling space per beef carcass. Ceiling space is used for this calculation because you will be hanging the carcass from the ceiling, and each carcass half will require

that may apply to your situation. It is easier to obtain permits and make changes while your plans are on paper rather than later when partial or full construction has been completed. It may be a good plan to construct a building that is larger than needed at the beginning, especially if you are committed to a long-term business. It is easier and more cost-effective in the long term to construct a

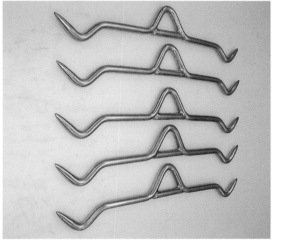

Stainless-steel gambrels can be used for lambs, goats, pigs, and deer. They are not adjustable, but they are sturdy for use with smaller-sized animals.

Any home-butchering business should have an adjustable gambrel with hooks. Being width adjustable will give it flexibility to be used with different-sized animals.

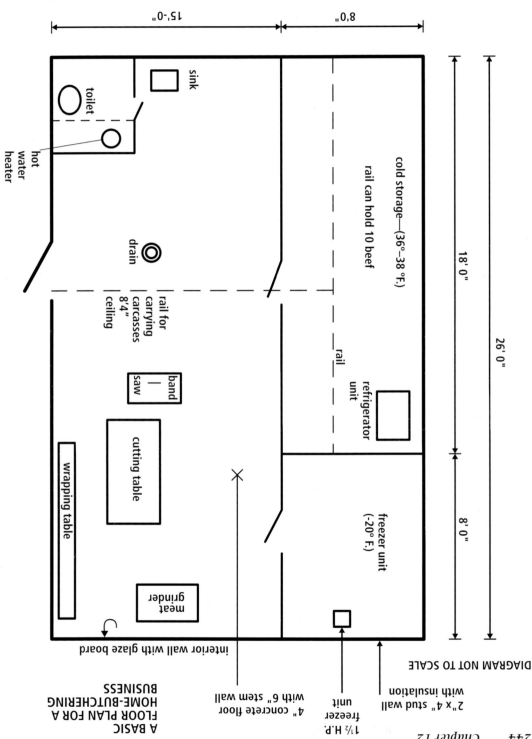

A BASIC
FLOOR PLAN FOR A
HOME-BUTCHERING
BUSINESS

23'-0"

15'-0"

8'0"

sink

toilet

hot
water
heater

cold storage—(36°–38° F.)

rail can hold 10 beef

drain

rail for
carrying
carcasses
8'4"
ceiling

band
saw

cutting table

wrapping table

rail

refrigerator
unit

18' 0"

26' 0"

freezer unit
(-20° F.)

8' 0"

meat
grinder

interior wall with glaze board

6" stem wall

4" concrete floor
with

1½ H.P.
freezer
unit

2"x 4" stud wall
with insulation

DIAGRAM NOT TO SCALE

a hook. You will also need to be able to space them apart to avoid possible contamination between carcasses.

Cooler

The cooler is the most important room in your building and should be kept between 36 to 38 degrees Fahrenheit when in use. The importance of quickly cooling a carcass after slaughter was discussed elsewhere in this book. A cooler that measures 8x16 feet should allow enough room to hang up to ten beef carcasses. The room should reach and be maintained at those temperatures before any carcasses are brought in for cooling.

Freezer

A freezer will be needed to quick freeze wrapped packages of meat to a temperature of minus 20 degrees Fahrenheit. The freezer size will depend on the amount of meat needing to be frozen at one time or stored until customer pickup. Generally, it requires about 50 cubic feet of freezer space for the meat cut from one beef carcass. Be aware that as freezer units increase in size, so does their construction cost and subsequent maintenance costs. A small unit is the most economical, and you should install only what you need.

Cutting Room

The cutting room is where you will cut up the carcasses, wrap the meat, grind hamburger, and make sausage. It needs to be large enough to accommodate the floor equipment you'll need, such as a band saw, grinder, cutting and wrapping tables, and room to maneuver a hanging carcass from a ceiling rail to cutting table. Cutting up meat in cramped quarters may not be an ideal situation for you. Also, having windows that allow in natural light should eliminate or minimize any claustrophobic effects. However, avoid southern light exposure to the cutting room, as this may increase the temperature through solar heating.

Barrels or tubs can be used to collect unusable parts including hooves, legs, hides, heads, and other unwanted body parts. They should be washed before and after use as should the floors and walls. Have a good supply of hot and cold water available.

Stainless-steel trays can be used to place internal organs, such as kidneys, livers, hearts, and lungs, on for later work. With rollers attached to its base, the tray can be easily moved from workspace to cooler.

wire baskets to place packages in, a tenderizer to score minute steaks, and a meat grinder or sausage stuffing machine. Depending on their size, the grinder and sausage stuffer can be placed on separate tables in another area of the room if needed. Be sure to buy only equipment with safety features to avoid accidents. All tables should be sturdy, made of materials that are easy to wash and sanitize, and have smooth surfaces to avoid depressions, which may harbor bacteria.

It is likely that your state will require an inspection of your facility before you can begin a business processing meat not exclusively for home use. State inspectors can provide guidelines for their requirements, and you should check with them about those and any licenses or permits that may be required.

If you are only offering a home butchering service, your customers will bring their carcasses to your facility. Carefully inspect the carcass before you accept it to determine if it has been bruised or damaged, that it appears to have come from a healthy animal, and that the meat has not soured or appears spoiled before it arrived. Discuss any concerns you may have with your customer before they leave. Once you have accepted the carcass for processing, you will likely be held responsible for any quality issues that may arise later, even if you were not at fault.

Seasonal Variation

The volume of your business may vary with the seasons. Traditionally, fall tended to be the time when most home butchering was done. This was for several reasons, including the animals were fatter and gained weight during the lush spring and summer growing periods, and the cooler temperatures made it easier to keep the meat from spoiling.

A separate wrapping table should be used for packaging the meat cuts. It can also provide space for a meat scale to weigh packages, wrapping paper rolls, meat stamping pads to identify cuts within the packages.

A wood table that measures 8x3 feet will allow enough room to lay out a carcass to begin the primal cuts. It also allows room to lay out any knives and saws as needed.

A wrapping paper roll can be attached to the underside of the table where you package the meat cuts. It has an edge for tearing the required amount of paper needed.

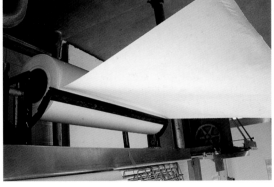

An accurate scale is necessary for packaging your customer's meat or weighing out spices or ingredients for sausage making. Some models have printers embedded within them that can be programmed to print labels for different cuts.

Refrigeration has helped alter that, and animals are usually slaughtered when they reach target weights rather than at the end of the growing season. Butchering can be a yearlong business.

Overwrap machines will offer flexibility in your packaging plans. They can be used for all kinds of cuts and seal the packages to minimize air exposure and increase shelf life. Vacuum packaging will further increase shelf life.

Income Example

While a number of factors will influence your potential income, you can use some assumptions to determine what that income level might be in developing your business plan. Below is only one example that may or may not fit your particular situation. However, the formula still can be used for the different variables and prices you decide to apply.

Let's assume that you can cut up 25 beef, 50 hogs, and 15 midsize animals, such as lambs, goats, and deer. If you have a beef carcass to weigh 500 pounds, pigs at 150 pounds, and lambs at 50 pounds. Say you have 20,750 pounds of meat. If you charge 30 cents per pound for cutting, wrapping, and freezing. This amounts to $6,225.00 gross income. This will need to cover expenses including electricity bills, which may be large because of the cooler and freezer.

Heavy string has many uses, including tying boneless roasts and trussing dressed birds and small game. The string should be kept in a clean, sealed container until used.

You may be able to expand your business to include poultry and other fowl, as well as other animals used for meat mentioned elsewhere. Developing a work schedule that keeps you busy will increase your gross income. Days not butchering or slaughtering are days when income is not generated. Butchering is a labor-intensive business, and you should be prepared for a lot of handling and lifting. However, using good equipment, keeping good records, and communicating with your customers may lead to a satisfying and rewarding business venture.

GLOSSARY

Aging: The time process involved that causes a maturing or ripening of meat enzymes that increase flavor and has a tenderizing effect.

Aitchbone: The rump bone

Anterior to: Toward the front of the carcass, or forward of.

Antioxidant: A substance that slows down the oxidation of oils and fats and helps check deterioration.

Backstrap: Connective tissue composed of elastin that is found in the neck. In most animals the backstrap is inedible.

Blade meat: An inedible, yellowish-colored connective tissue composed of elastin running from the neck through the rib region of beef, veal, and lambs, and also the base of the ribs.

Bone-in cuts: Meat cuts that contain parts of bone.

Bruising: An injury that does not break the skin but causes discoloration in the muscle.

Butterfly: To split steaks, chops, cutlets, and roasts in half, leaving halves hinged on one side.

Carcass weight: The weight of the carcass after all the butchering procedures have been completed.

Collagen: A fibrous protein found in connective tissue, bone, and cartilage.

Creatine phosphates: Amino acid molecules that are an important energy store in skeletal muscles and the brain.

Cubed: Refers to the process of tenderization using a machine with two sets of sharp pointed disks that score or cut muscle fibers without tearing.

Cure: Any process to preserve meats or fish by salting or smoking, which may be aided with preservative substances.

Cutting yield: The proportion of the weight that is a salable product after trimming and subdivision.

Dorsal to: Toward the back of the carcass, upper or top line.

Dressing percentage: The proportion of the live weight that remains in the carcass of an animal, sometimes referred to as yield. It is calculated as: carcass weight ÷ live weight x 100 = dressing percentage.

Elastin: A yellow, fibrous protein that is the basic constituent of elastic connective tissue, as in a lung or artery.

Epimysium: The sheath of connective tissue surrounding a muscle.

Fabrication: The deconstruction of the whole carcass into smaller, more easily used cuts.

Fillet: To slice meat from bones or other cuts.

Foresaddle: Unsplit forequarter of a veal or lamb carcass.

Forequarter: The anterior portion of a beef side, including ribs one through twelve.

Freezer burn: Discoloration of meat due to loss of moisture and oxidation in freezer-stored meats.

Fright or flight response: A behavioral reaction by animals to a stressful or threatening situation that increases heart, lung, and muscle activity.

Gambrel: A frame shaped like a horse's hind leg, used by butchers for hanging carcasses.

Glycogen: A polysaccharide produced and stored in animal tissue, especially in the liver and muscle, and changed into glucose as the body needs it.

Grade: A designation that indicates quality or yield of meat based on standards set by the United States Department of Agriculture (USDA).

Herbivores: An animal that feeds mainly on grass and plants.

Hindquarter: The posterior portion of the beef side that remains after the removal at the twelfth rib forequarter.

Hindsaddle: Unsplit hindquarter of a veal or lamb carcass.

Intoxication: When microbes produce a toxin that is subsequently eaten and sickness results in humans.

Lactic acid: An organic acid produced by the fermentation of lactose by certain microorganisms.

Leaf fat: Fat lining found along the abdominal wall in pork, commonly called kidney fat in beef and lambs.

Live weight: The weight of the live animal at the time of purchase or the time of harvest.

Marbling: The streaks and veins of fat interlacing meat cuts.

Muscle pH: The acidity or alkaline level in the muscle. It generally declines after harvest and the rate of decline is an important factor affecting meat quality.

Mutton: Meat from mature sheep carcasses that are usually identified by the absence of break joints.

Oleic acids: An oily, unsaturated fatty acid present in most animal and vegetable fats and oils.

Omega-3: A family of unsaturated fatty acids that appear to have healthy benefits in diets.

Omega-6: A family of unsaturated fatty acids that may increase the probability of a number of diseases and depression.

Omnivores: A person or animal that eats food from plant or animal sources.

Palmitic acids: A colorless, crystalline, saturated fatty acid found in animal fats and oils.

Parturition: The act of bringing forth a young offspring; birthing.

Perimysium: Connective tissue covering and holding together bundles of muscle fibers.

Petcock: A small faucet or valve for releasing gas or air or draining.

Porcine stress syndrome (PSS): A term that covers a group of conditions associated with a recessive gene in pigs that causes acute stress and sudden death.

Posterior to: Toward the rear of the carcass; behind.

Primal or wholesale cuts: The large subdivisions of the carcass that are traded in volume by segments of the meat industry.

Render: To melt down the fat.

Retail cuts: The subdivisions of wholesale cuts or carcasses that are sold to consumers in ready-to-cook or ready-to-eat forms.

Rigor mortis: The progressive stiffening of muscles that occurs several hours after death as a result of the coagulation of the muscle proteins.

Salt pork: Pork cured in salt, especially fatty pork from the back, side, or belly of a pig, often used as a cooking aid.

Side: One matched forequarter and hindquarter, or one-half of a meat animal carcass.

Shrinkage: The weight loss that may occur throughout the processing sequence. It may happen due to moisture or tissue loss from both the fresh and the processed product.

Silverskin: The thin, white, opaque layer of connective tissue found on certain cuts of meats, usually inedible.

Subprimal cuts: The subdivisions of the wholesale or primal cuts that are made to make handling easier and reduce the variability within a single cut.

Yield: The portion of the original weight that remains following any processing or handling procedure in the meat-selling sequence. It is usually quoted in percentages and may be cited as shrinkage.

METRIC EQUIVALENTS AND CONVERSION

Conversions between U.S. and metric measurements will be somewhat inexact. It's important to convert the measurements for all of the ingredients in a recipe to maintain the same proportions as the original.

General Formula for Metric Conversion

Ounces to grams	multiply ounces by 28.35
Grams to ounces	multiply grams by 0.035
Pounds to grams	multiply pounds by 453.5
Pounds to kilograms	multiply pounds by 0.45
Cups to liters	multiply cups by 0.24
Fahrenheit to Celsius	subtract 32 from Fahrenheit temperature, multiply by 5, then divide by 9
Celsius to Fahrenheit	multiply Celsius temperature by 9, divide by 2, then add 32

Approximate Metric Equivalents by Volume

U.S.	Metric
1 teaspoon	5 milliliters
1 tablespoon	15 milliliters
¼ cup	60 milliliters
½ cup	120 milliliters
1 cup	230 milliliters
1½ cups	360 milliliters
2 cups	460 milliliters
4 cups (1 quart)	0.95 liters
1.06 quarts	1 liter
4 quarts (1 gallon)	3.8 liters

Approximate Metric Equivalents by Weight

U.S.	Metric
0.035 ounce	1 gram
¼ ounce	7 grams
½ ounce	14 grams
1 ounce	28 grams
16 ounces (1 pound)	454 grams
1.1 pounds	500 grams
2.2 pounds	1 kilogram

Metric	U.S.
1 gram	0.035 ounce
50 grams	1.75 ounces
100 grams	3.5 ounces
500 grams	1.1 pounds
1 kilogram (1000 g.)	2.2 pounds

Weight Conversion of Common Ingredients

1 pound salt = 1½ cups
1 ounce salt = 2 tablespoons
1 pound sugar = 2¼ cups
1 ounce cure = 1½ tablespoons

Conversion from Ounces to Tablespoons

¼ ounce = 1¼ tablespoons
½ ounce = 2½ tablespoons
¾ ounce = 3¾ tablespoons
1 ounce = 5 tablespoons
2 ounces = 10 tablespoons
3 ounces = 15 tablespoons
4 ounces = 20 tablespoons

Equivalent Measures and Weights

3 teaspoons = 1 tablespoon
4 tablespoons = ¼ cup
16 tablespoons = 1 cup
2 cups = 1 pint
4 cups = 1 quart
2 pints = 1 quart
4 quarts = 1 gallon
16 ounces = 1 pound

INDEX

Recipes

ACKNOWLEDGMENTS

I wish to thank my wife, Mary, for her constant support. Her comments and suggestions helped improve this book from beginning to end.

Our son, Marcus, did the photography for this, his fourth book for Voyageur Press. He and our daughter, Julia, were active 4-H and FFA members—a great satisfaction for their parents.

A sincere thank you to two men with whom I became friends over the course of the five months I worked with them: Dr. Jeff Sindelar and Ronald Russell.

Dr. Jeff Sindelar is an assistant professor and extension meat specialist at the University of Wisconsin–Madison. I appreciate his assistance, critiques, and interest in this project.

Ronald Russell, senior lecturer at the University of Wisconsin–Madison, is actively involved in teaching and as coach for the UW–Madison Meat-Animal Evaluation Team. Both gave freely of their time, expertise, and experience, and both provided a pleasant atmosphere in which to observe their interaction with students. Without their help, this book would have a much different appearance.

Jonathan Campbell, an extension program specialist at Iowa State University, conducted an excellent seminar in carcass fabrication, which he allowed me to attend. His knowledge and easy explanations to my questions were most appreciated.

Several other people deserve my thanks for their assistance to my request for help. They include Oris Dilley, Bill and Tara Kindschi, and Tom and Virginia Kraft.

Jerry and Ruth Apps have been friends and mentors for many years and have always taken an interest in my writing. Their initial encouragement and recommendation was the catalyst for me to write this fourth book for Voyageur Press. A simple thank you does not adequately convey my gratitude.

A special thank you to my editor, Margret Aldrich, who stepped in to shepherd this book to completion with the assistance of Kari Cornell. Also, a thank you to Leah Noel for her close attention to the manuscript and identifying points to strengthen it.

About the Author

Philip Hasheider is a fifth-generation farmer presently raising pasture-grazed beef with his wife and two children in southcentral Wisconsin. His interests in production agriculture and history has allowed him to write ten books, including Voyageur Press' *How to Raise Cattle*, *How to Raise Pigs*, and *How to Raise Sheep*.

His diverse work has appeared in numerous local, regional, national, and international publications, and he was the writer for the *Wisconsin Local Food Marketing Guide* for the Wisconsin Department of Agriculture, Trade, and Consumer Protection.